It's Not About the Badge

Critical Acclaim

"Until you have walked in the shoes of a rural police officer, you can't understand the challenges, range of emotions and satisfaction of the job. John DiGirolamo brings those stories to life in *It's Not About the Badge* so the reader can walk along with the officers, stride for stride in these compelling real-life tales. The author delves beyond the police work and into their personal life, family situations and faith journey, creating a captivating reading experience."

Jimmy Tidwell - former Chief of Police for the town of Buena Vista, CO. Mr. Tidwell was the police chief for over 24 years and his law enforcement career spanned 34 years and one day.

***

"Given the current wave of unwarranted, irrational hatred of cops by leftist radicals, demagogic politicians and their liberal-media echo chamber, this book couldn't be more timely and valuable. John DiGirolamo humanizes six actual police officers in a compelling mixture of true-crime drama, personal insights, motivations, and dedication."

"Cops are ordinary people with families who have extraordinary jobs that can put their lives on the line each day. As you walk in their shoes, you'll appreciate the pressure of making split-second decisions in life-threatening encounters with dangerous criminals. As a cop, under-reacting can take your life from your family; over-reacting can cost others their lives and put you in jail. Good cops, the vast majority, should be defended not defunded."

Mike Rosen - longtime host of the *Mike Rosen Show*, KOA 850 Radio, Denver, CO; author of *Reality, A Plain-Talk Guide to Economics, Politics, Government and Culture*

***

"Sometimes gritty, *It's Not About the Badge*, gives a graphic account about the nature of policing in Central Colorado. From their relationships with family and friends, to the tragedies they witness daily, and sometimes rewarding success stories, John DiGirolamo offers a glimpse into a cop's world. In this creative non-fiction piece, he draws his characters from police officers in Central Colorado and stories from real-life incidents, lending it an eerily accurate and believable depiction."

DiGirolamo writes about the many reasons why those who walk the blue line continue to do so. He illustrates the difficulties and the uniqueness of doing police work, but he also shows the humanity of the people police serve daily. And he writes candidly about the blow cops felt during the summer of 2020 when demonstrations around the United States were aimed at cops.

Paul J. Goetz - Managing Editor, *The Mountain Mail*, Salida, CO

It's Not About the Badge

John DiGirolamo

Deer Track Publishing
Centennial, Colorado

First Edition

Library of Congress
   Control Number: 2021901277

ISBN: 978-1-7365088-1-7

Published by: Deer Track Publishing
               Centennial, CO
               Email: deertrackpublishers@comcast.net

Cover Design: Andrew Duffy, Longmont, CO
Front Cover Photography: Megan DiGirolamo, Buena Vista, CO
Back Cover Photography: Phreckles Photography LLC, Salida, CO

Dedication

This book is dedicated to the past, present and future police officers who risk their lives daily for the betterment of our communities. It is especially dedicated to Jesse Cortese, Dean Morgan, Jamey Murray, Lamine Mullenax, Megan DiGirolamo and Jesse Mitchell. They opened up and allowed me into their professional and personal lives so I could share their stories with my readers.

Also, to my wife Kathy, without whose love and support this book would not be possible.

Contents

Prologue

As the summer of 2020 raged on with daily protests, riots, looting and calls for defunding the police, I only saw one version of police officers portrayed in the media. And that portrayal was all negative; depicting the police as part of the problem and actively seeking to discriminate against minorities.

They were often portrayed as racist, power hungry egomaniacs, who chose their profession for all the wrong reasons. Many large cities had mayors and council members calling for their police force to be reduced or even eliminated and replaced with rapid response social workers. The "reimagine the police" trend gained traction.

Rarely did you hear from the police officers themselves, especially from rural America. I wrote this book to give six officers a voice to tell their stories and provide the reader a peek into their everyday lives. These stories offer a glimpse of what it is like to walk in their shoes and what policing is really like. They are ordinary people doing extraordinary things for their communities.

The daily acts of heroism and the dangers police officers face is seldom reported or make the headlines. These stories are the experiences these officers remember the most and which had an impact on them in personal and profound ways. They are more than just police officers; they are real and interesting people.

Read about what motivated these regular people, from different backgrounds and demographics, to become law enforcement professionals. Join their journey and experiences and get to know the human spirit behind the badge. It's not about the badge, but instead it's an inside view of those who stand in the gap between good and evil in our society today.

***

The names of witnesses, victims of crimes, the accused and criminals have been changed to protect both the innocent and the guilty. All of the stories are based on real events. The author has added details for context and illustrative purposes.

***

I.

Hard Wired

June 2020

"A what?" he asked.

"A dog bite complaint," dispatch repeated.

"Yeah, OK," he sighed into his radio. "All my guys are busy on calls, so I'll go check it out." He put his radio microphone back into the holder and stared out his patrol car window. "Unbelievable," he muttered to himself. With everything going on, this was what he had to go check out? There was a pile of paperwork waiting for him, which seemed more appealing than dealing with a neighbor's unfriendly dog.

It was tough to get out of bed today. With the protests of George Floyd's death dominating the airwaves and internet, it seemed like every media pundit assumed all police officers in the country acted with excessive force. And they did that all the time, especially to minorities.

Protests turned to riots and each day seemed to bring a new call to "Defund the Police." Cops were now the enemy. The guys in blue were now the problem. It didn't matter if deaths like George Floyd were rare. It was tough enough to do this job, but without public support, it was becoming less than its usual thankless job.

He sighed aloud again and started his patrol car. As usual, another was meal interrupted, and he wrapped up half of his burrito. It didn't matter now since his appetite was gone and he placed it on the passenger seat.

3

Eating would have to wait. He was getting tired of every news headline and social media post portraying police officers as out of control racists. He was frustrated. It simply wasn't true. It wasn't true statistically and it wasn't true of the people he worked with every day, and that frustration led him to lose his appetite more than the call to check on someone bitten by a dog.

But the social media narrative was too strong. Average citizens gave him dirty looks or the one finger salute. Nobody seemed to remember that he was there to protect them. They seemed to have forgotten that their boring day at the office was only possible in a civilized society; it was only possible with law and order. The more he thought about it, the more frustrated he felt. The worst part: it didn't seem like it was going to get any better. He tried to push those thoughts from his mind.

He realized his teeth were clenched the whole time. He purposely tried to relax his jaw and shook his head slightly. He flipped his turn signal on and pulled out of the Brown Dog Coffee shop in Buena Vista and headed south on U.S. Highway 24.

Fifteen minutes later, he slowed down on the dusty dirt road and turned into the driveway of a small one-story country house. It was white but needed a paint job and the driveway was long enough to be a big chore to shovel in the winter if you had to do it by hand.

It wasn't the best neighborhood in the county, so it's likely that snowfall was cleared with only a shovel, or not at all. Luckily, the snow was long gone this time of year. He opened his door and in the fading light of sunset, he saw a lanky man in his late sixties ready to greet him with an agitated face. The sergeant felt a slight surge of annoyance with this low-level incident and the old man's upset look on his face.

"Thanks for coming," the man said and before he could reply, the old man continued. "My grandson was bitten by their dog." He was clearly worried and pointed towards a neighbor's house.

"And you are Randy Neddleson?" the sergeant asked.

"Yes, I called the sheriff's office earlier."

"When did this happen?"

"Two days ago."

"It's been two days?" he asked, thinking it would have been better if the old man called it in right after it happened. "How old is your grandson?"

"He's 19."

"An adult?" the sergeant asked.

"My grandson can't always defend himself. He's a special needs kid," Randy replied. "You'll have to go slow with your questions. If he gets overwhelmed, he'll shut down."

The sergeant's slight annoyance disappeared.

They entered the house and saw that Michael was anything but an imposing figure. He was only about 5' 7", skinny with sandy brown hair, and fidgeted from nervousness. He recognized Michael as the kid who worked at a local store, but hadn't ever met him. He was always friendly and seemed to have a permanent smile pasted on his face.

He also was pleasant and courteous. Michael was the kind of young man who would offer to bring your purchases out to your car and help load it. He was just brought up that way. He didn't mind the extra work. In fact, he enjoyed it. It gave him satisfaction when he could be helpful and useful. It gave him a sense of purpose. But one interaction with Michael would reveal his flaw: he had a learning disability.

"Michael, this sergeant is here to talk about what happened the other day," Randy told him, and Michael's smile vanished.

"Can you tell me what happened?" he asked them both.

"I don't know," Michael said in a sheepish tone, looking down at his feet.

5

"One of Michael's chores is to get the mail every day," Randy stated. "But for the past month, the neighbor's dog has been harassing Michael. The dog isn't on a leash, and Michael finally told us that he'd been bitten three times."

The sergeant turned his head to Michael, but he didn't make eye contact. "Tell me exactly what happened," he said in a coaxing manner, but Michael didn't say anything.

"He grabbed the mail and started coming back to the house and the dog ran off of his porch, and came down the street and lunged at Michael, isn't that what you told me?" Randy asked.

"Hmm," was all Michael could muster.

"The dog lunged at him, knocked him down and that's when he bit his leg," Randy continued.

"Yes," Michael said in a low voice, still looking down at his feet.

"Show him the bite mark," Randy requested. Michael turned around and the sergeant could see the wound on the back of his leg, just above the knee. The bite mark still looked fresh, was red and was an ugly wound. It would eventually heal, but he'd probably be left with a permanent scar.

"That's from two days ago," Randy replied. "We didn't know about it until this morning. I was helping him with his bathroom routine after he got out of the shower and that's when I noticed he'd been bitten. Michael told me it had happened before, but never this bad. I guess he was too embarrassed to mention it."

The sergeant could see the look on Michael's face change as he recalled getting bit. His eyes got bigger and his face tightened; the sergeant recognized the look of fear.

"Michael can't run real fast, and he had no time to defend himself," Randy continued. The sergeant got a closer look at the bite.

"You need to keep cleaning it so it doesn't become infected. He'll need to see a doctor if it gets worse," the sergeant told Randy.

"It's a mean dog," Randy replied. "That dog is nasty to everyone who comes around. They don't tie it up and the split rail fence doesn't do any good. Michael isn't going on their property, and the mailbox is at the end of our driveway. That dog has no right to attack my grandson. And they just let it. They don't care and laugh at him." Michael again looked down at the ground and shuffled his feet.

The sergeant could feel his blood pressure start to rise. He unconsciously balled up his fist. Here was this kid, who clearly never hurt anyone. Here was this kid who always said "hello" and "have a nice day" and *actually meant it*. Here was this kid who was physically awkward and uncoordinated and had a hard time running. Here was this man who had the mind of a child. Here was this kid who was probably teased his entire life for being "slow" or a "retard" or even worse names.

Here was this kid whose only crime was being an easy target to be picked on. In all ways, he was defenseless. This sparked something deep inside the sergeant. He'd seen just about every type of crime and every type of criminal. He'd seen more victims than he'd like to admit, more physically hurt than Michael. But something gnawed at him deep inside. This was a clear case of *right vs. wrong*. There was no reason for this kid to be scared to simply get the mail. Someone needed to defend this kid. Someone needed to stand in the gap between good and evil. He had a good idea of who that could be.

"It ain't right," Randy said. "Can you talk to them or something?"

"Absolutely," the sergeant stated emphatically. He turned to Michael and said, "I will take care of this."

"Thank you, sir," Randy offered.

7

The sergeant turned and headed toward the front door, down the driveway and towards the neighbor's house. As he approached the house, he could hear the dog barking and growling. He was unafraid and even more determined. The switch had flipped.

There was nothing more disturbing, nothing more unnecessary and nothing more wrong than to intimidate the weak. As he walked up to the front porch, and woman in her late 20s walked out of the house.

"Do you know Michael, the boy a few doors down?" he asked, all 5'9'' and 180-pound frame standing tall and solid like a brick wall.

"Yeah, what of it?" she replied.

"Two days ago, your dog bit him. I saw a teeth marks and a nasty wound on his leg."

"Well, he didn't exactly attack him," the woman snickered and slightly rolled her eyes. This just added fuel to the sergeant's anger. But he just stood firm with controlled emotion. "That kid is just a weirdo, yah know?" she scoffed.

"It's not a joke. Your dog is a menace and is terrorizing an innocent kid. You know that kid can't defend himself. He shouldn't have to," he added. He turned back to the woman in front of him and his face was clenched tight and he stared at her with no emotion in his brown eyes. The "look" communicated that without a doubt there was nothing funny about the situation.

"Yeah, OK, I guess," was all the woman could say and looked off in the distance. She avoided the sergeant's glare.

"Has it had a rabies shot?"

"Yes, it is up to date."

"Show me the tag," he instructed, and she went back into the house. He noticed a man standing behind the window in the house. The husband or boyfriend wasn't coming out anytime soon, and the sergeant just glared at him. The woman returned and showed him the up-to-date vaccination tag.

"Let me tell you how it's going to go," the sergeant stated. "I am writing you a Vicious Dog citation. You're going to keep that dog in the house or rope him up outside. You are going to keep that dog under control. Whatever that dog does is completely your responsibility. You understand?"

"I guess so."

"If it happens again, the charges will be amped up, potentially including hate crime charges against the mentally disabled. Do you understand?" he repeated.

"Yes."

"If this happens again, I will personally intervene on behalf of Michael or anyone else your dog harasses for your personal entertainment."

"Yes sir," the woman replied quietly. The sergeant took her name and finished writing the ticket. "Don't make me come back here," he coldly stated. The sergeant handed it to her and walked away and returned to Randy and Michael's house. They walked out of their house to greet the sergeant.

"That dog won't be bothering you anymore," he told them.

"OK," Randy said, nodding his head and Michael's face softened.

"Yes. Your neighbor is very sorry and said it won't happen again," the sergeant stated, and Randy gave him a quizzical look, doubting that his neighbor was apologetic. He turned to Randy and handed him a business card. "If it happens again, you call me personally and I will come out to deal with the situation."

"Thank you," Michael cheered and hugged the sergeant, surprising him. Michael's face was lit up with a broad smile. A simple, innocent smile. That's all it took to melt the frustration of the sergeant. He felt a sense of calm and peace.

The sergeant walked back to his patrol car and started the engine. "Thank you, God, I needed that call," he said aloud. For the first time in weeks, he felt good, really good at work. This is what it's all about. Defending those who can't defend themselves. That's what separates us from the animals. That's what makes us a civilization. This is why he went into law enforcement. His sour mood had changed in a mere half an hour. He felt refreshed and pumped up.

He was grateful for the reality check. There was nothing "heroic" that he'd done, it was just an ordinary call. No one will make an action movie based on this call, but it was important to Randy and Michael. And that made it important to him. It didn't matter that the media fueled the cries to "Defund the Police." He was going to remember this call for the rest of his life. There was something extraordinary about this ordinary day. After 10 years on the force, he needed a reminder about why he loved being an officer. And thank God he got it.

***

Two weeks later

"It worked!" the voice excitedly said. "It really worked."

The sergeant looked at his cell phone and didn't recognize the phone number. He didn't have a chance to ask who it was.

"Every day I can walk to my mailbox and guess what? No dog. I can even stroll to the mailbox!"

"It's Michael, right?"

"Yes."

"That's great news."

"Thank you so much! No one bothers me at all, all thanks to you," Michael said excitedly, and the sergeant could almost see the smile coming through his phone.

"You're welcome. I'm really glad," the sergeant responded and grinned for the first time that day. "If you ever need help, you know who to call, right?"

"I call Sergeant Cortese."

***

Meet Jesse Cortese, age 38

Follower of Christ
Man
Son
Brother
Husband
Father
Uncle
Daddy
Patriot
American
Musician
High school state basketball champion
High school state football champion
Deputy Sergeant, Chaffee County Colorado
SWAT team commander

11,945 days earlier

September 1987

"Don't forget to finish tying your shoe," his mother, Donna, said. First grader Jesse Cortese was looking forward to his soccer game as he jumped into the car. His first year of soccer was especially fun and he looked forward to it since he didn't have a gym class, as he was being homeschooled by his mother.

"I will," Jesse replied as he reached down to redo one of the laces on his cleats that had come undone. He liked having cleats for soccer, and not just wearing sneakers. It made playing soccer just a little bit special. His mother smiled at him as she pulled out of the driveway. A few minutes later, they arrived at the Buena Vista soccer field. It was a warm summer afternoon, with the breeze helping to keep everyone from overheating. He noticed that several other kids on his team had already arrived.

There were other teams too, older boys up to the sixth grade. He walked towards his group on a corner of the field and noticed one of the third graders, Wayne talking with some other boys. He did not like Wayne; he was not a nice kid. Most of the younger kids were afraid of Wayne because he would bully them. He'd call them names, and also push them around. Five-year-old Jesse didn't understand why Wayne did that. He'd picked on Jesse's little brother Luke too. The kids he picked on weren't doing anything to Wayne. In fact, they weren't doing anything at all, but that didn't stop Wayne.

Coach O'Leary had them practice some ball handling skills before the game. The game was fun, although sometimes it seemed like he just stood on the field not doing anything, waiting for the action to come to his side of the field. After winning the game, the coach told them to get some water.

Jesse went to the water fountain and drank a few gulps. When he finished, he headed back towards some of the kids on his team. That's when he saw Wayne grabbing the shirt of a second grader. He was yanking on it hard, and he could see Tommy being flung around.

He stood and watched for about two seconds. He could hear Wayne yelling at Tommy, calling him an "idiot" and "why don't you change your diapers, you little baby?" He continued with, "Don't shit in your pants, you stupid moron."

"What word did he just use?" Jesse thought to himself. Then he found himself running. He didn't remember his legs starting to move, but he now suddenly found himself at full speed towards Wayne and Tommy. He felt anger towards Wayne and even at five years old, he knew when he saw an injustice.

During the scuffle, Wayne's soccer cleat came off. But he kept teasing Tommy and yanking on his shirt. He stopped for just second and Tommy's face eased up and relaxed, thinking it was over. But it wasn't. Wayne grabbed his cleat and swung it hard at Tommy, missing his head. Tommy's face immediately cringed, and his eyes got wide and his mouth slightly puckered with fear. Wayne had picked on him before, but never like this. Maybe a shove or a punch in the arm, but never with the blunt force of a soccer cleat.

Then Wayne swung again, this time connecting on the top of Tommy's left shoulder, then bouncing off of it and smashing square on his ear. He yelped in pain and shock when the cleat stung the tender skin of his ear. Tommy was helpless and his face was contorted with pure fear. The cleat smashing his ear stung like a bee and his first reaction was to flee, get away from Wayne and just run. And keep running until Wayne gave up.

Jesse knew of Tommy, who was one year older, but was a smaller kid. They weren't friends, but he seemed like a nice kid, and certainly didn't deserve the punishment Wayne was dishing out.

14

Where were the coaches and parents? Where were the other kids? It seemed like no one noticed what was going on. Was it really up to Jesse to intervene? Jesse couldn't take it anymore; Wayne needed to be stopped.

This compulsion kept Jesse running towards the two of them and let out a scream as he knocked into Wayne as he was about to take a third swing with the cleat. Wayne saw him at the last second and was surprised that any kid, let alone a kid in a younger grade had dared to stop him. Both boys fell to the ground.

Jesse wasted no time and jumped on top of Wayne, his knees digging into his stomach. "Get off of me," Wayne protested. Although he didn't realize it at the time, it was official; this was Jesse's first fight.

Jesse made an awkward swing and his fist landed and Wayne immediately cried out. "How do *you* like being punched?" But before Wayne could answer, instinct took over and Jesse hit him again with his right fist which landed just below his eye. Wayne cried out again and tears started to flow and his mouth opened wide for more air.

"Why are you so mean?" Jesse asked and stared into his eyes for an answer that never came. Jesse was upset, and about as mad as a five-year-old could get. He breathed in deeply and raised his fist again, but he was snatched up by Coach O'Leary.

"Break it up boys," his Coach yelled. By this time several of the parents came rushing over, including Jesse's mom. "Stop fighting!" coach continued as he slowly lowered Jesse down to the ground. Coach towered over the five-year-old and scolded him, "You're done! And you'll sit on the bench at our next game."

"But…" Jesse tried to protest.

"No 'buts' young man."

"Jesse Reed Cortese, what has gotten into you?" his mother asked.

"You need to take him home," Coach told her.

"Oh, I will!" she stated emphatically. Jesse recognized that tone in his mother's voice. And it was bad news for him.

"But he was beating up Tommy," Jesse protested some more.

"I don't care. It is not OK to fight," she countered and grabbed him by the arm. "Let's go." She kept a firm grasp on his arm as they headed back to the car. It was a long and silent fifteen-minute car ride. Finally, once inside, she brought him to the kitchen table.

"Why were you fighting?" she asked.

"Because Tommy was getting beat up."

"By Wayne?"

"Yes. Someone had to stop him."

"OK, but that is not the way to handle things, and you should have gotten a parent or a coach. You know fighting isn't the answer."

"But he needed help right away."

"Yes, but you should have gotten an adult to help," she repeated with a more stern voice.

"I don't know why I am getting in trouble, when I was the one helping," Jesse countered and crossed his arms, pouting. "What about David?"

"David?" she asked, unsure which David he was talking about.

"Yeah, David versus Goliath. He had to stand up to that bully too."

"Ahh..." she answered and smiled slightly. "I see you have been paying attention to some bible studies. It is not the same thing," she continued with the smile gone.

"The bible also says to turn the other cheek. Do you remember that story?" she countered.

"Yeah, but…" he said and trailed off.

"No more fighting, OK? You don't want to get kicked off the soccer team, do you?" she asked and waited in silence.

"Can I go to my room?" he asked without acknowledging his mother's question.

"Fine," she answered. He got out of the chair and marched towards his bedroom. He understood *what* his mother was saying, and he understood *why* she was saying it, but it still didn't make sense. He *had* to help Tommy. He wasn't sure why, but he felt it with conviction.

Wayne avoided him at the next soccer practice and Tommy never said another word about it. The fight and his actions got seared into his memory. He was born that way. He just didn't realize it until now. He wasn't sure exactly what it meant, but he was certain it wasn't going to change. Jesse was just hard wired that way.

***

March 2009

"Well, you finally made it for a ride-along," Officer Justin Pikul stated with a wide grin.

"Yes, I am ready to roll," Jesse Cortese answered. The two had been lifelong friends since grade school. It was a crisp evening in Manitou Springs, a small town on the outskirts of Colorado Springs. The town was best known for being the launching point for the historic Cog Railway that took tourists to the top of Pikes Peak in the summer. Summer weather was still several months away for the 14,114-foot elevation of Pikes Peak.

Officer Pikul had been on the police force for five years when his best friend had complained about his boring job, so he suggested that Jesse join him for a ride-along, where a civilian accompanies an officer and observes what he does on patrol.

Typically, the ride-along occupant was someone interested in law enforcement as a career, and that person could see what a regular patrol shift would be like. Occasionally, a reporter, politician, writer or other interested citizen might participate.

This evening, Jesse joined the 8:00p.m. to 6:00a.m. shift, which is also the time when more officers are assigned for duty. That's usually when the bad stuff happens. Your mother always told you that nothing good happens after 2:00a.m., and just about every police officer would agree.

A few hours into the shift, Officer Pikul responded to an incident at a bar. One of the patrons was intoxicated and was harassing several people both inside and outside the bar. Manitou Springs is a small town, so it took them less than five minutes to get to *The Crossbuck*. The *crossbuck* is the "X" shaped symbol on the sign displayed just before a road crosses a railroad track, and that symbol was prominently displayed on the front door and several walls inside the establishment.

Officer Pikul parked in an open spot across the street from the bar and Jesse watched him approach a man in his early forties just outside the bar's entrance. Jesse tagged along, but at a distance. Ride-along participants are allowed to observe, but not engage or interfere in the police officer's work.

As he approached the man, Officer Pikul could hear him singing 'Happy Birthday' to himself. And singing badly. "Hey, pal, what is going on?" The man ignored the officer, who then stepped in a little closer.

"Hey, what are you doing?" he asked again. "You out drinking tonight?" The man kept singing and Officer Pikul could smell liquor on his breath.

"Officer, this is the guy who was harassing people inside *The Crossbuck*," stated a late twenty-something woman, who was standing a few feet away.

"What was he doing?"

"He just came over and sat in our booth and started saying, 'Hi Melissa, it's my birthday.' My name is Rachael. I've never seen him before, and he wouldn't leave our table."

"Then what happened?"

"A waiter came over and asked him to leave. He left our table but did the same thing to someone else," she continued.

"Is that what happened?" Officer Pikul turned his head to ask the man.

"Happy birthday tooooo me!" was all he could answer and started to slump on the bench.

Then a couple walked out of the bar. There was a little bit of ice on the sidewalk, and they walked slowly with cautious steps. They were both looking towards their car parked just a few spots down the road. The guy was grabbing something in his coat pocket and pulled out some keys. This caught the attention of the birthday boy. His eyes focused on the keys and then the woman walking along the side of him. He immediately stuck his arm out and grabbed her rear end.

"Hey!" she yelled in disbelief.

"Melissa, why don't you give the birthday boy a kiss?" he asked, his hand still outstretched.

Before anyone else could react, Officer Pikul placed both hands on the man's shoulders and lifted him off the bench and guided him towards the nearby wall. The drunk man was surprised and let out a whimper as he was forced up against the brick wall. Officer Pikul then grabbed his handcuffs and in two quick motions, the man was immobilized.

"Come on, let's go," he told the drunk, and guided him across the street, one hand on his shoulder and one hand on the cuffs, making sure the man was going exactly where and how fast the officer wanted him to go. Several observers thanked the officer and they headed back to the patrol car. They brought him back to the police station and prepared to book him. An hour later, they were back on patrol.

"I get a few of those obnoxious drunks every weekend and sometimes during the week too," Officer Pikul replied.

"Yeah, I bet that is pretty common," Jesse replied. "It's good that you're getting these people off of the streets, so they are not harassing anyone or getting in their car afterwards."

"A good part of this job is knowing you're making the town a little bit safer," Officer Pikul said. "So, how is your job going?"

"Snoozeville," Jesse answered. "It is so boring just driving around, especially trekking up mountain roads in the middle of a snowstorm." Jesse was working as a driver for Loomis, the armored car service making pickups and deliveries in mountain towns such as Aspen and Breckenridge. "The only interesting part is when we drop off cash to a celebrity. Their weekend play money," he continued. "I am literally ringing their doorbell holding a bag of cash."

"How much money are we talking about?"

"Sometimes as much as a few hundred grand."

"Whew, that's a lot," Officer Pikul responded with a whistle. "What do they do with all of that cash?"

"I have no idea. That's about the only excitement I get on that job. But it's not like they give you a delivery tip or anything."

"Well, being an officer won't be boring, I can tell you that much."

"That, I believe. You're making a difference out there," Jesse answered.

"Hold on," Officer Pikul said as he quickly made a U-turn and started following a beat-up old truck. There are drugs in there."

"Oh, really?" Jesse asked.

"We just passed the house of a known drug dealer, and that truck pulled out of its driveway. And it's almost 3:00a.m., so that usually means they just bought something. We're going to tail them for a bit." The patrol car followed 50 feet behind the truck on the relatively quiet neighborhood road. After a few minutes, the driver did what the officer was looking for.

"You see that? He completely went through the stop sign. I've got probable cause now," Officer Pikul stated as he turned on the flashing red and blue lights and the siren. A few seconds later, he saw the truck's taillight brighten as it slowed down and then it moved to the side of the road.

Officer Pikul radioed dispatch and asked for them to check the status of the truck's license plate. The pile of scrap metal posing as truck belonged to Frederick Canute. Mr. Canute had a criminal record of drug possession, several drunk and disorderlies, and a restraining order against him from a year ago. Officer Pikul went to go find out if Mr. Canute was in the driver's seat.

He adjusted his duty belt and stretched out his back for a quick second as he closed the door of his patrol car and started the twenty-five foot walk to present a ticket for failing to stop at the red octagonal sign. Not likely to be dubbed the crime of the century, but as he took the long and lonely walk from the relative safety his patrol car to the truck, his stomach tightened just a little.

That twenty-five feet represented the distance in which his life could go from a routine night on patrol to instant chaos.

No traffic stop was "ordinary" anymore, and Officer Pikul knew that as well as any officer.

The officer approached the truck's window, which was rolled up, so he knocked on it. He quickly noticed a driver and a front seat passenger. Both were scrawny males, both in their early twenties, and both looking like they hadn't slept in over 48 hours. As the driver rolled the window down, a small amount of smoke came out.

It wasn't as dramatic as a scene from 'Cheech & Chong,' but it was the undeniable smell of marijuana, which was illegal in Colorado at the time. He asked them to produce identification first and Mr. Canute was indeed the truck's driver. He then asked both of them to step out of the car, and they complied without incident.

After backup arrived to help arrest and escort them back to the police station, he checked the truck and found a few grams of LSD and *mushrooms*, both hallucinogenic drugs. It was going to be a low-level offense, but there was satisfaction in getting any amount of drugs off the streets.

When Officer Pikul's shift ended just after 6:00a.m., they decided to go out to a diner for breakfast. When they were settled, the officer asked, "So what did you think of your first ride along?"

"It was great. I wasn't sure what to expect, but it was the most exciting 10 hours of my life," Jesse answered. "You were busy the entire time. You are really making an impact, all while most of the town was asleep. It's like you are hunting evil."

"Do you think you might want to join the brothers in blue?" Officer Pikul asked.

"I've already decided. I am all in. I should have been doing this job five years ago. This really fits in with my personality." The next day, Jesse Cortese signed up for the police academy.

July 2012

"9-1-1, what's your emergency?"

"Hey, a guy has been stabbed in here and he's bleeding pretty bad."

"What is the location?"

"I am at the *Golden Nickel*. It's a bar in downtown Leadville. I'm the bartender," he said and waited for a long two seconds.

"I've dispatched the police and EMT. They should be there soon."

"OK, tell them to hurry. This guy is bleeding all over," Mark Gallegos stated and hung up the phone. He'd been a bartender for almost four years, and working at the infamous *Golden Nickel*, he'd seen just about every type of crime.

The Colorado saloon had been there for a century and catered to tourists during the day as an old authentic mining town watering hole. But after 9:00p.m., it attracted locals, drinking hard and getting rowdy. Just last week, there had been several local gals dancing on the bar and they damn near broke it in two.

It had been eight days since Mark had to deal with a scuffle, which was a long time at the *Golden Nickel*. Most of the time, he convinced them to take it outside so he didn't have to deal with it, or have to explain it to the owner. Luckily, he had the folksy, "aw shucks" way of talking that calmed most people down. But it didn't work tonight.

Four minutes later, it was Leadville Officer Jesse Cortese who first arrived at the scene. He saw a bartender standing next to the man, making sure no one got near him. Mark nodded to the officer and stepped out of the way. He muttered something under his breath when he realized that no one was going to pay this guy's tab.

Officer Cortese saw blood already soaking through the 52-year-old man's ripped up t-shirt. He bent down on one knee to get a closer look. He tried to avoid putting his knee in the pool of blood, but quickly realized that it was going to be unavoidable. He surmised that the victim had been sliced up several times through his stomach and chest. The blood kept coming and seemed to go *everywhere*. He was not going to be able to stop it.

In his first year in law enforcement, Officer Cortese hadn't seen this type of wound. He wasn't medically trained, but he knew some of the basics of treating trauma before the ambulance showed up. He used both hands to put pressure on the cuts, but they were just too long across the man's body. The blood continued to ooze out of the man's body and through the officer's fingers.

Then he noticed something squishy and it felt almost rubbery with an off-white color that was poking through his stomach. It was the man's intestines. Officer Cortese's hand flinched and he wasn't sure what to do. He stared at the guts, literally hanging out from the man's body.

This wasn't television or a movie, and it wasn't pictures from a biology class. How is he supposed to help this man? Does he put the intestines back in the man's body? He didn't want to damage the organ by putting downward pressure on the body. But it just kept bleeding. The blood felt warm and he couldn't stop it and this guy was going to die right in front of him if he didn't do something else.

"They're here," an unknown voice said. For a moment, Officer Cortese shuddered when he interpreted that to mean the person or persons who attacked this man. He had been so focused on the guy's stab wound that he forgot that the perpetrator could still be in the bar. He could hurt someone else or attack the officer. He looked up and yelled to the bartender.

"Where's the guy that did this?"

"He ran out the back," the bartender replied and pointed to where the restrooms and exit-sign were. He noticed the bartender's gaze shift behind the officer.

"Where's the knife?

"I think he took it with him," the bartender guessed.

"We've got this officer. Thanks." the EMT told Officer Cortese. He looked up at him, nodded and told him about the type of knife wound. He then stood up and stepped back and the second EMT took over. He headed towards the bartender and was handed a towel.

"I appreciate that," he replied and tried to clean up as best he could. Now that the victim was in better hands, he could go back to being a police officer. "Can you tell me what happened?"

"Well, they started arguing, over money I believe," the bartender stated. I was serving another customer and then I turned around to see Raul stand up and get in the other guys face. I never saw him before tonight."

"So, you recognized the suspect?"

"Yes, he lives in town, Raul Sanchez. He's a regular."

"I am aware of him," Officer Cortese answered. Raul was a low-level drug dealer in Leadville, and not surprisingly, had previous run ins with law enforcement. "What happened next?"

"Raul raised his voice, and you could see that he was pissed off. He said something about 'getting what he was owed.' I was about to try to calm him down when I see the other guy give him the middle finger and shrug his shoulders. That made Raul even more mad. It's like the summer heat puts people on edge, ya know?"

"Continue."

"Then he pulled a knife from his back pocket and took a long swipe at the guy, and then he flicked his wrist and did it again, although this time the guy jumped back a little and screamed in pain."

"Next thing I know, the guy was covered with blood and he fell off the barstool. It all happened in a matter of seconds."

"And you say he ran out the back?"

"Yup. By that time, me and several people had looked over and saw the whole thing."

"Who are the other witnesses?" Officer Cortese asked, and the bartender pointed them out. He went over to the four people to take down their statements. The EMTs placed the victim on the stretcher and were ready to take him to the ambulance.

He knew where Raul lived, and it was within walking distance from the *Golden Nickel*, and his apartment was the obvious first place to look. In the winter, walking a few blocks could be treacherous this time of night. But it is an easy few minute walk in mid-July.

After calling it in to his sergeant, it was determined that Officer Cortese and two county deputies would look for the suspect. Leadville is a town of only 2,600 people sitting high in the Rocky Mountains at 10,152 feet above sea level and is the only incorporated municipality in rural Lake County, which has just under 9,000 people. It was an old mining town and throughout the years, always had a "rough exterior" reputation. The police force was just a handful of officers and the town and county often backed each other up.

It was nearing midnight when they arrived at the apartment building of Raul Sanchez. Even in the dark, the building looked beat up and worn out by years of harsh winters at high elevation. The wooden stairs were in need of repair and didn't seem to be up to code.

Halfway up the stairs, Officer Cortese had a thought jump into his head: this is not a place of tactical advantage. In the middle of the rickety stairs he was vulnerable from an attack. There was nowhere to take cover, and an assault could come from anywhere.

His senses heightened and his concentration rose, quickly scanning the area above, below and each side. He steadily and quickly moved up the stairs. The two deputies were right behind him. When they reached the apartment door, Officer Cortese knocked and identified himself, but no one answered. He nodded to the county deputies and they went in.

Officer Cortese was the first one through the door, followed by Corporal Marius and Sergeant Dillard. He immediately noticed that the place was a dump. Drug users had many things in common and not caring about their living conditions was definitely one of them. He immediately noticed a small mirror, razor blade and white powder on the kitchen table, along with empty beer bottles and what looked like two-day old pizza.

The scene was familiar, this was the home of a cocaine user. Raul was a dealer that used his profits to feed his own habit. Who knows how much he had taken and whether he was coming down from his high. Either way, the only thing you could predict with certainty was the unpredictability of the situation. Would the suspect give in easily, or run and try to escape or fight back? It took less than two seconds for the answer to be revealed.

Raul was like a rat caught in a corner. The 41-year-old grabbed a knife from the table and pointed the 4-inch blade at the police. He wasn't going to give up, *he was going to fight*. Officer Cortese's training kicked in and he immediately aimed his Glock 19 directly at the man's chest. There was a small kitchen counter and a table separating the two. He was only fifteen feet away, so there was no chance he'd miss the shot.

"I'm going to kill someone," Jesse thought to himself. All he could see was the barrel of his gun and Raul's chest. It was tunnel vision; there was nothing else in the room.

"Put your hands up and drop the knife, now!" Officer Cortese commanded.

As a law enforcement officer, Jesse knew that sometime in his career, he might have to use deadly force. He just didn't think it would be in his rookie year. He might have to take a human life.

It would be justified if the man made any move towards him with the knife. He would have to take the shot. There would be no other choice. You eliminate the threat. Officer Cortese calculated that it would take one and a half seconds for Raul to reach him and potentially slice him open just like the other guy in the bar.

Raul was a not a tall fellow and was 'chunky' by most people's standards. But Officer Cortese knew people jacked up on drugs sometimes surprised you with their physical capabilities. This was no time to underestimate a criminal.

Raul was not a choir boy, that's for sure. Maybe a drug dealer, probably high on cocaine, who just stabbed someone, would not be mourned. But he was someone's son, maybe a husband and father. Maybe he could turn his life around. Maybe this was going to be rock bottom for him and he'd change his ways. Maybe he'd find God?

Yet maybe he wouldn't. Maybe he'd live and continue to commit crimes and hurt people. But, if the officer doesn't take the shot, he'd have a chance. His odds of getting his life put back together were low, but it would all depend on what Officer Cortese did in the next few seconds. And if Raul attacked him, Officer Cortese would be the one forced to pull the trigger.

If he discharged his weapon, it would be loud. But he wouldn't flinch. That split-second decision would end this man's life and would change Jesse's life too. *Everything* would change; you can't go back. Jesse felt his heart start to beat up and adrenaline pumped through his body. Killing this man would irrevocably change him, the person, more than just Jesse the police officer.

He'd thought about *this* moment before. He'd imagined the moment before taking the shot. He'd reflexively rely on his training and the justification would be valid. Righteous, even. He'd imagined that he wouldn't feel guilty about it. But what if doubt crept in? But taking too long to think and react could be too late for his own life's sake. *Thinking* about pulling the trigger was so theoretical, and this was so *real*. Ultimately, on this night the decision wasn't his to make.

Deputies Marius and Dillard flanked Officer Cortese on his left and right. Raul hadn't dropped the knife and stared at Officer Cortese who was pointing a gun directly at him. The sight of a gun being held by a man willing to use it froze Raul's drug fueled brain for just a second. It made him hesitate just long enough for Sergeant Dillard to come from his right side and tackle the man. They both crashed to the floor and Raul dropped the knife in the process.

Corporal Marius grabbed his handcuffs, went over and kicked the knife away and then straddled the man with all of his 6'1" and 230 pounds. He cuffed his left wrist, and as he grabbed his right arm, Officer Cortese guided his weapon back into his holster. The deputies helped the man to his feet, who was now yelling obscenities. It didn't matter. The whole incident took less than a minute and would look routine in the report. It was anything but a routine evening.

All three officers brought the suspect to the Leadville police department headquarters to be placed in a holding cell, and it was after midnight. Jesse was still amped up and yet exhausted at the same time. It was a weird feeling. They needed to get the suspect processed and he started to fill out the paperwork, along with the county deputies.

"Good work tonight," Corporal Marius told him.

"Thanks," Officer Cortese answered with a sullen expression on his face.

"What is it?"

"I almost took him out."

"Yup, that will happen from time to time," he explained. "But you kept your cool and let everyone do their job," Sergeant Dillard chimed in.

"Yes, it is a team sport, I know."

"Everyone did exactly what they were supposed to."

"I know. It's just unbelievable to think I was so close to taking another life," Cortese said.

"Let me tell you young man, that's how I want you to think. We take the shot only when we need to. To protect the public or defend ourselves," Dillard continued. "You did fine tonight. I've been doing this a long time, and every incident is different, and can easily go sideways." Sergeant Dillard had over 25 years of experience in law enforcement and had the grey hair and experience lines on his face to prove it.

"Yes, sir."

"We don't discharge our firearm all willy-nilly."

"Yes, I know. It is a huge responsibility," Officer Cortese agreed. It struck him that he really had come so close to putting this guy down. To take his life. Intellectually, he knew that was a possibility each and every day, but this was the first time he came close to pulling the trigger, and he simply felt heavy with a real burden. Almost *too* real as he replayed the scene over in his mind.

"Yes, it is. That's why they drill you new guys with so much training. You know how to react and react fast to all kinds of scenarios. Lord knows I've seen them all. And the training you get now is so much more sophisticated than when I started," Sergeant Dillard stated.

"I can't believe how amped up I am. I feel like I drank a case of Red Bull."

"I'm not surprised, it is not always easy to turn it off, so to speak."

"I'm just glad we got him cuffed without a further altercation and…" Cortese stated and stopped when his cellphone rang. "It's my wife."

"Take it," Dillard told him and started to walk away.

"Hey hon, did you make it home alright?" he asked as soon as he answered the phone. He was expecting this call since his wife Catherine was flying in late into Denver from Minnesota. By the time she landed, found the car in long-term parking, it would then take another three hours to drive from the airport to their home in Buena Vista, CO.

"Yes, but I am beat," Cat replied.

"Well, you're home safe and sound now. You can sleep in tomorrow." Jesse thought about how he was going to explain the evening's events to his wife.

"I will. Did you take care of my plants?" she asked, and he could tell she was walking around the house.

"Sure did," he replied. There weren't many things she asked her husband to do while she was gone for 10 days visiting family, but watering the plants was one of them. She loved having small plants and flowers in the house. It added a little life and color and made it a home. It brightened her day when she walked by the various house plants and saw them healthy and thriving. There was a sense of satisfaction when she noticed a new shoot coming up. Soon, she wanted to take her green thumb and apply it outdoors. But maybe next summer.

"Good. So, how is your night going?" she asked.

"It's been a little crazy," Jesse answered.

"What happened to my begonia?" she asked, her voice suddenly annoyed and accusatory.

"The what?"

"The begonia, you know that is my favorite plant. The one with the red flowers? It's on the little table over by the front door."

31

"Uh, didn't I?" he answered hesitantly, and was scrambling to remember what plant she was talking about. "I thought I watered them all."

"Well, some look OK, but my begonia is dead. It is all brown and shriveled up. You killed it Jesse."

"I'm pretty sure I watered all of them."

"Well, you didn't," she stated with sternness. "I ask you to do one thing while I'm gone, come on."

"I don't know what happened," Jesse replied back with his own stern voice. He could feel his stomach tighten with frustration. She just didn't get it.

After everything he'd been through? He was still pulsing adrenaline, and she is worried about a $10 plant? Really? Who knows if the guy in the bar was going to live? He was being airlifted to Denver.

It could have easily gone bad this evening with Raul. What if Raul had lunged at him? What if he wanted a 'suicide by cop' ending? Jesse could have shot him. Or, what if Raul had tried to fight his way out of the situation. What if Raul had a gun, and he, Marius or Dillard had been shot. Or killed?

Jesse took a deep breath and sighed. "Look, I have to go. We'll talk about in the morning."

"Fine."

"Fine," he replied as they both hung up. "Are you kidding me?" he said loudly, enough that Sergeant Dillard started to walk over towards Jesse.

Dillard gave a little raised eye gesture, as if to say, 'what's going on'?

"I don't believe it. She is pissed about a stupid dead plant. We've got a dozen plants in the house that I was supposed to water while she was gone."

"And you killed them all?"

32

"No, just one." Jesse exclaimed, obviously his blood starting to boil. "But it was her favorite, of course. After the evening we've had tonight, am I supposed to get upset about a plant? Where are her priorities? That is just not going to happen," he stated even more animated, waving his hands like many with Italian heritage are known to do.

"Well..." Dillard tried to say but was cut off by Jesse.

"Well, nothing. That is just a stupid priority. That will *never* be a priority. How could it be?" he stated emphatically and loud enough that other officers in the building noticed. "Does she think I am an idiot? That is just so fu..."

"Jesse!" Dillard interjected with authority. "You just need to calm down."

"How am I supposed to calm down?"

"Sit down and listen," Dillard commanded as he pointed to a chair. Jesse complied.

"You know I've been on this job a long time," he stated.

Jesse just stared at him in silence. "Yeah, I know," he finally replied, staring back at the veteran officer, arms folded.

"And I am on my second marriage, which is already going down the tubes. Do you love your wife?" he asked, and Jesse nodded.

"And you want to have a happy marriage?"

"Of course, but that is not the point."

"Let me give you the point, son," Dillard said, his voice rising. He realized his frustration, took a deep breath and slowed down his talking. "There are going to be nights like this. There are going to be a lot more when you're on the job as long as I've been. Some will be worse. All will have varying levels of danger. None of that should follow you home."

"OK," was all Jesse could muster.

Dillard continued, "She has no idea what kind of night you had, and you don't want her to know. There is a transition you need to make each and every day to go back to your civilian family."

"Huh, are you saying I can't talk to my wife?"

"That's not what I am saying. If you don't master the skill of leaving your work in the patrol car, you'll ruin your marriage," Dillard said and could see the wheels turning in Jesse's mind.

"The reason we get into this profession is so others don't have to deal with all of this shit," Dillard explained, and Jesse nodded in agreement.

"Let me give you one piece of advice, whether you want it or not," Dillard continued. "Your time on the job is really important *when you are on the job*. But when you are not on the job, your wife's priorities *need to be your priorities*."

"But…"

"But nothing. Take it from me. Maybe I'll get it right with wife number three. The third times a charm," he said and cracked a wry smile.

"How do I do that?" Jesse asked.

"Look, I don't care how long you have to drive around tonight. I don't care if you have to drive to Kansas. But drive around long enough so that when you walk in that door, before you see your wife, you have one thing, and one thing only on your mind."

"What?"

"That dead plant has to be your number one priority. Period."

***

July 2019

"I heard you arrested your old school buddy "Wayne-O" the other day," said Justin Pikul.

"Yes, it's always a good time when you arrest the school yard bully," Jesse Cortese replied and thought back to the fight on the soccer field. "I hadn't seen that scumbag in several years, so it was nice to get him off the street for stalking his ex-girlfriend. What a loser."

"I heard he confessed after we used the old CSI Miami trick on him."

"Yes, he threw a rock through the woman's window and we told him we found his fingerprints on it. Of course, you can't really get fingerprints off a random rock but obviously he had been watching way too much television."

"You gotta love Hollywood," Justin replied.

"Okay, it's just about time to watch the video," Jesse stated. It was only last month when he was inspired to create a men's bible study group. Being a police officer can sometimes grind on you mentally as well as physically. So, when Justin Pikul's wife suggested that he watch a video from Jim Burgen, Jesse was intrigued.

Pastor Burgen was from the Flatirons Church in Lafayette, Colorado, a suburb of Denver. The Pastor had a YouTube channel that was specifically targeted to a male audience. Jesse decided to contact several of the male police officers in the county as well as some other first responders. He only expected a few people to be interested, but tonight as they met in the church auxiliary room, the group topped 20 men.

Tonight's topic was Prepare for War. They listened to the hour video about how God is the one who defines what is true and what is a lie and figuring out a plan to be strong and fully armed so that you are ready to go to war.

As police officers, they're always prepared for a physical altercation, which might occur at any time, even when it seems to be a routine traffic stop.

They were a warrior society within a civilized society. And just like in sports, most of this game was mental. Tonight, it was reviewing the mental war against the scheme of the devil. After the video was completed, the men would talk about their reactions in a free-form setting.

"There is evil out there. Tragedy and bad things happen every day. We see the depravity of man and we are exposed to it all the time and it changes us," Jesse said, starting out the conversation.

"It's tough enough to deal with that on the job, but it also weighs on you after your shift is over," added Rusty Barnes. "Sometimes it's hard to see the good in the world."

"There are days when I go home, and I think the only good people in this entire world are the ones living in my house."

"We have to fight the doubt. It will chip away at your faith if you let it," a different officer responded.

"Yeah, sometimes we just need to be reminded of what we already know."

"We have to remember what is true, that we are a child of the King of Kings, that he has a plan for you, and to trust in that. It doesn't mean everything will be perfect and you won't have tragedy. Let God be in control. There is hope. If you reject it, you won't get help. You know you can't do it by yourself," another officer contributed.

"Sometimes it takes another cop, or another paramedic to look at the expression on your face and know the kind of day that you had. Our civilian family members don't always get that, but I appreciate that you guys do. I may not even need to talk; I just need someone to recognize the difficulty."

"We need to let God be in control, but all of us know that's not easy."

"Yeah, giving up control is not a big part of my personality," Jesse replied, and was treated with laughter and heads nodding.

"Well, I have to say that I really like this men's group. I don't feel as if I have to always talk about my problems and spill my guts out. But being in this group I feel both renewed energy and a sense of peace."

"Amen, brother," Rusty said. The group continued talking about the video as well as their own personal struggles. It's easy to have faith but it's not always easy to keep it. Although he didn't know it, in three weeks Jesse's faith would be tested.

July 28, 2019

Sorry man, I can't do this anymore. I love you. It's just too much pain.

Officer Jesse Cortese was in the county police building doing paperwork when he read the text. He quickly replied:

That's not true! What are you talking about? Where are you? What are you doing?

He waited a minute and did not receive any reply. He called dispatch and asked them to ping the cell phone number. Within a few minutes, they replied back and said that it was located in the nearby town of Nathrop. That's where Micah lived. He left his desk, got in his patrol car and headed there.

Micah was two years older than Jesse, now 40 years old, and he was considered part of the family. Micah was adopted from Korea to a local family and he and Jesse grew up together. Micah didn't get along with the adopted family and he moved out and was on his own since he was fifteen.

Jesse's family took him in, occasionally into the house for shelter, but he'd also been incorporated into their family in an emotional way. He was loved by all the Cortese family, and Micah would typically be included for Christmas, Thanksgiving and other holidays.

When Micah was about 35, the family approached him and asked him if he'd like to be adopted into the Cortese family. Micah started using the Cortese last name for everything.

Although Micah was Jesse's older brother, it was Jesse who took care of Micah. Micah always struggled to find how he fit into this world. Since leaving his adopted family at fifteen, he always felt discarded, a burden, like he was a misfit. This caused bouts of depression, drug use, doubt, and his inability to find his purpose in life. He would bounce around jobs, relationships and residences, and the lows outnumbered the high points. You could say he was a little bit of a lost soul.

Jesse looked out for him and tried to help him throughout his life and demonstrated that support when his family wanted Micah to take the Cortese last name. But it was difficult convincing Micah. When you've gone through your whole life thinking you're an outcast and don't have any worth, sometimes love and support from family and friends isn't enough.

On the surface, it may recently have looked like Micah's life was getting on track. He was the head chef at a local restaurant, was engaged to be married, and was living with his friend, Officer Jesse Mitchell. But often as it is, what you see on the surface does not reflect the churning sea underneath. His fiancé also had mental health issues. It turned the relationship toxic, and finally, Micah decided to call it off.

Jesse Cortese was concerned about Micah, considering the breakup and the way that Micah viewed his current emotions as the absolute truth. Micah's depression frequently superseded any rational points that Jesse tried to make about how there was potential and good things in his future.

Jesse's cell phone remained silent, so he knew there hadn't been any texts from Micah.

Officer Jesse Mitchell was on his patrol in Buena Vista, so Micah would have been the only person at the house, located in an unincorporated part of the county. Deputy Sanderlin was close by, so dispatch asked him to go there and check things out.

"I see his car on the property," the deputy said over the radio. Officer Cortese flipped on his lights and sirens and hauled ass.

Officer Sanderlin went up to the house and knocked on it, but no one came out. It was about 10:00p.m., so he used his flashlight to peer into the house. He didn't see anything, so he walked around to the back of the house. But there was nothing out of order, and it appeared that no one was home. He shined his flashlight left and then right but didn't see anything unusual on the property. He started walking towards Micah's car and that's when he saw him inside.

There was blood, *everywhere*. There was blood on the windshield, there was blood on the seat, there was blood on the dashboard, there was blood on the backseat and there was blood on the steering wheel. *It was everywhere.* He opened the driver's front door and there was no doubt what had happened.

Officer Sanderlin looked at the radio microphone in his hand and pushed the button, but no words came out. He pushed the button again, slightly cleared his throat and said in a trembling voice with trepidation, "I have a code Frank."

Jesse Cortese did a double take when Sanderlin's voice came across the radio. The first thought that popped into his head was, *did I hear that right?* But deep down, he knew what he'd heard and understood every word. That code meant that Micah was dead. Jesse involuntarily stopped breathing and tried to convince himself that he had misheard what had come across the radio.

Maybe he got it wrong. Maybe it looks worse than it actually is. He started to feel a little light-headed and pulled over to the side of the road. *Is he really gone? No, it can't be. There must be some mistake.* He put his patrol car back in "Drive" and finished the long mile to the house.

Jesse pulled up to Officer Mitchell's house, parked in the driveway and headed over to where Officer Sanderlin was standing just outside the car.

"You don't want to go any closer," Sanderlin told him.

"I need to see."

"No, you don't, you don't need to," he implored, trying to protect Jesse from what was inside. But nothing was going to keep him from finding out the truth, no matter how hard it was going to be, he had to be sure. He had to know what happened.

There was a shred of uncertainty, and maybe it wasn't really Micah, maybe it was somebody else, maybe there'd been a mistake, or maybe this was all just a bad joke. So, he had to be sure. He had to hold on to some shred of illogical hope because that's all he had. But he knew deep down that hope wasn't going to be available today.

He peered into the window and saw a service weapon lying on the floor with blood splattered across it. It's not like what they show on TV or in a movie. That's because this was not some fictitious character, this was his brother. This was as real as it could get, and it was as bad as it could get. There was no coming back, and that's what hurt deep down. There's no second chance, there's no changing your mind, *there's just no more.*

Jesse's face was ash white and his skin seemed to lack its normal taught texture. It was drooping because he had just been punched in the gut. He looked at Sanderlin, who was visibly upset, but offered no answers. How could he?

Jesse walked down the driveway and stepped in a small pothole. It amplified his lack of balance. It was as if his feet were not on stable ground. His stomach was in a tight ball and he couldn't regulate his breathing, and that's when he started to cry. His throat felt raw. At first, he tried to hold it back, and then he just couldn't control the emotion any longer.

Thoughts raced across his mind. *Why? Why did you do it? Why did you do it today? Why didn't you answer my texts? We could have talked. We could have figured something out and we could have come up with something better than this.* The ranges of emotions were constantly changing. Instant sadness started to be replaced by his boiling anger.

You're a fucking idiot! Dammit! Why didn't you fight back? You didn't have to do this. You didn't have to do this to me and everyone else. I could have helped you. You know I've helped you in the past, and you know it's gotten better when we've talked. Why didn't you try that this time? Why did you have to make it so final? Why did you have to go through with it?

He started to hear sirens in the distance, and eventually Officer Jesse Mitchell came back to the house, as well as Catherine, a pastor and several other deputies. When the coroner arrived, there was a sense of finality.

He caught a glimpse of the body once again. And it wasn't moving. It wasn't going to move. He wasn't going to see his brother's smiling face anymore. It's just so *final*. *Why didn't I call him today? Or yesterday? Why didn't I see this coming?* There is no reset button. There's no 'undo' and there's no reversal and that's what ate at his heart and soul.

***

Two months later

> "To conquer you must suffer.
> Suffer, pain is not the enemy."
> **—Throwdown**, *Suffer, Conquer*

It had been a whirlwind two months. All the funeral arrangements we're left for Jesse to determine. His range of emotions continued from sadness to anger, to guilt and shock, to the beginning of acceptance. He was asking the obvious question of *why*? He lost his sister in a car accident in 2009 and several friends from cancer in their early thirties.

What is going on in this world? What's the point? It's hard to see the good. Good people are dying, and bad people are thriving. *Why is this world turned upside down? For being such a tough guy, why did he feel so weak,* he asked himself. *For such a strong man, why am I so broken? I am the person that others lean on, so what's wrong with me now?* At times he never felt so alone, and so abandoned.

Life had a dark undertone. He'd be riding in his patrol car on a beautiful summer day, seeing people outdoors enjoying their life, laughing, having fun with their family and friends and they had no idea what had happened to his brother. They went about their day as nothing had ever happened. They lived their life as if Micah never existed.

Jesse would occasionally see one of his friends, and a thought would pop into his head: the last time I saw this person Micah was alive. He breathed out a loud sigh; he had been feeling down. If Jesse were giving advice to a friend of his, he'd tell him that he needed to talk to somebody. At least get things off his chest, but that was not Jesse's way. All the talking that he did was in his own head, for better or for worse, but the result was leaning towards the 'for worse'.

But recently he'd been thrown a lifeline. He was at the courthouse a few weeks ago, responding to a subpoena. And that's when he ran into George Hill. After George introduced himself, and without much small talk, he told Jesse something that would forever change his life.

"I woke up today and God came to me. He told me I needed to meet you and that you needed help and that we should talk." Jesse stood there silent with his jaw slightly open, wondering who this guy was. His first instinct was to reject such a notion and say, "I'm doing okay, it's fine, trust me I'll be fine."

Jesse was about to say those exact words when his throat tightened and was unable say anything. And then Pastor George Hill of the Grace Church in nearby Salida told him that not only was he here to support Jesse, but more importantly, God has never left him. Jesse took his business card, placed it in his pocket, and a minute later they were walking in the parking lot towards their separate vehicles.

George told him about a book called *Search for Significance*, which helped remind him of his identity. It was a simple but powerful concept, and he fully believed with conviction that he was a child of God, and that's the foundation of his identity and worth. That was something Micah never believed. *Why couldn't I convince him? Why wouldn't he believe me?*

The book explained that if you were rooted in worldly things such as sports, physical appearance, or a job and if that's what you used as your identity, it was like building a house on quicksand. Pastor Hill helped Jesse understand that life was not going to be a bed of roses, but you had to believe that God had a plan for you, and that plan included eventually reaching salvation.

For a few weeks, Jesse kept looking at the business card, knowing what he ought to do, but struggling; he just wanted to avoid thinking about the entire situation. Finally, he made the call to George and they got together.

George understood that Jesse was always the strong one; he was the one who was the protector. He wasn't supposed to need protection, and he understood that it was hard for Jesse to ask for help.

But then he reminded Jesse that a key part of a relationship with Christ is that you must open the door to your heart, and once you do, God's grace will come flooding in. At last, Micah's suicide was not the very first thing he thought about when he woke up in the morning. And finally, Jesse let his guard down and allowed Christ to come back in.

Jesse reflected on all of this as he sat in his car, anticipating the first time that Pastor George Hill was going to talk to his men's group. He knew it would do some good for the guys. And at this moment he never felt closer to them knowing that he had their support, whether it was just a facial expression, a pat on the back, a text or someone picking up his shift during this difficult time. It felt good to have these guys, these men, on his side, giving him hope, and finally he didn't feel alone anymore.

***

June and July 2020

"I've got a dozen packs of beef jerky, candy bars and some dried meal replacements. That ought to do it for a while," sixty-year-old Jenny Mostra said to her son. "I should have brought you a bar of soap, you stink."

"Yeah, thanks ma," said forty-two-year-old Jimmy Mostra. "Just give me the damn food." He grabbed the packages of beef jerky and stuffed them into his large dirt-stained backpack. But his mother was right. He did smell and smelled bad.

But what do you expect when he hadn't taken a shower in over 10 days? He'd been in the wilderness of both Park and Chaffee Counties, trying to keep a low profile after busting up his Jeep on a rough ATV trail.

His low intake of nutrition was catching up with him. He was living on just a few Snickers bars over the last few days after his jerky ran out. His pint of whiskey was gone a week ago. His sleeping bag was full of holes, and half of the stuffing had fallen out. His unwashed hair was down past his shoulders, and included bits of grass, dirt and leaves. It was a matted mess.

The clothes on his back were the only garments he had, and they were starting to tear. There wasn't any time to pack when he abandoned his Jeep. And being in the wilderness for ten days without any toilet paper didn't help his hygiene situation. He'd also added an inch to his existing bushy beard. But he didn't mind any of that. He liked being in the wilderness and he didn't mind the solitude at all.

People just pissed him off. Any kind of people and all kinds of people put him in a sour mood. So, he didn't mind sleeping under the stars in an old miner's cabin he'd found. At least it was a roof over his head, well, sort of. Several planks of wood were missing from the roof as well as the walls, and only one small corner of the cabin would be dry in a rainstorm.

Jimmy was lucky it wasn't winter. But future cold-weather problems were the least of his worries. He was just trying to survive day to day. Each day he stayed hidden, he considered it a good day.

"I brought you a shirt too," his mother told him and handed him one of his own flannel shirts. He started to change shirts and tried to hand the old shirt to his mother. "Just throw that one in the trash." There wasn't a trash can around, so he just dropped it on the ground.

"Where's Troy?" Jimmy asked.

"He should be coming soon. I told him it's almost a mile past the Turtle Rock campsite. I hope he didn't make a wrong turn onto some trail. I told him we'd be on the Lenhardy Cutoff Road," Jenny said, and looked along the rough dirt road one quarter of a mile before it turned and went downhill, but she didn't see any approaching vehicles.

"I can't stay that long," he stated.

"They came looking for you the other day," she said in an 'I'm annoyed' manner.'

"Yeah so, I wasn't there."

"They told me there is another warrant out for your arrest. I can't keep count anymore," Jenny replied.

"Neither can I!" Jimmy laughed it off. "But I keep pretty well hidden, so they won't get me."

James "Jimmy" Mostra was wanted in Chaffee County for felony burglary, for stealing money out of locked Park and Recreation self-payment containers. He was also wanted for looting a local store and an illegal gun possession. As a previously convicted felon, it was unlawful for him to have any firearms.

He was also wanted in neighboring Park County for a different firearm possession. He had to abandon his Jeep when he hit a pothole large enough to break the axle. He left over 500 rounds of ammo and a shotgun in the Jeep, and escaped into the woods just outside of Fairplay, CO, barely evading the law. He'd been hiking and making his way back towards Buena Vista ever since.

"I filed a complaint about them officers coming into my house to look for you. But your stupid brother let them in, and they had it on body camera footage to prove it."

"There is nothing to be found at your place ma."

"Yeah, I know, but I didn't want them in the house. Look, there's Troy." Troy Gado rode up on his dirt bike and came to a stop.

"Hey," Troy greeted them.

"You got my stuff?"

"Yeah, I got it," he said and handed him a bag of pot. "You got money for it?"

"You know I'm good for it," Jimmy answered, and Troy scoffed at the notion. He wasn't getting repaid for the $100 he'd just spent and privately wondered why he kept helping Jimmy.

"I gotta go," Jimmy said and looked around, but saw no one else. It didn't matter since there was no use in taking the chance of being seen. "Same time next week," he stated, grabbed his backpack and nodded a 'goodbye' to his mother and Troy, and headed back into the wilderness.

***

Three Days Later

Sergeant Cortese parked on the street outside the home of Jenny Mostra. He grabbed the arrest warrant from the front seat, got out of the patrol car, and took the long walk to the front door. It was just two days earlier when one of their confidential informants, Troy Gado, told the Chaffee County Sherriff's department that Jenny Mostra was providing supplies to her son James so he could live out in the wilderness and avoid capture from law enforcement.

This was to enough justify the arrest warrant for 'harboring a fugitive.' It was the second time he'd been to this house. The first time he'd come looking for James, who wasn't there.

He approached the house and when Jenny opened the door, she rolled her eyes and said, "What do you want? Jimmy ain't here."

"I am here for you. We know that you have been supplying your son with food so he can camp out and avoid taking responsibility for his actions."

"That was someone else. I haven't seen him months," she lied.

Officer Cortese ignored her denial. He handed her a summons and told her that because of the COVID-19 restrictions, he wasn't going to book her and take her to jail. Because technically her offense was considered non-violent, she would just receive a court summons. She was not at all pleased.

"Go to hell," she told him and grabbed the paperwork and then said with disdain, "Now, get off my property!" Officer Cortese left without facial expression or comment. It was now common that people felt emboldened to rail against the police. He was getting tired of it all, but he didn't anticipate any show of respect from this woman. That attitude was passed down to her sons.

***

"The tree of liberty must be refreshed from time to time with the blood of patriots and tyrants."
--Thomas Jefferson

***

Six days later

The wind was increasing from the pressure system coming off Mt. Princeton in the Collegiate Mountain Range in Chaffee County. Several of the peaks were above tree line, and the local range has the highest density of 14ers in the state, a reference to mountains greater than 14,000 feet in elevation above sea level.

It was a pretty bold move, although some might classify it as stupid, for Jimmy Mostra to be parked in front of the house at 8:00p.m. on a clear and beautiful summer evening. The house was located down a dirt driveway over 100 feet long. He could see a play area for kids in the back, a small deck and a hand-built wooden doghouse on the side of the property. He wasn't sure what he wanted to do, but he knew he wanted to do something. Jimmy wasn't big on making a plan, so he'd just wing it, as he usually did.

At this moment, he didn't care if anyone saw him. It was payback time. At this moment, he wanted to make a point. At this moment, he wanted everyone to know that messing with him was a bad idea. It was even worse if you messed with his ma. It could get you hurt. It could get your family hurt. And Jimmy Mostra was going to be the guy to inflict such pain.

He puffed out his chest and imagined he was like Sylvester Stallone in a *Rambo* movie. Nobody messes with Rambo. Well, they could try, but they'd regret it. Revenge was sweet, he thought to himself. With renewed confidence, Jimmy moved the lever to the right and put two 12-gauge shells into his Remington double-barrel shotgun. He looked around the property that the Cortese family called home and took aim.

He sprayed two rounds of buckshot into the doghouse, splintering wood and ripping out half of the roof. "That ought to get noticed," he muttered to himself. He paused and wasn't sure what to do next. Then he saw the dog in the backyard, and it noticed Jimmy and started barking.

He wasn't sure who was at home and he thought about reloading and taking aim at a window. That would sure make his presence known. But then he got a little nervous when a thought crossed his mind: *I don't want to go back to jail.* As much as he'd like to stay and terrorize whoever was in the house, it was time to go. He made his way back to his car and quickly drove away.

Six days later

> *Hey Cortese,*
>
> *I just finished interviewing my confidential informant about a drug case, and your name came up. Jimmy Mostra is apparently out from hiding in the woods and is couch-surfing with some of his low-life friends. He's been popping off about how pissed he is that you issued a felony warrant on his mother. The CI heard him say that he was going to kill you. He knows where you live and described your house perfectly. WATCH YOUR BACK!*
>
> *Sergeant Rusty Barnes,*
> *Buena Vista Police Department*

Sergeant Cortese read the email with disgust. This confirmed what a completely different CI told a different law enforcement officer the day before. Jimmy Mostra was after him. He also saw vague threatening posts on Jimmy's Facebook. The CI also said that Jimmy told his friends that if he got caught, he was going to take down at least four police officers.

Maybe it was big talk from Jimmy, *but what if it wasn't?* Throw in drug use and the fact that Jimmy was bragging to his friends about what he was planning to do might embolden him enough to carry out his threat.

The threat was real, and a rat backed into a corner was unpredictable. Some criminals want to go out in a blaze of glory. The sergeant would have to be on high alert even more than usual.

Sergeant Cortese was not afraid for his life. He could handle Jimmy Mostra if he tried to attack him. Cortese was the quintessential warrior. But his family's safety was another matter. He couldn't watch over them 24-7.

He felt sick in his stomach thinking about someone hurting his wife, Catherine, or his two boys, Dominic, age 6 and Mikel, age 5. It was only yesterday that Dominic asked him why the doghouse was broken. When he looked at it, he knew it wasn't broken from a gust of wind; he could still see pellets in the wood planks. It was lit up by a 12-gauge shotgun.

One of the advantages of being in law enforcement in your hometown was that you knew every square inch of the area, its history and its people. In a small town, the police knew just about everybody.

Officer Cortese knew of the Mostra clan and was in high school the same time as Jimmy's younger brother. But on the flipside, everyone knew you, so it wasn't that hard for Jimmy Mostra to figure out where the Cortese family lived. It was time to implement Operation Hurricane.

Sergeant Cortese received a real threat to himself personally a few years ago, and it was afterwards that they decided to get a protective dog. Their choice was a Doberman Pinscher and they also installed security cameras. This was a common move for law enforcement officers. When he arrived home, Catherine saw the look in his eyes and knew that something was not right.

"We need to talk," he stated calmly. "Take a look at this," Jesse said and handed Cat his smart phone which displayed the email from Sergeant Barnes.

"Who is this guy?" Cat asked and Jesse explained the background and some of the latest activities of Jimmy Mostra.

"We need to do the Hurricane drill," he stated and called out for his boys. "It's time for a family meeting," and they all sat at the kitchen table. "Do you boys remember the Hurricane drill?" he asked the children.

"Yes, that's where we go and lock ourselves in the secret hiding spot if there is a bad guy in the house," Dominic replied.

"That's correct. You go and hide quickly *and* calmly," Jesse replied, nodding his head. "There is a bad man who doesn't want to go to jail. He broke the law many times and hurt people, so he needs to be put away. He wants to hurt Daddy, but you know I won't let that happen."

"And Mommy will be in the hiding spot to protect you too," Cat told them in a steady voice. Catherine was very comfortable with her pump-action 20-gauge shotgun. She was the daughter of a forty-year veteran police officer, and she'd also seen threats against her father.

She wasn't exactly used to having threats against her husband and their family, but she wasn't going to freak out. She was mentally tough, and her mama bear instincts came out in full force. She had resolve and would have no qualms protecting her family from Jimmy Mostra or anyone else for that matter. She'd give her life for them.

The Hurricane drill had the kids go to their secret hiding spot and Cat would call 9-1-1 and be on guard. The other part of the drill is for Jesse to clear the rooms in the house as well as to look for threats outside. He knew it was Jimmy Mostra that shot up the doghouse. But he didn't have any proof and was unlikely to get any.

Jesse was glad that his wife and children took these drills seriously, and had a warrior mindset like himself, but he hated that they had to do it in the first place. He was starting to wonder if it was all worth it.

Luckily, they were just drills, but this latest incident was definitely too close for comfort. He taught the kids early that there is good and evil in the world. And sometimes you had to fight to overcome the evil.

When they would be out in a store or a public place, they'd practice reading people, looking for nonverbal cues. He taught them to always be aware of their surroundings. Since he started them at a young age, it came naturally to them, and they were surprisingly good at it for kids who hadn't learned their multiplication tables yet.

Maybe it tainted their childhood innocence a bit, but he wanted those boys to be like Boy Scouts: *be prepared.*

Jesse and Cat taught them to also rely on the strength of God's goodness, and not just focus on bad things and bad people. Working in this job, it is easy to get cynical about people, and he didn't want that attitude passed on to the kids.

Jesse simply allowed all future events to be in God's hands. If he didn't have faith, he'd probably go crazy from paranoia and wouldn't be able to function. "I trust in you," he said silently. Luckily, the evening ended without incident.

Two days later, July 4, 2020

Sergeant William Plackner of the Chaffee County Sheriff's department headed towards the house that had been raided just yesterday. The confidential informant, Troy Gado had proven useful with identifying where Jimmy Mostra was hanging out. A neighbor had also provided a tip that Jimmy had been at the house for the last few days.

Yesterday, a warrant was issued to search the property of Richard Hoffman, one of Mostra's buddies, where they found a 12-gauge shotgun and more ammo, but no Mostra. The informant also told them that Jimmy had been borrowing Richard's moped.

The plan was to have Sergeant Plackner go back to the house to look for Jimmy, and he would be assisted by Sergeant Shane Garcia and Officer Megan DiGirolamo of the Buena Vista Police Department.

"I'm approaching the house," Plackner stated over the radio.

But before he could reach the house, he saw a man on a moped drive onto the street from around the back of the house. The man turned and looked at the sergeant's patrol SUV. He went in the opposite direction and revved the little engine for all it was worth.

"He's on the move, riding the moped, heading west on county road 306," Plackner stated. Within a minute, all three patrol cars were chasing Jimmy, with sirens blaring and lights flashing. There was no way a moped was going to outrun the patrol cars, but like a rabbit being chased, Jimmy Mostra was hoping to outmaneuver them.

Jimmy turned left into an open field, hoping the police would give up, but the patrol cars followed him. The field was relatively flat, but it was not a road and both Mostra and the police were bouncing around going a mere 12 miles an hour.

In the old days, one of the patrol cars could have tried to get ahead of Mostra and use his vehicle to block the path of the moped. But the "pursuit" protocols had changed, and the officers were no longer allowed to do that. They had to allow an "avenue for escape" to protect the safety of the person being pursued. This policy allowed Jimmy the opportunity to continue his quest to escape from law enforcement.

The field ended and Jimmy cut through someone's backyard and back onto a road, heading towards downtown Buena Vista. The three officers drove to the edge of the field, along a small fence line to avoid going through the backyard, and they were quickly able to return to the road.

"He keeps reaching into his jacket pocket for something, but I can't tell what it is," Sergeant Plackner reported as he was pursuing directly behind Jimmy.

All the officers were aware of Jimmy's threats to Sergeant Cortese personally, and his threats to take down police officers before being captured. He was ripe for shootout with the police and a 'suicide-by-cop' ending. Were there more weapons that they didn't find at the house last night?

The town of Buena Vista was proud to present its annual Independence Day parade, and it epitomized the nostalgia of small-town America. It was a favorite for both locals and visitors. But this July was like no other, and the town had barely started opening back up for business after the coronavirus shutdown. Many large events and festivals were already cancelled, and the town's parade was one of them.

Some local residents decided to create their own parade with their personal cars and trucks. It was not a formal event, but about 50 vehicles followed a designated route, waving flags and honking their horns. The streets were not shut down, so they just had to drive and obey the normal traffic signals. Jimmy Mostra had no idea that he was headed straight for the parade.

There was a lineup of cars at the corner of U.S. Highway 24 and Main Street and Jimmy came zipping by and started waving at the decorated cars going in the opposite direction. With the lights flashing and sirens blaring, some in the parade thought they were part of the festivities and waved back at Jimmy and the police. The three patrol vehicles were in hot pursuit, if you could call it that, at a measly 25 miles an hour.

But a crowded street is exactly the type of situation that made the officers tense. Would Jimmy try to dart in front of one of the parade cars to elude the police and cause an accident? Would he jump off the moped and try to carjack someone in the parade? Would he look to take a tourist hostage? Or would he just stop the moped and have a shootout right there in downtown, looking for an infamous ending?

Jimmy was confident that he could elude capture. He'd been successful so far, and he just needed to take his moped where the police would be unable to follow him. Main Street in downtown Buena Vista was barely ½ mile long, and Jimmy was soon headed towards the Arkansas River and the railroad tracks.

County Road 371 is a rough washboard dirt road that Jimmy knew well, and it ran parallel to the river and railroad tracks. He took it north. Just outside of town, the road became even rougher, so the pursuit was still at a 12 mile an hour crawl.

"DiGirolamo, this road will break your car. Go back to Highway 24 and see if you can get a few miles north of here to head him off," Sergeant Garcia instructed.

"Copy that," she replied and noticed that every piece of paperwork that was in a folder was now all over her front seat.

Jimmy had one more trick up his sleeve, so he drove his moped onto the railroad tracks.

"Garcia, go to the RV park and try to cut him…oh, boy!" Sergeant Plackner exclaimed as he bottomed out in a pothole.

Sergeant Garcia stopped his SUV and doubled back and headed towards the local RV park a few miles away to where he could access the railroad tracks while Sergeant Plackner continued his pursuit.

Jimmy continued on the tracks and then to a bridge over the Arkansas River. The bridge was barely wide enough for Plackner's SUV, but he continued to pursue. He'd come this far and this close to catching Jimmy, so he wasn't going to let him go unless it was absolutely necessary. Jimmy continued at the 12 mile an hour pace.

A mile later, Jimmy was looking for his next place to turn before reaching a small tunnel coming up. He could take County Road 375 and head towards the Turtle Rock campground. But looking for the turn-off meant that he took his eyes off of the front wheel of his moped, which turned out to be his crucial mistake as he crashed the moped.

Sergeant Plackner stopped his SUV, jumped out as Jimmy was trying to stand up. He took a swing at the sergeant but missed wildly and Plackner easily wrestled him to the ground.

Jimmy smelled like beer and he seemed to be high on something. It was quite the training day for a rookie deputy who was in the patrol SUV with Sergeant Plackner.

The two men soon had Jimmy subdued and cuffed. The 'high-speed' pursuit was over.

**

Deputy Dakoda Defurio and Sergeant Jesse Cortese

Five Fun facts About Jesse Cortese:

1. A fan of the pop music group, the *Spice Girls.*
2. Played Defensive Back at Nazarene University, Olathe, Kansas.
3. Graduated from Buena Vista High School with a 3.9 G.P.A.
4. The oldest of 6 children of Tony and Donna Cortese.
5. Former lead singer in a hard-core rock band.

II.

Through Smoke and Flames

September 27, 2007

"It's almost done," said the tattoo artist and continued, "it's going to look great."

He nodded to the artist in agreement and watched him grab a tissue and dab a small drop of blood that was coming out of the rose he had just created on his bicep. "Well, that's appropriate," he thought to himself.

He looked down again, seeing that his skin was red and slightly swollen from the creation of a rose, sword, and six leaves. It was perfect.

The tattoo also included a date and her name. He looked at the date that would be forever recorded on his right bicep. Of course, it took him back to exactly one year ago, and his mind flooded with the memories of a day that he would never forget. But the tattoo wasn't about him and his memories, it was about *her*.

For the past few months, he was at peace with everything that had happened, but it took a long time and many restless nights to get there. He knew that getting the tattoo was going to temporarily bring back the torment that he experienced for months.

He was right, those feelings were resurfacing as his heart rate became elevated and his mouth was suddenly dry. But he also knew in his heart, soul, mind, and most of all, in his gut that he needed a permanent reminder of what happened that day. He needed a *permanent reminder* of her. He was hoping that this reminder would also let him stop feeling guilty for wanting to move on.

59

In the aftermath, he was constantly thinking about the sequence of events. The counselors they provided allowed all of them to express everything they thought and felt. They were told to make peace with it. Not to forget, but to let it go. *Easy to say, but not at all easy to do.* He could never forget, but he also couldn't let it eat him alive. And he wasn't the only one, all the people in the group sessions had the same feelings, and some were dealing with it better than others.

He used to take out the memorial flyer every day and look at it. He would just stare at her picture. And it would weigh on him. Life didn't seem normal for a long time. What was *normal* anymore?

For months, he wasn't sure how or when he was going to be relieved of the burden. But at least he had the opportunity to move on, whereas she would *never* get that opportunity to get over it, find closure, move on, or get on with any kind of life. Her outcome was permanent.

He would also stare at her name on the flyer, wishing he could have met her. He frequently contemplated having just *five minutes* with her. He could learn so much about her and the light behind those bright eyes.

But he could only have the conversation with her inside of his head. Once again, thinking *why couldn't I have done more*? Why did this have to happen to you? It started out as a normal day that turned down a path that no one could have envisioned.

I wanted to help you. *I wanted to save you.* I was running on adrenaline and instinct and honestly would have given my life for yours.

That thought weighed heavily on his mind, and then the guilt shifted, picturing someone telling his family that *he wasn't coming back.* But he knew deep down that he wouldn't have hesitated to make the trade. That was just how he was built.

But he couldn't trade his life, because the evil one wouldn't let him. The evil one wouldn't let anyone help you, and his thoughts continued. I am sorry. Why am I here and you are not? Is that fair? He still couldn't make any sense of what happened. How could he? How could anyone? I am *truly sorry* that somehow, I let you down. *Can you ever forgive me?*

Then his thoughts shifted to his conversations with God. I need to make sense of this. I need to understand how it fits into the bigger plan. Tell me *why* it happened. But he knew that some things are a mystery, and God has a plan for all of us, but that doesn't mean that all of us understand it as it unfolds in our life. I can't understand it, but I trust in His divine will and judgment. *Can you at least give me the strength to carry on?* Will you please take care of her?

Somehow, he sensed a bit of strength and peace, and felt God's presence was with him, propping him up to face the world. He was calmer, and his heart rate lowered and because of his faith in Jesus, he knew where he was going when he died.

The man breathed heavily and took one more look at the artist's handiwork. The tattoo would be a constant reminder, but the constant torment was over. *Finally.*

It had six leaves for those who would continue to grow and live, and a sword for those who confronted the evil one. And finally, it had a red rose representing 16-year-old Emily Keyes who drew her last breath on September 27, 2006.

***

Meet Dean Morgan, age 46

Follower of Christ

Man

Son

Brother

Husband

Uncle

Father

Daddy

Patriot

American

High School Varsity Soccer and Baseball Player

Chief of Police, Town of Buena Vista, CO

Former SWAT Team Leader

"She was always something special
A diamond shining bright in the rain
Everybody dreams of angels
No one will ever know
How much I loved you so"
-- **L.A. Guns**, *Ballad of Jayne*

367 Days Earlier
September 25, 2006
11:15p.m.

"I'm sorry baby, I really am," she exclaimed. Peggy had seen that menacing look before, and she was afraid. When he got that look in his eyes, the rage could be set off by the smallest thing, the most illogical thing, and she knew that he just wanted to lash out at somebody. Unfortunately, she was that somebody. She's always been his punching bag.

"Sorry isn't going to cut it," he yelled at her. "I am sick of this shit, and I am sick of you!" he said, pointing directly at her. He could be mad at anything, the way she looked, if the house was clean or not, what television show she was watching, how the kids were behaving, the lack of money, her cooking or his assumption that everyone was talking about him behind his back.

That part was true, everyone knew her predicament, and they did gossip about him. And he deserved every bit of criticism because his behavior was mostly reprehensible. He wasn't a good husband, been mostly unemployed for almost a decade, doing odd jobs here and there until he showed up drunk and got fired. He certainly wasn't a good father, and nowhere near the role model she wanted her kids to have. They had been married for a dozen years and exactly 11½ of them being the worst years of her life.

So yes, it was true that she complained to anyone who would listen, for all the good that would do. She was always embarrassed at his behavior, which would frequently result in a black eye for her and something destroyed within the house. She stopped counting the number of times a window was broken from Rowland throwing something wildly at her in his drunken stupor. Broken windows weren't that bad in the summer, but it was late September in Bailey, Colorado which sits at an altitude of 7,739 feet, so it was quickly dropping below 40 degrees after sunset.

His ego was fragile, and just the thought of her and her friends gossiping about what a piece of trash he was, really got his blood boiling. And tonight's rage was no different. She had simply mentioned that her friend Janine was over watching a television program after she put her boys to bed. Janine was long gone before Rowland came home. Janine was no dummy, and she knew that Rowland wasn't going to come home in a good mood. He never does.

"Honey, why don't you just go to bed? We can talk about it in the morning," she tried to reason with him. He didn't notice her sad and lonely eyes.

"I don't want to go to bed," he continued to yell. "I want to teach you a lesson." Thirty-seven-year-old Rowland Burke told her and puffed out his chest, trying to make his 5' 7" and 195-pound portly frame seem larger and more ominous.

He pointed his index finger at her forehead and then moved his thumb upwards, so it was in the shape of a gun, and then curled his index finger to signify the pulling of a trigger. That scared her even more because she didn't know what he was going to do. And then her fear was justified.

From under his shirt, he pulled out a revolver and wagged it in front of her face.

"Put that away, you'll wake the kids," she cried, trying to appeal to some semblance of fatherly duty. If it weren't for her two little ones sleeping upstairs, *maybe* she would do something to make a change. She'd tell herself lies and make excuses for his behavior. She never truly convinced herself, but it was enough for her to continue. Maybe he'll change, maybe when the kids were older, maybe she could get a decent job. But it was always *someday*, and never today. In a rare moment when she was honest with herself, she would admit that she was scared to leave him.

She started to back away and move to the other side of the kitchen table, and that's when his foot caught on a chair leg and he stumbled and yelled "I am so sick of living with you." He then pulled out his revolver, pointed straight up towards the ceiling, and took two shots.

She flinched when the deafening sound reverberated throughout the small wooden cabin. She screamed in fright. He'd previously brandished the weapon when he was in one of his anger rages, but he never actually pulled the trigger. He was pointing it away from her, but the kids were on the second floor. She didn't have time to think about whether he was standing right below the boys' room or their own bedroom.

"No!" she screamed and move towards him, trying to push him towards and out the front door. But thirty-two-year-old Peggy Burke, weighing only 105 pounds, was not going to physically win any battles with Rowland. He was mean enough to push her around and beat her up, but was he crazy enough to shoot his own children? She didn't know and didn't want to take the chance. She managed to push him another few steps towards the front, but then he turned around and rested his back on the front door. Her momentum made her take another step towards him, he looked down and they were eye to eye.

He grabbed the back of her neck and moved it towards him and slowly pulled his weapon up to her face. He squeezed her neck and she involuntarily gasped and opened her mouth. That's when he put the pistol inside of it.

***

11:56p.m.

It took Dean and Andrea Morgan a little over two hours to drive the 125 miles to Buena Vista from his cousin's wedding in South Fork on the previous day. It was a long day and he was looking forward to crawling into his own bed and getting a good night's sleep. But that wasn't going to happen for a long time.

His phone rang, "Morgan?"

"I'm here."

"We've got a domestic violence situation in Bailey, shots have been fired and the SWAT team is getting organized so we need you to get on the scene as soon as you can."

"OK, I'm leaving now," he stated. Andrea gave him that look, as if to say, "Really? We just got home and you have to go out now."

After grabbing his tactical gear, he gave her a quick kiss goodbye. "Stay safe," she quietly replied.

***

September 26, 2006

12:15a.m.

Rowland's drunken rage continued. Peggy started to cry, but with the pistol stuck between her teeth, she couldn't enunciate her words. The steel felt cold on her tongue and she wondered to herself, is this really going to be the way it ends? Who's going to take care of the kids? *I hope they take them away from him if I'm gone.*

Rowland just stared at her, feeling pretty powerful that he got his wife in this position of complete submission, and her life was dependent on his whim. He could pull the trigger, or not. It was all up to him and no one else. And she couldn't do a damn thing about it.

The thought of her completely helpless and with him in total control made this the best part of his day. That twisted and cruel thought brought up a hearty laugh. It was the wicked laugh of someone who had no control over his own life, so the only thing he could do was take it out on his wife.

His laughter turned into a loud beer belch, which then caused him to laugh even more. This relaxed his arm and the gun slipped out of her mouth.

Peggy darted from him and towards the stairs with the goal of going upstairs to protect the boys. But even if she could get to their room first and lock it, he could easily bust down the door. What if in his fit of rage he went to hurt her and instead, shot one of the boys? She hesitated after reaching the fifth step.

"Get back here!" he yelled at her and stumbled towards her. In his drunken stupor, he tripped on his own feet and fell face-first onto the floor.

She looked around, thinking she had a moment to run away. Or fight back. She decided to run.

Peggy went to the front door, opened it as quickly as she could and ran outside. She had her car keys in her pants pocket and tried to get into the car, thinking she should drive towards downtown for help.

But it didn't take long for Rowland to get up and shoot at her while she was fumbling to open up the car door. And similar to an overused movie scene, the panicked female dropped her keys. But her clumsiness probably saved her life. He fired two shots at her but missed her high and wide, hitting the car instead. That's when she heard the sirens. She looked back at him and determined that he heard them too.

As several police vehicles pulled up the driveway, he went back inside and slammed the door.

"It's my husband, and he tried to shoot me. But I've got two kids in the house and I don't know what he's going to do," Peggy nervously said to the first SWAT team member that jumped out of the van. She was ushered to the team leader so he could get a sense of what had happened. She relayed the sequence of events to the officer in a hurried and somewhat frazzled tone.

Detective Dean Morgan was a member of the Park County SWAT team, who were surrounding the house and trying to get an assessment of what was happening inside. Detective Morgan had experience with domestic violence situations, and it was always the unpredictability and volatility of the situation that increased the danger for the victims and the officers as well.

The violent person was almost always in a highly emotional and agitated state, and frequently intoxicated or on drugs. What was this guy going to do? Was he going to shoot his kids? Was he going to shoot himself? *Was he going to do both?* Would he instead try to shoot at the officers through a window? Nobody knew, *and that was the problem.*

"Rowland Burke, we know you are in there. We don't want anyone to get hurt. Put your weapon down and come out of the house with your hands up," the SWAT team leader said over a megaphone. It was met with silence.

More silence.

Peggy watched from the end of the driveway and was hoping they would get lucky and he would just pass out. But *hope* is not an effective strategy. She wondered how they'd know if he did pass out since they didn't have good visibility into the house because most of the curtains were closed. There was tension building because of the unknown. What would Rowland do next? What was his anger level?

Tick, tock.

It could go in a multitude of directions, and most of them were bad outcomes. SWAT team member Dean Morgan prayed the guy would just give up, and not turn it into a bloody scene, especially with two boys under ten-years-old in the house.

Luckily, his wish came true. Rowland Burke slowly opened the door without his gun, put his hands up, and said "OK, I give up." All the SWAT team members breathed a sigh of relief. This was the desired outcome. This is what they wanted. This time they got lucky, and Rowland followed the SWAT commander's instructions perfectly.

***

11 hours later

After getting home at 7:00a.m., and after grabbing just a few hours of sleep, Detective Morgan was back at work in the police department building in Fairplay to get a warrant prepared. As the lead detective on the case, he wanted the warrant so they could return to the house and extract the bullets from the ceiling and the doors of the car.

He had heard Peggy's full story and also wanted to get a warrant for a DNA test on the revolver. He'd seen too many times where a wife or girlfriend would change their story, and try to take the blame herself. But if there was DNA evidence on the inside barrel of that gun, it would override whatever excuse she made for the useless piece of humanity that she called her husband.

***

September 27, 2006

11:41a.m.

<u>Actual audio recordings</u>
<u>(slightly edited for clarification purposes):</u>

Dispatch:	"OK, I have the teacher, hold on."
Sandra Smith:	"This is Mrs. Smith."
Dispatch:	"Mrs. Smith, what happened? You don't know who this man is?"
Sandra Smith	"No."
Dispatch:	"Do you know how old this man is?"
Sandra Smith:	"40's."
Dispatch:	"When did he come in and what did he do?"
Sandra Smith:	"He came into the classroom while I was talking to my class. He set a backpack down in the back of the class. I went back and approached him because I didn't recognize him and asked if I could help him with something. And he pulled a gun."
Dispatch:	"Do you know what kind of gun?
Sandra Smith:	"A black square-ish looking handgun."
Dispatch:	"Then what?"

Sandra Smith:	"He said to go to the front of the room and face the blackboard."
Dispatch:	"I'm going to have you hang on a second." Dispatch is relaying the information to the officers in route to the school.
Sandra Smith, talking to someone else:	"Are they still in my room? I shouldn't have left them." (she starts to cry and moan, with her voice audibly shaking.)
Dispatch:	"Ma'am if we didn't know about this, we couldn't help those kids. Don't beat yourself up, okay?"
Sandra Smith:	"OK." (in a trembling voice)
Dispatch:	"Hold on I'm talking to law enforcement." (pauses for a moment) "Go ahead and continue."
Sandra Smith:	"I resisted. I said I can't let you put all these kids in danger. Then he yelled and told all of the kids to go to the front of the room and face the blackboard. And they did. And I didn't. And he pointed the gun at me. I said I can't let you put these kids' lives in danger. He said if you don't want to be hurt, just do what I told you."

72

Dispatch:	"Hold on. I need to interrupt you. How long have you been out of the room? We have more law enforcement in route."
Sandra Smith:	"Five minutes. There are six kids still in my room!" (voice starting to tremble)
Dispatch:	"OK."
Sandra Smith:	"He started going down the line and started asking their names and then said, 'you get out of here,' and told probably half the kids to get out of there. And then he got to me and told me to get out of there. And I said, "I can't just leave these kids here." (starts to cry) "He pointed the gun at me again and said 'don't worry about it, just get out of here.' But make sure nobody gets back in."
Dispatch:	"OK, I need to relay this to the officers." (a few seconds of inaudible speaking.)
Dispatch:	"When you were leaving, what else did he say? Did he give any kind of explanation or reason?"
Sandra Smith:	"No, he said 'get out and if anyone comes back in this room, I have enough explosives in this bag to blow up the school.'"

***

Around 11:35a.m. the gunman entered teacher Sandra Smith's Honors English class in Room 206 at Platte Canyon High School. After the first time Mrs. Smith refused to leave, he pulled out a Smith & Wesson 40-caliber Glock 22 and shot it once into the ceiling. He ordered all of the male students as well as Mrs. Smith out of the room.

He then made all of the remaining female students face the chalkboard. He claimed to have a backpack full of C-4 explosives. His backpack was loaded with duct tape, handcuffs, knives, a stun-gun, rope, scissors, massage oil, sex toys, another handgun and many rounds of ammunition. At 12:15p.m., he released one student. Six now remained in Room 206.

As the SWAT van rushed down U.S. Highway 285 into the mountain town of Bailey, Colorado, team member Detective Dean Morgan got his first glimpse of the kids getting evacuated from the school. It was an eerie and surreal picture, and it instantly brought back memories of seeing a video of a similar scene at the Columbine High School shooting in 1999.

It was as if someone punched him in the stomach and he felt physical pain while watching innocent kids being led away from the school. His stomach churned and a thousand thoughts ran through his head, all of them trying to determine one thing: *How can we prevent this from turning into another Columbine?*

Detective Morgan rushed up the stairs to the second floor. Most of the kids on this floor were still hunkered down in their classrooms. Park County Sheriff Wagner started to evacuate the kids on the second floor, and Detective Morgan immediately noticed the fear in their eyes.

Some were crying, and although they didn't know exactly what was happening, they all must have heard the gunshot, so they know for certain that it wasn't a drill. They're wondering if their friends are going to make it out alive. Has someone already been hurt, or worse? Is there more than one gunman? How many gunshots would they hear that day?

He saw them plead with their eyes for help. And SWAT member Dean Morgan promised to be the help that these kids needed. He had a look of steely resolve that provided reassurance that most of the teenagers were too scared to notice.

There were seven Park County SWAT team members now on the scene. It would be a while before the Jefferson County bomb squad and additional SWAT teams drove the 35 miles to the high school. Morgan and the other team members were advised by dispatch about what Mrs. Smith knew of the situation before she was forced out. The team set up right outside Room 206.

"The guy is crouched behind a television stand in there with six girls in the room," Sergeant Glenn Hardey told the team. "He's got his arm around one girl's neck with the gun to her head. This is real." Someone tried to peer into the small glass window of the classroom door.

"I'm going to kill everyone if I see you!" the gunman yelled. "Don't try to come in here or everyone is dead." This immediately caused panic and there were screams of pure fright from the group of mostly sophomore girls. It also heightened the stress level of the SWAT members. The result was exactly what the *evil one* intended. They were all on high alert for another gunshot. After the screams stopped, the silence was deafening. The SWAT team patiently waited.

Tick, tock.

"What does this guy want? Has he made any demands?" a SWAT member asked.

"No, nothing yet," answered Captain Mark Hancock. "Look, it's going to be at least another half hour before those Jefferson County guys get here. We have to be ready for the possibility that this maniac starts shooting again. We must contain this if it turns active. We are going to take action and go in to stop everything. I want to negotiate first and keep this guy calm. I'll try asking again."

"Why don't you let the girls go? What do you want? I'm sure we can work this out," he stated at the door of Room 206, hoping that the gunman would respond with some answer. Perhaps then they would know what motivated him, or what could be negotiated in exchange for releasing the hostages.

The question was met with silence.

And more silence. Cold sweat and tension filled the air.

Morgan stated, "If he starts shooting, (Rod) Greeley you are going to open the door and I'm going to go in behind with our SWAT shield and Sergeant Hardey will be right behind me with the rest of the stack; we've got to take this guy out." The team would gather in "stacks", which is lining up behind the door, ready to enter one after the other. Entrance would be dynamic, fast, but with tactical intent to clear corners and press the target.

Sergeant Hardey gave Morgan the look of 'yeah, we'll get it done if that's what it comes to'. It would be each individual's long walk alone into the ring of danger.

They were ready to risk their own lives to try to save those kids. They knew from an intellectual and emotional basis that there was a good chance the gunman could easily shoot one of the officers.

None of them wanted to die or take unnecessary risks, but that was the mentality of the *sheepdog*. Every SWAT team member had that view of themselves. If they didn't, they shouldn't be on the SWAT team. The sheepdog protects the sheep from the wolf outside. They stood at the thin line, with no questions asked. With no hesitation. And with no reservations.

They would lay it all on the line for those kids, and each other. It is one thing to *say* you'd give your life trying to save those kids, but it is another thing to be in a position where that actual possibility is literally a few feet away. It was a cold sweat reality check. They understood and lived the brotherhood of the badge.

Detective Morgan's biggest fear wasn't for his own life, but the situation where the *evil one* is a moving target with a girl in a chokehold, using her as a human shield. He'd have to be careful. He'd have to be smart. He'd have to be deliberate. He'd have to be quick, and if he took a shot, he'd better be accurate. He was the sheepdog, but he didn't know what that was going to mean on this particular day.

Suddenly, the door opened and hostage #6 was released. The officers scuffled over to her to bring the girl to safety, which set off the gunman.

"Get away!" he screamed. He then made the girls start screaming again and tapping their feet on the ground, as if it was a drum roll with an anticipating crescendo. It was terrifying for everyone and added to the stress level, chaos, and feelings of helplessness. It was exactly what the *evil one* wanted, and he achieved the desired effect.

Then there was only silence.

And more silence.

Tick, tock.

***

"We remember our pain;
we remember our sorrow;
we remember our heroes.
We remember those who in selfless acts of courage,
who in sacrificial dedication
risk all in time of crisis and need."
--**Gino Geraci**, *Columbine High School Memorial*

***

He randomly released another girl. And then another girl came out 30 minutes later.

"Are you hurt? What's happening in there?" the officer asked.

Lynna Long, a 15-year-old sophomore told the officer, that he made the girls line up and face the chalkboard and then sexually assaulted all of them. She was groped above the waist but believes Emily 'got it worse.'

Lynna said that she was afraid to look, "but you could hear Emily saying, `No. Please don't.'" She could not see what he was doing, but she knew the other girls were being molested because "you could hear the rustling of clothes and elastic being snapped and zippers being opened and closed."

During the sexual assaults, the *evil one* held his gun to the hostages' heads and threatened to kill them if they did not cooperate. She had never seen this guy before, and no one knew why Emily was targeted.[1]

The SWAT team members were horrified. They became agitated. They needed to protect these kids, but they didn't want to make the situation worse. Negotiation was preferred and having him give up was the best solution. But the situation could change at any moment, and the unpredictability was almost unbearable.

***

---

[1] Lynna Long and her mother allowed the Rock Mountain News to identify her by name. (source)

1:50p.m.

<u>Last text messages:</u>

John-Michael Keyes: *R U OK?*

Emily Keyes: *I love you guys*

More hostages had been released and the fifth girl came out and told the officers that the *evil one* stated, "Everything's going to be okay; it's all going to be done by 4:00p.m."

4:00p.m. deadline? "What did that mean?" thought Detective Morgan. Was he going to kill the remaining two girls? Would he kill himself? Would he blow up the school and take the girls, himself and many officers with him? What was his end game? Was there a political motivation? Did he want fame? Nobody knew who he was, what his motivations were, or more importantly, what was his next move.

The Jefferson County SWAT team was in command and they put together a hostage-rescue plan. They had fiber-optic cameras to see inside the classroom. The gunman was sitting in a chair against the wall with Emily and another girl being used as a human shield.

A decision was made. The SWAT team had explosives to blow a hole in the drywall with the Jefferson County SWAT team going in first, then Park County, who had never trained with explosives.

They were not going to let 4:00p.m. come around and see what wickedness would be unleashed. They were going in. The plan was to enter Room 206 immediately after the explosives discharged, hopefully distracting the gunman for a second or two so the SWAT team could take a shot. They wanted to save those girls. The teams were running on adrenaline and never had a second thought or hesitation to confront the wolf. It all came down to the next 11 seconds.

3:15p.m.

The two explosive charges burst simultaneously, and each SWAT team rushed in. Emily attempted to escape. A shot was fired by the gunman through his own hand and into the temple of Emily Keyes.

The gunman was shot once but had enough time to turn the gun on himself and fire. At the same time, three more rounds from SWAT pummeled his body.

Actual audio recordings:

"He's down," a SWAT member said over the radio.
"One hit."
"He took the girl with him. Get in medical."
"Medical, go!"

The explosion caused dust and debris from the ceiling tiles to come down like snow. It continued and added to the haunting scene. Detective Dean Morgan had a hard time seeing, as there were just outlines of the tactical team. He turns on his flashlight to see a silhouette of long hair in front of him. He grabbed the second hostage and moved her towards the exit where another officer guided her out.

The medical team was working on Emily. He noticed a letterman jacket and several bras on the floor. They took Emily out of the room and a medical chopper flew her to Denver.

The room became eerie again with silence as dust and debris continued to fall. No bomb materials were ever found.

***

4:32p.m.

Emily Keyes was pronounced dead.

***

The memorial service for Emily Keyes was held on September 30, 2006, and Chief Dean Morgan still has the flyer from that event. About a week later, 5,000 motorcyclists took part in the "Columbine to Canyon Ride", which was dedicated to the victims of both the Columbine and Platte Canyon high school shootings. The procession of motorcycles was so long that the first rider to get to Platte Canyon High School arrived as the final motorcyclists departed from Columbine High School, with two riding alongside each other.

The *I Love U Guys* Foundation was founded in 2006 by the Keyes family and focuses on school safety, education, advocacy, and training. More information can be found at http://iloveyouguys.org/about.html

In Loving Memory

***

July 14, 2012

2:30a.m.

"Come here Digger, I need to talk to you, okay?" asked Sergeant Morgan. Digger responded with just a stare, and in his whiskey-fueled state, he was having a hard time focusing. He'd heard the question but couldn't quite decide what to do.

Dwane "Digger" Dawson was a veteran of the rodeo circuit. He never did make it big, nor was he going to, but he was good enough to annually qualify, albeit in the bottom percentile of wage-earners. Most of those earnings were quickly transferred to the local bartender. It probably would have served him better if he'd lost all of his rodeo skills and found something else to do with his life. But he was just good enough to continue on and have his 33-year-old body beaten season after season; such is the life of a rough-and-tumble rodeo rider.

And that life included lots of drinking and even more fighting. He couldn't even remember what the fight was about at the *Green Parrot Bar*. But he did remember hitting somebody, and then deciding he needed to hightail it out of there. He exited the bar and headed East on Main Street in downtown Buena Vista and that's when he heard his name called out by Sergeant Morgan.

Sergeant Morgan and another officer were called out to the bar for a routine DUI crash. Of course, it wasn't *routine* since he never knew what he was going to encounter, especially at the *Green Parrot Bar*. It had a reputation where locals sought solace in the bottom of a bottle. It was almost as crazy as Leadville's *Golden Nickel Saloon*. After working the DUI crash, he noticed Digger walking out of the bar.

He knew Digger Dawson and didn't think of him as a dangerous man with a dark heart. He was simply a guy who frequently drank too much, didn't make clearly thought-out choices and was easily provoked into exchanging punches.

Sergeant Morgan remembered seeing something about there being a warrant for Digger's arrest, so he decided to detain him. "Just wait here a second; don't be difficult," Sergeant Morgan told him. He contacted dispatch to see if the warrant was still open for Digger Dawson.

Digger recognized the sergeant but didn't want to deal with the police that night. He knew dispatch would come back and confirm that he was a wanted man. Then he faintly heard dispatch reply back to the sergeant, who briefly nodded his understanding. Digger looked over the officer's shoulder towards Main Street, then turned his head to see no one coming from the other direction. With the street empty, he decided to bolt.

Digger ran down the street as fast as he could, but there was a reason cowboy boots weren't the choice of sprinters and in his intoxicated state, he could barely make ten steps before Sergeant Morgan tackled him, both landing hard onto the pavement. Sergeant Morgan quickly rolled Digger over to his stomach, straddled him with his 6'2" and 185-pound frame, and in a few seconds had one arm handcuffed. A moment later, still in the middle of the street, he had both arms cuffed. Digger's entire escape only lasted 25 seconds.

Sergeant Morgan dropped off Mr. Dawson at the county jail in Salida since the town of Buena Vista didn't have jail cells, as is common in rural counties. The officer present for the DUI crash separately took the drunk to the jail in her patrol vehicle.

Sergeant Morgan noticed some scrapes, bruises and a little crick in his neck, so he decided to be prudent and get checked out in the local emergency room. The last thing he wanted was a neck injury that could cause problems months or years later.

After leaving the hospital, he saw the sun was starting to rise in the east. He was thinking about calling it a day after getting clearance from the doctors. It had been a long day, and although Sergeant Morgan didn't know it at the time, his day was about to get much longer.

Two hours earlier

It barely registered to Jerry that in a few months Colorado would have a ballot initiative to legalize marijuana. Jerry was going to score one way or another. Being only eighteen years old, if Amendment 64 passed, he wouldn't meet the twenty-one-year-old age requirement anyway. Not that he gave much thought about following the law. He threw a cold piece of pizza back into the box, took another toke from the bong, and then chased it with a warm beer.

He was feeling pretty good about himself since only a few hours ago he was chased by the Leadville police trying to pick him up on an arrest warrant. But he was able to elude them, outfox them, outsmart them, and quite frankly, been able to show off his superior driving skills. Little did he know that it wasn't his racecar driver talents nor the performance of his 2003 Ford Taurus, but rather his wild maneuvers on county roads in the middle of the night resulted in a decision by Lake County Deputy Bryce Hinton to give up his pursuit.

The deputy clocked Jerry going 18 miles over the speed limit on County Road 11, just outside of the Leadville city limits. He started to pursue with the intention of issuing a traffic citation, but Jerry decided to flee. It was just too dangerous, and policy dictated that Hinton should not continue pursuing for merely a traffic violation. He had pursued him long enough to recognize that the driver was Jerry Hernandez, so he decided to return to the Sherriff's office and write up a warrant for his arrest of trying elude an officer. He knew where he lived and he would look for him at the trailer park when daylight hit and he received his warrant.

But the truth and seeing a situation clearly wasn't something Jerry frequently concerned himself with. He was feeling proud of his ability to elude the law, but his relationship skills were another matter.

He arrogantly scoffed at the notion that his girlfriend was getting tired of his antics of teenage rebellion. Lisa Othello had seen too many of her four siblings marry a deadbeat.

She wanted something a little bit better, and she knew deep in her heart that Jerry was headed down a rathole future that probably included being a drug addict, a deadbeat dad, constantly unemployed, and perpetually poor. She was not impressed with his ability to outrun the long arm of the law. She'd skipped out around 2:00a.m., and Jerry guessed that he might not be hooking up with her anymore, let alone anytime soon.

Feeling a little overconfident after smoking a strain with high THC, he decided he needed a little fun. And what better fun could there be than to show the deputy again that he couldn't catch Jerry? *Catch me if you can.* At that moment, nothing seemed more fun than another chase where he outwitted the police. He also wanted to show off some of his recent Amazon Prime purchases.

It only took a few minutes for him to drive to the Lake County Sherriff's Office in the small mountain town of Leadville. He revved his car engine, turned the steering wheel and hit the accelerator. He started doing donuts in the police parking lot. After about fifteen seconds, he slammed on the brakes and the car skidded to a stop, but nothing happened, and no one came out. Frustrated, he honked his horn, waited a few seconds, honked his horn again and started doing more burn-out moves in the parking lot.

He was successful in getting the attention of Deputy Hinton, and as he opened the door to see what was going on in the parking lot, Jerry drove recklessly into the street. Deputy Hinton jumped in his patrol SUV and once again, the chase was on.

But Jerry's driving skills failed him this time because within two minutes, he went down a dead-end street. He realized his mistake and started thinking about his escape options.

He was soon instructed by the deputy to slowly get out of his car. He opened the door, stepped out and squinted at the bright lights in front of him. Jerry allowed the handgun in his waistband to be clearly visible to the deputy. Now he needed to decide whether to give up or run. He decided on the third option

After being instructed by Officer Hinton to get down on the ground, he pulled a grenade out of his pocket, and threw it at the patrol vehicle.

Hinton, who was standing in front of his vehicle, saw the grenade come towards him wide right, but it was going to land close enough to potentially hurt him in an explosion. He drew his weapon, took a step back while still keeping an eye on Jerry, fired two quick shots and crouched behind the car. Putting the engine block of his SUV between him and the threat provided the most protection from a grenade explosion or any shots fired at him. He curled his body up into a ball, expecting the blast.

It had cost Jerry less than $20 to buy authentic looking toy grenades from Amazon. And in the dark, they looked even more real to Deputy Hinton. Throwing the grenade gave Jerry enough time to get back into his car, start it up and escape out of the dead-end street.

Hinton was expecting a blast that never came. Maybe it was a dud, he had no idea, and the only thing he knew is that some kid just tried to blow him up. This *kid* had now committed a felony and was a public threat that must be pursued. This eighteen-year-old was no kid, and his actions were the stuff of hardened adult criminals.

He saw Jerry's car barely squeeze by his patrol SUV on the narrow road. It looked like blood was coming from Jerry's right shoulder and the back window of the Taurus had been shot out. Hinton fired two more shots at the vehicle, but it kept on going and he heard the engine whine from Jerry's Ford Taurus as he headed south on U.S. Highway 24. The chase was on once again.

The Taurus sped out of Leadville and immediately entered a sparsely populated area and a long straightaway section of the highway. The only thing that was going to stop him now was hitting a deer or a moose. "Caution and prudence" were not part of his vocabulary, so he continued to rip down the highway at 115 miles per hour.

Soon Jerry had to decide, either try to take Colorado Highway 82 and its windy two-lane road over Independence Pass towards Aspen, or go straight south towards the town of Buena Vista. He decided he would go with speed and continued south.

Deputy Hinton was in an SUV that had a difficult time keeping up with the Taurus. Another Lake County deputy and a Leadville police officer joined him, and he asked the dispatcher to see if anyone in Chaffee County could help.

A few minutes later, the Taurus crossed into Chaffee County. The only officer on duty at 6:30 a.m. was Sergeant Dean Morgan. He was informed that Lake County was calling for mutual aid and that shots have been fired. He rushed to the north side of town with the intention of setting Stop Sticks near a secluded area, but because they were moving so fast, he didn't have time to set up the maneuver.

Stop Sticks are used to puncture the tires when its hollow spikes break off into the tire, forcing air to be vented quickly but without causing a blowout. Hard plastic Stop Sticks replaced the bulky metal Spike Strips that were more difficult to deploy.

Sergeant Morgan crouched behind a guardrail with his rifle. He could see the Taurus tearing down the highway, the public threat coming towards him. Policing protocol allowed the sergeant to attempt to stop the felon; he took two shots but missed. He jumped in his Dodge Charger and joined the pursuit. The Taurus traveled the 39 miles between Leadville and Buena Vista in under 20 minutes.

The Taurus blew through the stoplights in Buena Vista, miraculously not causing an accident and merged onto U.S. Highway 285, still heading south on the mostly straight highway towards the small town of Poncha Springs, just 24 miles beyond. Sergeant Samuel Livingston of the Buena Vista police department was also called in from his residence to help pursue the fleeing car, which was just ahead of Morgan.

As every minute clicked by, Sergeant Morgan knew there would be more people on the road as the county started to wake up on this sun filled Colorado summer morning. The Taurus started weaving back and forth in order to pass cars and trucks on the highway. And at almost double the speed limit, the Taurus was an accident waiting to happen with a high likelihood of causing a fatality.

Poncha Springs is too small of a town to have its own police department, so the nearby town of Salida was called in to help, as well as a Colorado State Patrol Officer Boccaccio. He was informed that the perpetrator had used a grenade, which his wife overheard. She did not want him to go, but duty called.

But this wasn't a fanciful and funny chase scene like in *Smokey and the Bandit*. This wasn't comedic car maneuvers by an anti-hero or a good ole boy from the *Dukes of Hazzard*. He wasn't driving a cool classic muscle car or a fancy Lamborghini as in the *Cannonball Run*.

This was anything but entertaining. This was a guy impaired by drug use, fueled by youthful bravado and carelessness, creating a real and imminent danger for the public, the officers and himself. This was an eighteen-year-old who believed he had nothing to lose. The kind of person most dangerous to law enforcement.

Sergeant Morgan in his Charger and State Patrol Officer Jim Boccaccio in a Ford Crown Victoria were able to keep up with the Taurus, so they took the lead in the pursuit. The Taurus kept moving south, going through more stoplights, and passing other vehicles on the road.

A Salida police officer had set up Stop Sticks just before entering the town of Poncha Springs, but the Taurus veered off and went through a gas station instead, avoiding damage to his tires. The Taurus continued on U.S. Highway 285 towards Villa Grove, now entering Saguache County and Jerry Hernandez had no intention of stopping.

It was getting later in the morning and all the officers knew the number of vehicles on the highway was only going to increase, so the decision was made to try and stop the Taurus. Trooper Boccaccio had asked to assist because he was recently trained to execute a Tactical Vehicle Intervention, also popularly known as a "PIT move", where an officer deliberately tries to spin out another car. The Pursuit Intervention Technique (PIT) occurs when the police vehicle gently bumps the side of the target vehicle near the back, causing its tires to lose traction and spin out. If successful, the target vehicle comes to a stop, pointing sideways. If unsuccessful, or performed incorrectly, it could be dangerous and cause both cars to be in an accident.

Trooper Boccaccio passed up Sergeants Morgan and Livingston and hit the side of the Taurus, which then bounced into the opposite lane and onto the dirt shoulder causing a huge cloud of dust. For a moment the other officers couldn't tell exactly what happened, and there was an immediate concern that both of the vehicles had crashed.

Neither one crashed, but this maneuver significantly slowed down the Taurus to 30 miles per hour and Jerry attempted to continue down the highway. Trooper Boccaccio saw the opportunity to perform another PIT move at a more favorable speed. Boccaccio performed it perfectly, and the Taurus and Boccaccio both came to a stop in the middle of the highway.

"We need to box him in," stated Boccaccio on the radio. Only a few seconds behind was Sergeant Morgan who approached the Taurus at a 90-degree angle, slowing down in front of it. That's when he saw Jerry with a gun.

The sergeant passed in front of the Taurus and turned to become parallel to the Taurus. He quickly got out of his car with his gun drawn and pointed it at Jerry, who already has his handgun pointed directly at Sergeant Morgan.

That moment became *the* moment that every law enforcement officer knows is possible and regularly trains for. It is the moment that every officer *dreads:* the moment an officer is staring down the barrel of a gun. It is the moment that can *forever* change an officer's life. It is the moment that can do more than change an officer's life, *it can end it.*

Sergeant Morgan is not merely thinking that any second, he could take several gunshot rounds. *He is expecting it.* At this close range, Jerry wouldn't have to be an expert marksman to hit Morgan and the loud *"Pop", "Pop"* from the gun would be the last sounds he would ever hear.

He is just a few feet away from Jerry and yells," drop it." but Jerry does not drop the gun. "Drop it!" he commands again, and a split second later repeats it a third time "Drop it!"

He has no time to think and contemplate the situation. In that instant, Sergeant Morgan's training kicked in; he aimed his service weapon and took his first shot. He took four shots in rapid succession, all hitting the target. It all happened in an instant. Although he was aiming to stop the threat, his first shot went into the criminal's hand that was holding the gun. It is common that an officer could have "tunnel vision", where the only thing he could see was the barrel of the criminal's gun. The other three shots proved to be fatal.

There was no time to be scared. There was no time to be thinking about dying, there was no time to be hesitant, and there was no time to wait for any further response from the perpetrator. The time you need to read this sentence is how quickly Sergeant Dean Morgan needed to decide what to do about the threat to his life. That's it, less than a second to decide and two more seconds for training and instinct to take over. The threat was nullified.

A few weeks later

3:18a.m.

Dean Morgan woke up with his hand balled up in a fist, punching his pillow. He's been dreaming, angry at what happened just a few weeks earlier. Jerry was in the front seat of his patrol car, but he looked more like a zombie from a Hollywood movie set. He started to fight with the zombie, but it wasn't clear who was winning. He simply felt anger towards the guy and somehow woke himself up from the short dream.

Dean was angry at the zombie, for making him shoot him. He thought him a coward, the outcast kid who wanted to end it all in a twisted blaze of glory, with suicide by cop. Jerry's gun turned out to be an airsoft gun that was a replica of a Sig Sauer handgun. The local paper ran a picture of a real gun side-by-side with the airsoft gun, and no one could tell the difference. Jerry Hernandez clearly knew what he was doing and knew what was going to happen if he pointed it at an officer and refused to drop his weapon.

Dean was still mad at the kid, for making him pull the trigger and putting him in his grave, but he had no choice in the matter. Jerry put everyone at risk, and his actions were the epitome of reckless behavior. It was frustrating that he'll never know what was going through Jerry's mind and why he did what he did.

Dean reflected gratefully that he wasn't a rookie, but rather a 12-year veteran on the job who would be much better suited to handle such a situation and the fallout afterward. Shooting at a suspect is always a serious matter, and even more so when it's fatal. He was also grateful for the many hours of training that he had received as an officer.

This incident solidified in his mind the requirement that every officer has to be prepared to pull the trigger when you need to. That moment can come on any day and in any situation.

Nothing is ever *routine,* nor is a quiet mountain community immune from dangerous police actions. He had no idea the gun wasn't real, nor the grenades.

Ultimately, those facts were not relevant, as the District Attorney's examination of the facts concluded that Sergeant Dean Morgan's actions were an appropriate and a justified use of lethal force. He did what he had to do based upon the circumstance, and Jerry could have changed the outcome but chose his own ending. *Such a waste of life,* he thought to himself.

Dean may have pulled the trigger, but Jerry was ultimately responsible. Resolving and working through that thought process can be a burden. Dean knew he could stand before God and honestly say that he did the right thing. It was resolved in his heart and mind. Knowing that provided some comfort and he never dreamed of Jerry again.

***

June 17, 2020

"At the end of the day when you go home and hug your loved ones and taste that meal prepared with love, it will have a flavor the protected will never know. The sheep spend a lifetime eating grass, but you taste the flavor the protected will never know. That may be the warrior's greatest reward."
—**Dave Grossman**, *On Combat: The Psychology and Physiology of Deadly Conflict in War and in Peace*

"I can't believe her!" Andrea Morgan said, starting to tear up.

"Who?" Dean asked, getting concerned after seeing the look on his wife's face. She appeared distraught combined with frustration.

"My old classmate Jordan."

"What did she do now?"

"You know that Las Vegas police officer that was shot by the rioters two days ago? She posted on Facebook, supporting Black Lives Matter, who of course want to defund the police. They are telling lies about the police hunting down black men," Andrea continued trying to control her emotions.

"She said what?" Dean asked incredulously while shaking his head. He peered outside the kitchen window, noticing the beautiful view he had of the Rocky Mountains. "What is this world coming to?"

"It's gone crazy, that's for sure. She is repeating the lie that the police are a bunch of racists."

"Oh, geez," he said still shaking his head, "what's wrong with her? Does she know that BLM is a Marxist organization? I bet not. And I suppose all of her friends were in agreement?"

"Yes, and I replied on Facebook that the police risk their lives every day, and she didn't seem to care. She knows about the day you were at the Platte Canyon High School hostage incident. Did she conveniently forget that?"

"She knows full well what you and other officers are up against. And now she wants to defund you?" Andrea drew in a deep breath and continued, "I see what you go through every day, and I know how tough it is, and they just don't want to hear about it. Jordan didn't have an answer when I mentioned that you put your life at risk at Platte Canyon High School."

"She is just clueless."

"I know, but there are so many other people out there that think like her. And when I tried to defend the police on Facebook, her and her liberal friends started attacking me and calling me a racist."

"Yeah, they hate the police until someone is breaking into their house and then, all of a sudden, they need one."

"They didn't seem to care one bit about the police officer shot in Las Vegas."

"She and her friends are just as bad as these hypocritical politicians," Dean retorted and continued, "If you've never had to stare down the barrel of a gun, than don't tell the police not to defend themselves."

"I didn't see her risking her life for strangers," Andrea pointed out. "She gets to sit behind her computer and criticize the almost one million cops in this country. I've had to wash a victim's blood and hair out of your clothes. Do you remember that girl that got run over by the truck in Fairplay?"

"Unfortunately, I do."

"Well, I was the one who had to wash those clothes. You literally had to pull her out from underneath a truck at night in the in the middle of winter. I can't imagine doing that!"

"That must have been horrible. Those are not grease stains that need to get cleaned when your husband is a mechanic. This is blood belonging to a teenage girl, and she's never going to be able to live out her life. And I had to wash her blood down the drain. Jordan will never have to do that! And she never will."

"I know, I'm sorry you had to do that," Dean answered.

"I'm upset that Jordan doesn't understand that those types of things are part of our life. It's only cop families that know about stuff like that, we have to deal with stuff like that, and she has no appreciation for it. When I was a dispatcher, I thought my job was stressful, but the police are the ones going out on these calls and don't know what they are going to find."

"She has not seen the worst of humanity like I have."

"Yes, she doesn't make the connection that cops have to deal with this every day. It is not like an office job," Andrea continued.

"They all want to second guess the police in every incident, like a Monday morning quarterback."

"It might be good to block her on Facebook."

"Yeah, you're probably right. She said that she wasn't talking about you specifically, she has been supportive of you in the past, it's all the other officers that are part of a systemic racism culture and use excessive force."

"Which of course is a complete lie," he said sternly, now also getting frustrated. "Last year, 13 unarmed black men were killed by police. That's not an epidemic and that doesn't tell you the context of the shooting. The media just hypes it up and influences an unsuspecting public.

"I know, I can't watch television anymore."

"We've both lost some friends over the years because of their attitude towards cops. But it has never been worse than it is today."

"Well not only that, but they also don't understand even the basics about having an officer for a spouse. Being on call for holidays, going out to work in the middle of the night. I know it's hard for you to find real down time."

"Sometimes it is just easier to only hang out with other officers. They get it. Some friends and family members do of course, but many do not. Even some people at church seem to be giving me dirty looks. Even good Christians put anti-cop stuff on social media," Dean said and then continued, "Crime doesn't seem real to average people. Most people think all we do is chase down people stealing their Amazon packages."

"Yeah, or chasing Sasquatch," Andrea teased him and lightened the mood, reminding the almost-newly-minted chief about the time he thoroughly investigated and reported on a Big Foot sighting (nothing was found).

"Four different people reported that sighting, so I don't know..." Dean answered with a smirk.

"I'm sure glad that you are not doing police work in Denver or some other big city, but most people don't know that there's plenty of dangerous crime situations in small towns like ours," Andrea stated.

"I'd love to take Jordan for a citizen ride-along. Then she'd see what really happens, and that might open her eyes. Everyone should do a ride-along and there would be no question that the devil is real. You have been on ride-alongs, you have seen it firsthand."

"People who think like that don't understand the emotional toll it takes on officers. I have seen how it has affected you," Andrea stated.

"She is sheltered from that. But it is supposed to be that way. If I do my job right, the average person doesn't have to deal with criminals. They sleep easy at night, oblivious to the evil that is out there."

"Don't get me wrong, that's how I want it to be, but it would be nice to get appreciated for that instead of treated like we are the problem," Dean stated.

"I don't think my husband should have to die for citizens who hate him. Some days I wish you still were just a security guard at Hewlett-Packard."

"I would have been bored out of my mind," he said smiling and they both laughed.

"At least around here, the community appreciates the police. I know there are still plenty of people who appreciate you Dean."

"Yeah, I know, but you don't hear those stories on the news. I still don't know why God selected me to be in these situations. I still love my job and there is a sense of pride to carry the burden," Dean stated and continued, "But on a brighter note, someone bought my lunch yesterday."

"That was nice."

"Forget about Jordan."

"I will. I'm done."

"I can't wait until the next class reunion," he said in jest, and they both laughed again, as Andrea's blood pressure subsided.

***

A New Dawn

"Well, this is the morning." Andrea told her husband, checking his tie to make sure it was straight, just one more time.

"Yes, I almost don't believe it myself. After all these years of being out on patrol, I'm going to be spending most of my time behind the desk."

"You deserve it, you're going to make a great Chief."

"I've got big shoes to fill. Jimmy Tidwell has been our Chief for 24 years and has done a great job in the community of Buena Vista," Dean replied.

"He sure has, and he couldn't have handed the torch to a better man."

"I still remember being a teenager and watching William Shatner run around on *T.J. Hooker*. That's when I knew I wanted to be a cop. But I'm afraid I'm going to have a lot more paperwork than T.J. Hooker ever had."

"That's for sure," Andrea stated and laughed.

"Luckily, I've got some great new sergeants, so that will really help out. It's a huge learning curve, but I'm looking forward to the challenge. Except for the budgeting process that is," he said and smiled to his wife. "Who would ever want to be an accountant, sheesh!" Dean said in jest.

"I don't consider myself old, but I'll let these young guys do some high-speed chasing and some of the other crazy stuff that we do."

"No, you're not old but this work does take a toll on your body," she stated. "This is your time. The world needs more levelheaded leaders like you. You were chosen for this line of work. There are a lot of officers under your command that you are going to impact in a positive way. I am very proud of you. The kids are too."

"Thanks," he replied, not always comfortable with compliments. "This is a great community that really supports the officers, and an important part of the job as Chief is going to be to bridge the gap between the community concerns and policing concerns. There should be police oversight, but also a lot of training and communication with the community."

"These times that we're in, this is all part of God's plan."

"I believe that. I'm going to continue Jimmy's legacy. It's all going to be all right. I have faith."

"So do I."

On July 24, Sergeant Dean Morgan was promoted by the Buena Vista Town Trustees to Chief of Police, a 20-year veteran officer.

***

Sent to the Park County Sheriff's Office by the survivors of Room 206 at Platte Canyon High School after the shooting on September 27, 2006.

Five Fun facts about Dean Morgan

1. Favorite food is macaroni and cheese.

2. Favorite holiday is Halloween (no, he does not dress up as a cop).

3. Loves 80's heavy metal music.

4. History buff, especially the Civil War and the Middle Ages.

5. Still sleeps with his stuffed silverback gorilla, *Mongo* (from the Congo).

III.

In the Batter's Box

The First Week of November, 1976

"All right everyone, please settle down," requested Mrs. Nasanovich. The first graders were still shuffling a bit after returning from recess. They were getting back to their seats a little slower than the teacher would have liked, and she prodded them. "Come on kids, let's return to your desks."

The mid-morning recess had just finished at Buffalo Ridge Elementary School in Cheyenne, Wyoming. It was a bright and sunny November morning, although the breeze was kicking up, which made it seem a little colder than the outside temperature of 45 degrees would indicate.

"All right kids," Mrs. Nasanovich continued as all 24 children were finally seated. "Yesterday your homework assignment was to think about what you want to be when you grow up.

"And I told you that it can be anything you want. Maybe one of you will be President of the United States. Who knows?" she queried, which elicited a few chuckles from the kids.

"Each person will come up to the front of the class for a minute and stand behind my desk and tell the class. Would anyone like to go first?"

"Barbara," Mrs. Nasanovich stated after she was the first one to raise her hand. The six-year-old was in the front of the class only a few steps from the teacher. She walked behind the desk, slightly cleared her throat and looked at her classmates.

"I want to be a kindergarten teacher," she stated with confidence, as if saying her lines in a theater production. "They are a bunch of little kids, not like us first graders who go to school all day. So, I want to teach them to get ready for Mrs. Nasanovich's class," she replied and smiled, looking over at the teacher for approval.

"Oh, isn't that interesting," the teacher responded with a bit of laughter, not at all surprised by Barbara's answer, who was already known as the teacher's pet.

"Yeah, me too. I want to be a teacher," said one of Barbara's friends. "Well, you can't all be teachers," Mrs. Nasanovich told them.

"I don't want to be a teacher, I want to be a cowboy," Jack said with pride, "like my Dad." Many of the kids in the surrounding area came from ranches, so it was an expected choice.

"Thank you, Jack, but you're supposed to come up to the front of the class to tell people what you want to be when you grow up. Okay, let's get another boy up here, but don't tell us until you are at the front of the room," the teacher told them.

Only one boy raised his hand. "Come on up," she said and motioned him to the front of the class.

The boy got up to the desk, looked at the class, and hesitated for just a moment, immediately noticing that it was different standing in the front of the class versus simply answering a question from his desk.

He momentarily glanced down at the desk. Then he looked straight ahead and clearly stated with purpose, "I want to be baseball player and a police officer."

"Oh, that's nice. Is anyone in your family a police officer?" the teacher asked.

"Well, my uncle Leon in Colorado is," the boy answered.

"Is that why you want to?"

"I don't know about that. That's not why," he stated, after thinking about it for a moment.

"Can you tell the class why?" asked Mrs. Nasanovich.

"I just want to help people. I want to stop the bad guys. When someone's in trouble, they call the police, and I want to be the one they call. That's what I want to do," the boy answered.

***

Meet Jamey Murray, age 50

Christian

Man

Son

Brother

Husband

Father

Daddy

Patriot

American

2nd Baseman in the 1991 Junior College World Series

Outdoor Enthusiast

Bourbon Connoisseur

Road Patrol Officer, City of Bellevue, NE

12-year member of the Cheyenne, WY Police Department

9 years as a member of the SWAT Team

7,569 days later, August 6, 1997

4:59p.m.

It took exactly 94 seconds for 29-year-old Darrell Wharton and his best friend and roommate, Rick Reed, to drive the silver minivan from the bank parked on 18th street in downtown Cheyenne, Wyoming to their actual getaway car parked on O'Neill Avenue. It was in a quiet industrial section of town.

They had stolen the minivan three hours before, but it wasn't the minivan that they were after. It was the money that was stuffed into their backpack that they were interested in.

They didn't have a chance to even count it. Darrell had recently seen a quote from the notorious Willie Sutton when he was asked about why he robbed banks, "Because that's where the money is." The simplicity of the statement wasn't lost on Darrell, who soon after planned their first bank robbery. However, the fact that Willie Sutton was arrested and sent to prison for half of his life never seemed to register with Darrell.

The two men had entered the bank six minutes before five o'clock and just as they expected, there weren't many people on a Wednesday afternoon near closing time. As a matter of fact, they were the only customers in this particular bank, which did not employ a security guard.

Rick watched the door while Darrell walked up to the teller, lifted up his shirt just enough to reveal the .38 Special handgun that was stuffed into the front of his jeans. He quietly instructed her to put all the money from the drawer into a small backpack. He knew from watching Al Pacino in *Heat*, that it would only be minutes between the time she pressed the panic button and when the police were going to arrive.

Darrell decided that a smaller amount of money stolen in a quicker amount of time would work out in his favor. And he was right. She stuffed almost $15,000 into the backpack while the other teller was a mere 15 feet away, wrapping up her daily paperwork logs.

Darrell knew that as soon as he turned around, she was going to press that button, but that was OK because their minivan was parked right in front of the bank. This was done on purpose so the silver minivan would be identified as the getaway vehicle. Unbeknownst to everyone else, Rick had his 1984 Ford F-150 parked just a few blocks away. All they had to do was drive away in a cool and calm manner, switch vehicles and go the six miles out to their apartment on the north side of town.

"That was almost too easy," Darrell exclaimed and let out a howl. "I told you it would work. Speed is the name of the game when it comes to bank robbery," he stated, suddenly seeing himself as an expert in the subject.

Rick slowly eased his car out onto the street and headed south towards Lincoln Way, the main thoroughfare that would get him to the interstate in less than a mile.

"You should have seen the look on the teller's face," Darrell wickedly laughed, "I know they have more money in there, but it might have taken too long."

"I'll give you that," Rick replied, "I was getting nervous that it'd be just our luck that they close up early or worse, some cop would come in trying to deposit a check or something."

"It's 5:00 o'clock, so it's happy hour! Time for us to get home and count this loot and go get some beer."

"Let's do it," Rick replied emphatically.

***

5:09p.m.

"I didn't expect a bank robbery to happen for my ride-along," stated Janelle.

"They are pretty rare," replied Officer Jamey Murray, "this is the first one that I have seen since being on the force." Officer Murray had been with the Cheyenne Police Department for two years and his sister joined him for her first ride-along at the beginning of his afternoon shift. Regular citizens were able to join an officer for a shift to see what real police work looked like.

"Dispatch told us that the gunman was armed, so if we see them, you will absolutely need to stay in this car," he continued.

"I understand, of course." she answered.

"We don't know much about them, but so far eyewitnesses have said that it was two white males in their late twenties; the guy who stole the money from the teller is about 5 feet 10 inches and the lookout guy was about six feet tall. That's not much to go on until we get a sketch artist over there.

Dispatch told us that the bank teller saw them get into a silver minivan, maybe about seven years old. She thinks it was a Chrysler."

"Maybe they left fingerprints or something," Janelle suggested.

"Maybe, but we won't know that for a while. The first two officers were on the scene in less than five minutes, but the perpetrators were already gone."

The teller said that the entire robbery only took a few minutes, and they only robbed the money in just the one teller's drawer. They were in and out fast, so the best thing we have to go on right now is the silver minivan.

"Unfortunately, we don't have a license plate number," Officer Murray stated.

"Well, I'll keep an eye out from here," Janelle replied.

"We're still about 15 blocks from the bank," he stated, going slowly down Pershing Boulevard.

"OK," she said, and another minute passed.

"Hey, look what we have here!" he said, his voice rising, as he recognized what was in front of him. He couldn't believe it but staring him right in the face was a 1991 Chrysler minivan, silver in color, fitting the description perfectly. He flipped on his flashing lights and siren. The minivan's brake lights briefly came on and then off. A few seconds went by and then they turned red again when it had started to pull over to the side of the road.

Officer Murray had a heightened sense of alertness as the minivan pulled over. They knew that at least one of the bank robbers had a gun, but maybe the other one had a gun too. For a moment he was expecting the van to pull away and try to escape, but it didn't move. Were they going to try to shoot at him? It wasn't likely they would be taken easily. He immediately called dispatch to run the license plate.

"Slouch down in the seat," he told her. "I don't want them to see you in the car." He kept his eyes focused solely on the vehicle, looking for any movement whatsoever. Within one minute, the dispatcher had run the license plate, although it seemed like it took forever. The minivan was registered to Thomas and Teresa Karter. Was Thomas Karter one of the bank robbers? Of course, they could have stolen the vehicle, so it might not be the owner driving the van.

He had to be extremely cautious and dispatch had already instructed another patrol vehicle to the scene for backup. Once backup arrived a few minutes later, he was going to approach the driver. Officer Murray got out of the patrol car and took the long and lonely walk from the relative safety of his police vehicle towards the minivan, which potentially held armed criminals.

He slowly approached the minivan on the driver's side with his right hand gently resting on his service weapon pressed against his thigh. He was ready for whatever might be in front of him. This type of patrol stop was more than just an unknown situation because it bordered on what officers would categorize as a high-risk felony stop. He involuntarily raised his eyebrows slightly when he saw the driver.

"I'm sorry officer, but I didn't think I was speeding," she said before he could say anything.

"Please provide your license, registration and insurance card," he calmly requested. He noticed that there was no one in the passenger seat, and his steely brown eyes quickly scanned into the back of the van and saw two young children; a boy about five-years-old and a girl that was probably nine.

There was no one else in the car, and he refocused his eyes on the woman driving the van, a petite gal who looked to be in her early 30's. She opened her purse and handed out her license, and then started fumbling in the glove compartment to find the registration and insurance card.

Officer Murray studied the license and quickly confirmed that it was Teresa Karter, who lived only a few miles away. "Is this your minivan ma'am?" he asked.

"Yes, it is, I know this registration is in here somewhere," she replied nervously.

"Take your time," he said.

She finally found the paperwork at the bottom of the glove box and handed it to him. "Here it is."

It appeared to be in order with an up-to-date registration and current insurance card. The car's registration was in her name and Thomas Karter. "Is Thomas Karter your husband?" he asked and continued, "This vehicle is registered in both your names."

"Yes, we bought this minivan used, a few years ago. Is something wrong with it?"

"No. The reason why I pulled you over is that about 15 minutes ago there was a bank robbery, and the getaway car was a silver Chrysler minivan, just like yours."

"Oh wow, I had no idea. We were just coming from the library and we're headed home," she gasped. "I can show you the books we checked out, if you want me to," she offered.

Officer Murray noticed a few books on the floor in the back of the van. "There's no need, it was just a coincidence that they used a vehicle like yours. It's a very common make and model, and you just happen to be in the area."

"I was going straight home."

"I understand. I'm sorry for the inconvenience, and you have a nice evening ma'am, and you too kids," he stated and waved at the two little ones in the back seat. They both waved back.

He took a few steps away from the van, and then dispatch came back on the radio. "Who is driving the van, was it Thomas or Teresa Karter?"

"It was Teresa Karter," Officer Murray answered. "Oh, and you can call off my backup."

"She's got an active warrant," Dispatch told him. He immediately turned around and walked back to the minivan.

"Hold up a second," he told Teresa.

Speaking back to dispatch, he asked, "What's the warrant for?"

"It's an expired pet license, issued by Animal Control. The warrant was automatically processed about three months ago."

"OK, thanks," he stated and looked back at Teresa Karter, who had a confused look on her face as she was able to overhear most of the conversation.

"Ma'am, are you aware that there's a warrant out for your arrest?"

"My arrest? No, I had no idea. What's going on?" she asked. Her face turned the shade of light ash and her jaw literally dropped from the surprise when Officer Murray told her that she was wanted by the police. "I've never even had so much as a speeding ticket!" she tried to counter argue.

"The warrant was issued by Animal Control for a failure to stay current with your annual pet license."

"What? You can get arrested for that?" she asked in a voice tone which was starting to show panic.

"The license expired last December 31st, so now it's eight months late.

It is a Wyoming law that a failure to pay will automatically result in a misdemeanor warrant. It also includes a penalty fee of 50% plus the regular license fee."

"Wait, you're kidding right? I never got a bill," she replied, frantically trying to process what she was being told.

"Ma'am, I wish I was," he stated with empathy written all over his face.

That look scared Teresa even more, because she knew that he was serious. But she still couldn't believe that she was going to go to jail for this.

"Can't I just pay the fine or something? I promise to go and pay first thing tomorrow morning."

"I really wish it were that simple," stated Officer Murray.

If an officer encountered a person with a known arrest warrant, they were required by state statute to immediately arrest the person. He understood the predicament that Teresa Karter was put in. But this was not an option, even for a $25 fee and the $12.50 penalty fee, the requirement was the same as a more serious offense.

He didn't want to violate any of his department rules even though it seemed silly to place someone in handcuffs and drive them downtown to the police station because they forgot to pay their dog license fee. He was a sworn officer of the law, but he didn't want to be cold-hearted and traumatize the woman, who had an otherwise completely clean record. There had to be a better way.

"What about my kids, we can't leave them here?" Teresa asked as she began to cry, as reality started to sink in. She was shaking a little bit and really looked distraught. She was shell-shocked, and offered, "I've never been in trouble before."

Officer Murray guessed that she'd never been pulled over or had any kind of negative interaction with the police. Her hand was nervously twitching, and her brow was sweating. She was obviously getting stressed out, and she kept looking back at her kids, who were also getting agitated. Even the youngest child sensed that his mother was very upset.

"It'll be alright kids," she told them, but was also trying to convince herself. She grabbed a tissue from her purse to dry her eyes.

Strict protocol would require that she be put in handcuffs and placed in the back of his squad car. He'd then have to call Children's Protective Services to take the kids. Next, he'd inform the towing service to take and impound their minivan.

And that was just the beginning, she had to be fingerprinted, photographed and booked at the city jail. And since it was after 5:00p.m., she might be spending the night in jail if she didn't have enough cash on hand to pay the fees. And her kids would also probably spend the night in a facility.

Not only would it cost them much more than the mere dog license fee, but the experience would be an emotionally traumatic experience for both Teresa and her two young children. Obviously, that was not the intent of the law, but the law was clear on what an officer is supposed to do in this situation.

Officer Murray had an idea. "There is no way around this situation, but I do have some thoughts on how we can come up with a reasonable solution for everyone," he stated.

She nodded with a silent reply. She was desperate, and the last thing she wanted to do was leave her kids with strangers, but she knew she was at the complete discretion of what officer Murray decided.

"Does your husband have a cell phone?"

"No, but he should be at home. He works the night shift," she told him.

"Let's try giving him a call. We'll have him drive here and pick up the kids."

"We don't have another car. I'm sorry," she stated and started to cry again. Her stomach was in knots, thinking that their lack of a second vehicle was going to ruin the plan.

"Hmmm, that's OK, let's try to call him. If he's home, I'll follow you to your house and you can drop off the kids with him," Officer Murray suggested. "I'll then have to take you to the police station, and we can get you processed. I'll call in before we get there and let's see if we can get your fine paid today.

"Your husband and kids can follow us and pick you up when you're done. We should be able to get all this done in an hour, two at the most. If you can pay in cash, you should be able to take care of it today."

Officer Murray dialed the phone number and identified himself. He asked if he was speaking to Thomas Karter. After confirming that it was him, he briefly explained the situation to Mr. Karter and based on the address that Teresa had on her license, they could be at the house in about 10 minutes.

When they arrived, Teresa pulled into the driveway, jumped out of the minivan and hugged her husband. And that's when she really melted down.

Tears were streaming down her face uncontrollably, while trying to explain to her husband what had happened. The kids also exited the vehicle and went to go hug their parents. With Teresa crying, the kids also started to cry.

"I'm so sorry," she told the kids.

Officer Murray reiterated the plan to Thomas, and he agreed that would be the best solution for everyone.

"Thank you, officer, and you can call me Tommy," he stated and put out his hand. The two men shook.

"Yes, thank you so much for being so understanding, and letting me bring my kids home," Teresa chimed in.

"No problem. I'm glad we were able to figure something out," Officer Murray told them. There was no reason to make this situation any worse and upsetting than it already was. She was not a criminal and was a threat to no one. And the commonsense approach resulted in an outcome that would satisfy both the city and the citizen.

"OK, Mrs. Karter, we need to go now," he stated. Teresa, Tommy and the kids did a group hug. He decided that handcuffs were not necessary, and he simply escorted her to the back seat of the squad car.

Janelle had observed everything, and her brother Jamey updated her in the car while they were driving to the Karter's house. When Mrs. Karter got into the back seat, Janelle wasn't sure whether she should say anything to her or not. She decided that silence was the best option.

Officer Murray had already called into the police station and explained what was going on and ensured that he was able to escort Teresa Karter directly to the person who could do all the processing. Teresa Karter brought enough cash on hand to pay the fees, and she was safely back at home by 7:00p.m.

***

January 2004

"This isn't even close!" Eugene told him, with his voice rising in volume from obvious annoyance. "You will have to do it over, and I need it now."

"Um, what color do you want again?" Kyle asked, unbothered by the customer's agitation.

"It's the same color I gave you yesterday afternoon. I've circled it right here," Eugene stated, emphatically pointing at the sample paint card with dark forest green circled. His patience was wearing thin.

"You made ten gallons of this lime green stuff and it looks like crap. The house that I am building is 20 miles out of town, half of which is on a dirt road, and now I'm wasting my morning coming back here because you couldn't make the right color paint," he told him, pointing again to the sample of the paint versus what was in the ten gallon can.

Kyle Parker furrowed his brow and appeared to be trying to concentrate, trying to understand what this man was telling him. But he was having a hard time being friendly and responsive since he was running on about two hours of sleep after a hard night of partying. He didn't want to be at work today. Truth be told, he didn't ever want to be at work.

He was 20 minutes late for work today, which didn't make the owner very happy. George Wheaton, the owner, was a friend of Kyle's parents, which helped him get hired. He'd been working at the paint store for almost six months, which was long term employment in Kyle's experience. He was surprised he lasted this long.

He'd previously worked at a tire store, gas station, a pizza restaurant, Subway and a grocery store. He even did a stint at the public library before getting fired. Since barely graduating high school seven years ago, he bounced around mostly minimum wage jobs, in between bouts of unemployment.

For some reason, his bosses never seemed to treat him as a valued employee. His bosses always failed to express their appreciation for him, and it was easy to demoralize Kyle. It was difficult to get him motivated for work. His bosses never seem to understand the skills he brought to the job.

Perhaps that was because he didn't have many skills, didn't add much value, and was late to the job almost every day, that is, the days he actually showed up for work. But to Kyle, the world was just out to get him. They didn't understand him. No one did. Besides what was the big deal with the paint? It was just paint.

"Yeah, I guess I could do another ten gallons for you," Kyle finally managed to mumble out. "I think we can do this one at half-price."

"Half price?" Eugene asked in shock. "First of all, I come in here all the time for paint for the houses I'm building. And secondly, you didn't make the right color. It was your fault."

"Well," was all that Kyle managed to say.

"I've got to trim this house out," Eugene continued. "I've got a schedule and there's no way that I'm paying again," Eugene told him, with his agitated voice now rising enough to get the attention of the owner.

"Good morning Eugene, what's going on?" George asked, hoping he was mistaken that Eugene was about to lose it with Kyle. It didn't take long for Eugene to reiterate what had transpired yesterday afternoon and this morning. And, as he did, he was getting himself more annoyed at the situation.

"I don't know what happened," was all that Kyle could muster up for an explanation.

"I am already behind schedule for this build, and now I am wasting half of my morning here," Eugene stated.

"I will personally take care of you and mix up that paint right now so you'll be on your way as soon as possible," Wheaton told him. He hadn't been in business for 22 years by providing lousy service, especially to local contractors. "And of course, they'll be no charge for the replacement, and I'll throw in a couple of paintbrushes for you."

"I guess that would be OK, because I gotta get back to the job site."

"Kyle, can you go grab a couple of brushes?" Wheaton asked. Kyle nodded and shuffled his way towards the shelf with the brushes. "I am sorry about all of this, Eugene," he said, turning his attention to his customer. Eugene still looked displeased and didn't answer him.

Fifteen minutes later, the paint was mixed, and Wheaton showed Eugene a sample of the color. Eugene nodded and shrugged his shoulders and as he grabbed the handle to the paint bucket, he told Wheaton, "that kid reeks of pot."

***

A few hours later, Kyle couldn't wait for the clock to hit 1:00p.m., his scheduled lunch hour. In fact, he couldn't wait at all, and at 12:56 p.m., he told Mr. Wheaton, "Hey, I'm going on lunch break."

"Kyle," George Wheaton stated, and Kyle stopped a few feet from the door, and slowly turned around. Wheaton continued, "I don't think this job is working out for you. There is no need to come back from lunch." Wheaton was expecting to hear a list of excuses, but Kyle nodded once and headed out the door.

***

Nine hours later

"There he is!" someone shouted above the loud music and pointed to the door. The six people crammed into the trailer cheered and raised their cans of beer with an honorary toast. They were cheering Henry Wesson's arrival because he had their score.

"BG, my man!" Kyle shouted and smiled with a wide grin, happy to see his new friend. "BG" was Henry's nickname and stood for "Big Gun," as in Smith & Wesson. Everybody called him BG, and he liked having the tough guy and gangster image.

Kyle met BG just a few weeks ago through a mutual friend after Kyle's pot dealer flaked out on him one too many times. BG was more reliable, so to speak. BG always had dime bags available for sale, and that's what made them friends.

"Show me the money," twenty-seven-year-old BG said with a hearty laugh and watched as six of the seven partyers grabbed for their cash. "Don't worry, BG will take care of you." It wasn't long before the trailer was engulfed in a thick haze of smoke. BG shuffled over to the small kitchen area.

"Kyle, my man, what's going on?" BG asked.

"You know, the same old stuff," Kyle answered and then took a long inhale from his bong, held his breath a second, and then exhaled. "Well, actually, I quit my job at that stupid paint store," he lied. "My boss was a real jerk; you know what I mean? And they weren't paying me any money anyways, so I was just wasting my time."

BG nodded, stared off into space somewhere for a moment, and then had a thought. "You know, I could use some help. You wanna make some quick cash?"

"Yeah, sure," Kyle responded. "What do I have to do?"

"Your car still works, right?"

"Yeah, it's fine."

"I just need you to make a pickup from Greeley and Denver," BG told him.

"Nah, that doesn't sound too hard," Kyle replied and slightly shook his head.

"I'll pay you $500 bucks."

"I'm in," he said with enthusiasm

"OK, come by my place tomorrow and we'll talk about the details."

You got it man." Kyle answered, grinned, and went to take up another hit from the bong. After exhaling, he smiled again, forming his ear-to-ear grin in slow motion.

He was feeling mellow and relaxed. He felt the reverberation of the base, thumping from the stereo. *Life was good*, he thought to himself, taking in the view of the smoke haze, his friends, and the whole party scene. Life was going to get better now that he was going to make $500 in one day, which would take him a couple of weeks if he were still working at the paint store.

He can drive down to Colorado once or twice a month and still make more money than he did before. *Life was good.*

***

The next day

So where am I going?" Kyle asked as he entered the trailer.

"Come in and keep your voice down," BG instructed him.

"I have two packages for you, one to pick up from some business associates in Greeley and another in North Denver. It's really simple, all you have to do is to pick up the package from the guy I tell you to. It has to be him and no one else, do you understand?"

"Yeah, that doesn't sound too hard."

"It's not hard so don't mess it up," BG said, his voice no longer resembling last night's jovial and friendly tone. His smile was gone too, and his eyes told Kyle that he was serious. This was business.

Cheyenne, Wyoming is split by two major freeways, Interstate 80 going east and west, and Interstate 25 going north and south. Denver was only 100 miles directly south on I-25, with Greeley even closer. It was the perfect distribution hub for drugs.

BG was a small-time dealer in Cheyenne and was trying to expand the places he bought his product. Cheyenne was the largest population center in Wyoming, but at less than 60,000 people, it was still small. Denver was ten times larger and too close to ignore the business opportunities.

He was always looking for new drivers, somebody who the cops might not recognize, but there is always the risk that a newbie could screw it all up. Pick up had to be precise and the package weight had to be perfect, otherwise the deal could go south very quickly.

He had to emphasize with Kyle to take this seriously. His problem was, of course, that most of the people he knew were also drug users, and reliability was not a skill on top of anyone's resume. But that was the nature of his business.

BG would have a separate person unbeknownst to Kyle drive to a nearby location for the money part of the exchange. The idea was to arrive there simultaneously so the gang members could confirm both the drug and money transfer so it would separate the transactions. BG had seen this done on a television show one time and it seemed like it was a safer way of doing business.

"When you leave, you drive directly to the address I'm giving you. You don't stop for gas, you don't stop for something to eat, you don't take a piss and you don't do anything except drive to Greeley, do you understand? And you get there exactly at 4:00p.m." BG coldly directed. "Do you understand?" he asked again.

Yeah, I got it." Kyle responded.

"You don't make small talk with these guys, you pick up the package and that's it, then you leave."

"Yeah, I said I got it. I'm not an idiot, you know?" Kyle replied, suddenly getting defensive. He was getting concerned too, as BG was usually joking around, being Kyle's fun-loving friend. But, standing before him wasn't the BG that *he* knew.

"And when you're done, you're going to go directly to the second address," BG commanded, and Kyle understood that the fun and games were over.

***

March 2004

"But I was just down in Greeley yesterday," Kyle protested. Not that he disliked his new job being a well-paid delivery boy for BG. He'd been doing the Greeley and Denver run for a couple of months, and each time it had gone smoothly. He and BG we're becoming closer friends, but it was clear who is in charge, and it wasn't Kyle.

"I've got some new product for a delivery tomorrow."

"Oh?" Kyle asked with some inquisitiveness, but he also had learned not to ask too many direct questions.

"Yeah, I've got a sample from my buddies in Greeley," BG said and did a long slow inhale on his joint and handed it to Kyle. "I need to get more of their stuff."

"OK, I can go," Kyle responded as if he really had a choice. He inhaled a quick hit before handing the joint back to BG.

Kyle went from being a mostly heavy drinker and a weekend pot smoker to a daily pot smoker and weekend binge drinker. His pastime was playing video games and was known to remain in his apartment for days.

He'd make his drive down to Greeley and Denver, but only because he had to, not because he really wanted to. The real motivation was to keep in BG's good graces. BG was a great friend to have, but he wasn't the kind of guy you wanted to get on his bad side. His temper could flare at the drop of a hat and he frequently flashed his .357 Magnum revolver, constantly reminding Kyle who was in charge.

"Why don't you try some of this," BG suggested and retrieved a small crystal shard from a bag and put it in a 3-inch glass pipe. "This is the sample I got from Greeley."

"What is it?" Kyle asked innocently, but he had a pretty good guess that it was methamphetamines. BG didn't respond, and just handed him the pipe.

"Oh, why not?"

Kyle grabbed a lighter from the small table and he lit the bottom of the pipe with the crystallized shard inside. A white smoke started to appear, and Kyle inhaled.

"Woah, this is some good shit!" Kyle responded.

"Yeah, the Greeley boys have some good stuff," BG stated, and that's all the time needed for the methamphetamine to take over Kyle's brain.

Kyle slumped in the chair, smiled and never felt more joy and euphoria than he did *at that exact moment*. He didn't win the lottery, but he felt like he picked the winning ticket ten times in a row. It was unbelievable. Previously, Kyle's mood was neutral, but all of that had changed. Kyle didn't care why or how his mood had risen to 100 on a scale of 1 to 10. He simply knew that everything was great. Actually, it was more than great, *it was perfect*.

Everything was going to work out exactly in Kyle's favor, he just knew it. He felt better than he ever did in his entire life. Each part of his body felt good, as his heartbeat started to accelerate, and his blood pressure rose. In an instant, Kyle didn't have any worries. His life was problem free.

"This stuff is amazing," Kyle thought and couldn't keep himself from smiling. "I've never felt like this. It's different from pot. *It's way better!*" he exclaimed. All of a sudden, he felt smarter and confident. All kinds of thoughts raced through his head and he could barely keep up with all of the new insights that he had just discovered.

Whether it was about his life, or why he suddenly noticed a bunch of lint underneath the chair, why was it there, what did it mean, and would it be there forever? These were now important things that Kyle needed to know, and needed to know now, but then his thoughts bounced around even more.

Colors seemed more vibrant, and sounds seemed crisper, and the music sounded better. Better than he ever heard it before, clearer, and it just touched him deep inside, even though he had a hard time recognizing the song. The singer was singing it just for Kyle! This was utopia, this is what perfection was all about, this is what truly made him happy.

***

21 minutes later

"Dude, do you have any more of that stuff?" Kyle asked, now that his high had worn off.

"Yeah, but it's gonna cost you, this ain't no charity outfit, you know?" BG responded.

"Can you take it out of the payment for my pickup from Greeley tomorrow?" Kyle asked in a hopeful manner.

But Kyle's next hit would never be as good as the first time; *it never is for anyone.* And that was a certainty. But Kyle needed that next high, he needed it with every fiber of his being. He craved it, his body wanted it, he wanted it really bad, and one way or another he was going to get that next hit, sooner rather than later.

"Sure," BG said, smiling and handed Kyle another shard of meth. He leaned back in his chair, clasped his hands behind him head in a relaxed motion and watched Kyle light up the pipe. He just created another customer for life.

***

July 2004

"I'm smart enough to make my own meth. Do you know how much money I can make if I produce it instead of buying?" BG asked.

"Yeah, why not?" replied Kyle, and scratched a small sore on his cheek. He had just taken another hit of meth 15 minutes ago, but the days of feeling euphoria were long gone.

He always craved it, but he didn't seem to get as much out of it. Increased pot smoking didn't help either. Nothing he did came close to the first high from four months ago.

His meth use was starting to make him nervous and intense. Instead of wasting his time playing video games, now he would try to physically take the game console apart. He'd leave piles of parts and components all over his place, as well as anyone else's place he happened to be in. BG already got ticked off at Kyle yesterday when he took apart his boom box, and of course was unable to put it back together.

"We're going to have to figure out the supplies," reflected BG.

"OK, as long as we don't blow up your trailer," Kyle commented, half serious.

"Kyle, we're going to build it at your place," BG said sternly, and there was no doubt between the two of them that's what they were going to do. If anyone's home was going to blow up, it would be Kyle's. If anyone's place got raided, it would be Kyle's. If anyone was going to take a risk, it would be Kyle. But all the profit belonged to BG, that was crystal clear.

"OK," Kyle replied and looked away for a moment. "What do you want to do, go to the hardware store or something?"

"First we need to see if we can get a load of anhydrous ammonia. A lot of ranchers around here use it, so we're going to go scope out some places and then figure out when we're going to steal it."

"Yeah, that sounds like a solid plan," Kyle retorted, as if he really knew if that was a good idea or not. "When do you want to go?"

"Pretty soon; we'll chill here for a little bit."

"Cool."

***

Detective Jamey Murray was on his second rotation through the Cheyenne police department's narcotics division, his ninth year as a police officer. It was common practice for the 100-person department to have some officers rotate between road patrol, narcotics or as a general detective for three-year rotations. By doing so, this allowed many officers to develop a cross-functional skill set and avoid burnout. Narcotics was the coveted department of 15 detectives, and only officers passing the rigorous testing would be considered for openings in the rotation.

The Cheyenne narcotics division was coordinating their activities with the federal Drug Enforcement Agency task force to crack down on the drug trafficking between Cheyenne and Colorado.

Murray arrived at the DEA task force building just before 4:00p.m. He was joining his partner to interview a confidential informant. After entering the building, he went up to the 4th floor and sat down at one of the open desks.

A few minutes later, Detective Jason Moon of the Cheyenne police department brought in their confidential informant and they went into an interview room. As per protocol, they would do the interview without their weapons. Detective Murray removed the magazine case from his 9-millimeter service weapon and slid back the case to remove the bullet from the chamber and added it to the 14-round capacity magazine of his .40 caliber Glock 23. He placed the weapon in a designated locker.

"Alright, what do you have for us?" asked Detective Moon after they sat in the interview room.

"I was at a party, and I overheard this dude saying how he was making a ton of money selling pot and meth he got from Greeley and Denver."

"And who is this *dude*?"

"It was Henry Wesson," the CI stated.

"You mean Big Gun?" asked Detective Murray.

126

"Ah, so you know BG, do you?"

"Definitely. So, when is he making his next run?"

"I don't know. But I got something new for you," the CI replied with a sheepish grin.

"Go on," Detective Murray told him, unimpressed by the CI's obvious open-ended comment. He'd seen too many "hot tips" from CI's that went nowhere.

"He kept talking about getting a bunch of anhydrous ammonia...I think that is what it's called. I think he's gonna try to set up his own lab."

"Did he say how and where he was going to get it?"

"No, just that he was looking to grab some."

Detective Murray nodded to his partner and they told the CI they would be right back and left the interview room.

"He didn't give us a lot of specifics, but it's probably worth checking out and see what BG is up to," Detective Moon suggested.

"Let's cut this guy loose and head over there," Murray replied. A few minutes later, they escorted the confidential informant out of the building. Detective Murray went to retrieve his Glock from the gun locker, put the 14-round magazine into the weapon and put it back in his holster. He was ready to go.

There was only one way in and one way out of the Happy Trails Park that was home to about 40 mobile trailers. Everyone on the Cheyenne Police Department knew about this place, since there were almost nightly calls that ranged from noise complaints, to domestic violence, robbery, drug dealing, fighting and sometimes even murder. It was the definition of a rough neighborhood. It was also home to Henry "Big Gun" Wesson.

Detectives Murray and Moon were in an unmarked car about fifty yards from the entrance to the trailer park. They were well aware of Mr. Wesson's previous illegal activity, and they were waiting to see what he was up to.

After being parked for about an hour and 45 minutes, they saw an old Lexus pull out onto the street and in the passenger side, they saw it contained Mr. Henry Wesson. They let him go a few yards up the street and then started to follow him.

They were waiting for a legal reason to pull him over. At the moment they didn't have probable cause and they did not know who the driver was. They surmised it would only be a matter of time before the driver would commit some type of driving infraction, or even better, lead them to where they were looking to buy or steal anhydrous ammonia.

**

"We'll take your car, "BG stated.

"OK," Kyle responded, and they headed out in his luxury sedan. Kyle used some of his drug-running money to buy a Lexus LS400. However, this 1990 sedan was worn out long before Kyle purchased it. The vehicle included a variety of unique features including a ripped up backseat, numerous scratches and dings, along with electric locks that no longer worked. But to Kyle, it was still his *luxury sedan.*

"Head towards Interstate 80, we're going east," BG told him. It only took BG about two minutes to figure out that they were being followed. "You see that brown Buick behind us, they are police narcotics."

"What?" Kyle asked, and started to become nervous. He'd made a total of 23 deliveries between Cheyenne and Colorado, and never had the police near him. And here he was, without any drugs in his car and now they were being followed by the police.

Both Kyle and BG both had drugs in their system, which was already starting to make them a little paranoid, but now with an unmarked police car behind them, Kyle was convinced they were out to get him. And being nervous and distracted, Kyle never saw the stop sign.

"There it is, that's all we need," stated Detective Murray. They observed the traffic violation, which would be justification to pull them over. Normally, they would request a marked patrol car and a uniformed officer to make the routine traffic stop for them, as most people responded better to an official police car rather than an unmarked car with a small magnetic flashing light suddenly put on top of their roof. "We are less than a mile from the freeway, so we're going to have to pull them over ourselves," Murray stated.

"And this guy is always known for being armed, so we need to be careful," Moon warned.

***

"What do I do?" Kyle asked, looking into his rearview mirror and seeing the unmarked police car's flashing lights behind him.

"Step on it, we're almost to the freeway," BG told him. Kyle continued to hesitate though.

"What do you think you're doing?" BG asked, wondering why Kyle didn't do as he was told. Kyle drove slowly but not yet pulling over. He went another block and then decided to give up and pulled to the side of the road. BG was not happy.

"We're not going to get arrested today," BG said emphatically. Kyle saw stone cold eyes when he glanced over to him. That's when he noticed the .357 Magnum revolver in BG's hand, resting on his lap.

"What do you mean?"

"You pull over and when he comes up to you, lower your window and lean back. I'm going to blast him," BG stated without emotion.

***

Detectives Murray and Moon saw the Lexus pull over to the side of the road. They stopped behind it and radioed dispatch, who reported back that the Lexus belonged to Kyle. Kyle Parker had a clean record and was not someone that they were familiar with. But if he was hanging out with BG, he was probably a criminal, just one that hadn't been arrested yet. They both approached the car, with Detective Moon heading to the driver and Detective Murray on the passenger side.

"Did you know you went through a stop sign?" asked detective Moon.

Detective Murray was on the passenger side looking into the car to see if there was any obvious drugs or drug paraphernalia.

"Did I?" Kyle asked nervously.

"I'll need your driver's license, registration and insurance card."

Detective Murray was trying to get a better look of what might be on the floor near the passenger seat. He verified that the passenger was Mr. Henry Wesson, who let out a big exhale and then leaned further back in his seat. As he shifted his weight, that's when Murray saw what was under Wesson's thigh.

"GUN! GUN!" Murray shouted and both he and Detective Moon immediately drew their service weapon and pointed it at BG and Kyle.

"Put your hands up," he commanded, "put them up right now." Kyle immediately put his hands up, while BG hesitated a moment, grunted something inaudible and slowly put his hands up.

"Don't move until I tell you to," Detective Murray stated. Detective Moon got Kyle out of the car, put the handcuffs on him, searched him for weapons and put him in the back of the unmarked police car. They instructed BG to slowly get out of the car while making sure they both had eyes on exactly where his hands were.

"Let me see those hands, and don't do anything stupid," Murray instructed. After a tense couple of minutes, BG was then also handcuffed. They requested backup and a patrol car was soon bringing BG to the police station.

Two hours later

"That was a close call," Detective Moon stated, "you'll never guess what Kyle told me when I was bringing him back to the station."

"What did he say?" Detective Murray asked.

"Kyle was stressed out and nervous the entire time he was in the back of my car. He told me that they didn't realize there were two officers in our unmarked car. BG told Kyle that they weren't going to allow themselves to be arrested, and that BG was going to shoot the officer as soon as Kyle lowered his window."

"Oh crap," Detective Murray stated incredulously.

"That would have been me," Moon stated. "But when BG saw you in his side mirror walking up to the car, he didn't go through with it, and tried to hide the gun underneath his leg."

"That's why he had his gun, seemingly ready to go," Murray commented.

"Yes, otherwise he probably would have stashed it in the glove box or under the seat or something."

"We're lucky that we didn't get a patrol car to pull him over, since it's typically just one officer per vehicle. Who knows what could have happened?"

"Yes, it's a bit eerie now to think about how close we could have come to a shootout," Detective Moon commented in a serious tone.

"Yes, but it's worse than that," Detective Murray flatly stated and clenched his jaw.

"What do you mean?"

"Before we interviewed the confidential informant, I unloaded my gun as we're supposed to do, but when we left, I totally screwed up. I put the magazine back into the Glock, but I didn't chamber the bullet. I only realized it when we were here processing those two."

"Oh, wow." Moon commented as the weight of the dangerous possibilities sunk in. *This could have gone down much differently.*

"Yes, I might not have had enough time to properly load the weapon if BG tried to shoot one of us. I can't believe that I made a rookie mistake," Detective Murray stated and shook his head in obvious frustration. "It's embarrassing." His stomach tightened in a knot and he felt nauseous again, just as he did an hour ago when he first realized what he'd done. It was the definition of an *"oh, shit"* moment. It was now an even worse feeling, knowing that a loaded weapon was so close to being used by a desperate criminal.

"Wow, we really got lucky today," Moon replied, also realizing the gravity of what could have been. Both officers gazed in the distance for a moment.

"I was just so stupid!" Murray stated in anger. "I'm a field training officer, I've been on the SWAT team. I should have known better. I can't tell you how mad at myself I am. I am sorry I let you down, partner," he said beating himself up and disbelieving he made such an error.

"Look, we all make mistakes, I'm just thankful that it didn't cost us anything."

"Yeah, it just makes me *sick* knowing that I might have had to defend myself, only to realize the gun was not ready. I would have lost a precious second or two. *One or both of us might not be standing here if BG decided to start shooting. We got very lucky."*

***

August 2006

4:32p.m.

Detective Jamey Murray of the Cheyenne narcotics division waited for two hours in an unmarked police car near the house of Steven Tolentino. Mr. Tolentino had an arrest warrant for delivery of methamphetamine and felony possession of a gun. In layman's terms, he was a dangerous drug dealer.

The Cheyenne Police Department had already arrested Mr. Tolentino several times but that did not seem to deter his drug activity. As best as the police knew, he lived alone. Finally, Tolentino showed up and parked in the driveway. He lazily got out of the car and entered the house through his front door and was the only person to get out of the car.

"He showed up," Detective Murray stated, "Sorry, your dinner plans will have to wait," he told Detective Jason Moon.

"Fine," Detective Moon answered with a loud sigh, "I'm on my way."

A short time later, Detective Murray was also joined by Sergeant Simmons, who was in charge of the narcotics unit as well as Officer Greg Robinson. All four officers were members of the SWAT team, so they had worked together frequently and were ready to come up with their tactical plan.

When an officer is on road patrol, anything can happen, but when you are on a SWAT call, you are signing up for battle. Only those with a strong desire to combat evil, and be the person that can stop destruction and help people, join the SWAT team. They put themselves in harm's way, *on purpose*. Most SWAT calls aren't to save their family or friends. They are doing it for people that they don't know.

A few minutes later, Detectives Murray and Moon went to the back door while the other two officers went to the front door. Sergeant Simmons knocked on the door and identified themselves as the Cheyenne Police Department and they waited. Nothing happened.

"I hear movement inside the house," Sergeant Simmons said over the radio. In this situation, the police had a confirmed arrest warrant, and if they know the person is inside a residence, the police can enter the premises to make the arrest without needing a search warrant. This is common in many states, including Wyoming.

Although no one else entered the house when Steven Tolentino arrived home, that didn't mean that it was empty. Even just one person in the house makes the situation volatile and unpredictable. Yet with additional people, some of which could be criminals, can potentially create chaos.

The officers treated the situation as if they were on a SWAT incident and were on high alert as Sergeant Simmons busted down the door and entered the house. It didn't take long to clear the 900 square foot main level of the house. That left the basement, which had no means of escape.

The advantage of being a member of the SWAT team was the availability of additional firearms and tactical training. The officers cautiously walked down the basement stairs, anticipating everything and anything that could happen.

"This is the Cheyenne Police Department. We know you are in there. Come out slowly with your hands up," shouted Detective Murray. His command was met with silence.

What was Steven's state of mind? Was he going to try to hide? Was he armed? Was he going to come out with his hands up? Was he going to try to shoot his way out to avoid being arrested? Were there other people downstairs? If there were other people, were they criminals or not?

What if there were family members or a girlfriend? Would he use them as a hostage? Any one of those situations could be dangerous and potentially deadly.

When Detective Murray got to the basement, he saw a closed door on his left and a hallway leading to a larger opening on the right. Detectives Murray and Moon stayed near the closed door, while Simmons and Robinson continued down the hall to the larger room. They only found a few storage boxes and an old couch, but no Steven Tolentino.

Boom! They heard the sound of a gunshot going off and it echoed multiple times, but in that small basement it was difficult to determine where it was coming from. Immediately afterwards the basement was completely silent.

"Did you have an accidental discharge?" Detective Murray asked over the radio.

"No, we thought maybe you might have," replied Sergeant Simmons, "I don't see any signs of a bullet hole."

"No, it wasn't us." That only left one logical conclusion.

"This is the Cheyenne Police Department, Steven Tolentino put down your weapon and come out of that bedroom with your hands up!" Detective Murray shouted into the closed door. He was standing just to the left of the bedroom door and Detective Moon was on the right side. Silence.

Policing and especially a SWAT team are a highly trained group of officers who have a specific mission, including protecting the safety of the other officers. Similar to baseball, it is a team sport, but there is nothing the team can do to help the player when you are alone in the batter's box. It is all up to the individual.

Jamey Murray's philosophy as a baseball player was to be the player at bat in the bottom of the ninth inning with two outs and bases loaded and you need three runs to win the game. He's wants the pressure. He wants the opportunity. He wants to be the one in that situation because then it is 100% on him. That's the mentality of a winner in baseball and a member of the SWAT team.

More silence from the bedroom. It doesn't take much power to blow through a cheap hollow bedroom door, and Steven Tolentino's sawed off 12-gauge shotgun was more than enough to blast splintered wood into the hallway. The sound was deafening and reverberated throughout the basement for a long additional two seconds.

It only takes one mistake, one wrong move, one wrong decision or one unlucky step to the left or to the right to result in injury or death. Tolentino's shotgun pelted lead into the hallway.

"He's is trying to shoot his way out of here," thought Detective Murray and there was an immediate concern for Detective Moon standing only a few feet away. Luckily, the officers weren't hit.

Immediately, Detective Moon returned fire with his MP5 submachine gun, emptying his entire magazine within a matter of seconds. The smell of gun powder permeated the basement and there were multiple holes in the flimsy door.

The SWAT team listened for any response or movement from Steven Tolentino. There was silence followed by a faint sound coming from within the bedroom that indicated he was moving to the corner of the room. Even with holes in the door, there was no direct line of sight of where Tolentino was hiding.

Now, they had to decide their next tactical move. The smart play was to have the rest of the SWAT team deployed to the scene. That's exactly what they did, and they knew Mr. Tolentino wasn't going anywhere.

There were multiple attempts to entice Steven from the sole basement bedroom. But Tolentino wasn't interested in surrendering. He *was* interested in smoking the meth that he had in his pocket, so for the next three hours, he got high. He knew he was trapped and that he wasn't going to escape.

Rather than risk the lives of the SWAT team members with a bull rush, after three hours they decided to use tear gas in order to get Steven out of the bedroom. In a purposely loud voice, one of the SWAT team members started talking just outside the bedroom so that Steven could hear what he had to say.

"OK, since he won't come out peacefully, we're going to have to use gas on him." The strategy was to let him know what was coming and give Tolentino the choice of how he wanted it to end. Finally, Steven was out of meth and decided it was time to simply give up. He was then taken into custody without incident.

After it was over a few hours later, Detective Moon stated, "I just reacted. He shot through that bedroom door, and I just turned and shot back, but I was putting myself in harm's way. That wasn't too smart."

"It's a split-second decision," Detective Murray responded. "You stood your ground and when I heard the gunshot, I took a step back up the stairs. It was the training kicking in telling me to get out of the line of fire. I thought the wall in the stairwell was concrete, but it was actually just painted to look that way. He could have shot through the wall and easily hit me."

"That's pretty scary to think about."

"Yeah. You were more like Rambo," Detective Murray commented. "Which sounds brave and all, as long as you don't get hurt."

"This time it worked out for both of us," replied Detective Murray. "It's controlled fear in the heat of the moment, but when it's over, you realize how different the outcome could have been."

"If you always do what you've always done,
you'll always get what you've always gotten"
--Popularized by **Tony Robbins**, Unknown source

Bellevue, Nebraska

April 2019

"Mom and Dad may not have noticed, but I did," he said as his brother walked into their bedroom.

"What are you talking about?" Drake asked, and looked away, trying to appear busy.

"You're not fooling anybody. It looks to me like you got in a fight at school," stated fourteen-year-old Colin Chesterson, looking at his little brother as he put the backpack down on his bed.

"Well, sort of," eight-year-old Drake admitted to his brother. Colin came over and looked at his face a little closer, noticing some swelling and a touch of redness on his left cheek.

"Alright dude, I hope you kicked his butt," Colin replied and let out a big laugh.

"It's not funny," Drake retorted. It was the first time the second grader had been in a fight and it had lasted less than a minute before the teacher broke it up. He didn't like the way the kid at school was making fun of his mother.

"Look bro, if someone is bullying you at school you need to just punch his lights out, that'll send him a message of *who's in charge around here.*"

"No, it wasn't a bully, it was my friend Paul."

"That nerd, you let him beat you up? What's wrong with you?" Colin asked teasingly and punched his little brother in the shoulder, knocking him off balance where he tripped and fell onto his twin bed.

"It wasn't like that. You don't know anything," huffed Drake, and rubbed his shoulder. Colin's punches were not play fighting.

"Yeah well, you'll be explaining it to mom and dad; wait until they find out what their precious little boy did."

"No, don't tell them!" Drake protested.

"Why not, doesn't mom deserve to know what her perfect little angel is up to?" Colin retorted with an obvious strain of jealousy.

"No, they don't need to know. Besides, they're not going to do anything about it anyways," Drake responded with the reality of having uninvolved parents.

"Yeah, I guess you are right about that. Neither one of them are going to be winning any *parent-of-the-year* awards," Colin retorted.

"They're not that bad, they're just busy," Drake defended.

"Busy? Are you fooling yourself!" Colin jested. "They both sit around the house all day. Dad hasn't had a real job since I was your age," he snapped.

"Yeah, well..." Drake trailed off, unable to think of anything to contradict Colin. He knew his parents weren't the greatest, but he didn't doubt that they loved him. But *they did* have a lot of stuff going on, so what could Drake really complain about? Besides, on a day like today it was to his advantage that they didn't pay attention too much.

"So why did you and Paul get in a fight?" Colin asked. Were you fighting over a girl?" he asked mischievously.

"No," he answered and shook his head, "he was teasing me all day long and he kept doing it at lunch, so I threw a fork at him. And that's when we started wrestling on the ground."

"What was he teasing you about? That you're such a dork?" Colin asked and laughed again.

"He said mom's a tweaker, and I didn't like it," Drake responded.

"Well, she is," Colin laughed and continued, "What do you think she and dad do all day? They're just looking for their next score."

"Well, I didn't like when Paul said it, and I don't like when you say it either!" Drake exclaimed.

"Bro, you're just going to have to get used to it," he replied and trailed off.

"Well, I still don't like it. Colin, can I ask you something?" Drake asked and got noticeably quiet.

"Sure," Colin replied, suddenly calm and without the older brother's teasing tone.

"What's a tweaker?"

***

Six Months later

October 2019

"Where's Dad?" Drake asked his mother. He was standing in the kitchen holding his fishing pole in one hand and a tackle box in the other.

He was wearing his father's old fishing hat; it was olive in color with several hooks and lures attached to it. The hat had several rips and a few stains on it, showing its age and frequency of usage over the years. But Drake loved it because it made him feel like a real fisherman. *Especially* when he went fishing with his father.

But those outings were happening less and less. Drake could barely remember the last time he went fishing and wanted this day to recapture the father-son bond.

"I don't know," his mother replied without looking at him. It was 10 o'clock in the morning, and she looked like she hadn't slept in days. There was a reason for that, and it was *because she hadn't slept in days*. The partying started four days ago and hadn't stopped.

"I'm going fishing today with Dad," Drake stated with a smile. He was saying it with the pride of a son who loved his father and needed that special time to feel important in his father's life.

It didn't matter how big the lake was, and it didn't matter if the weather was too hot or too cold. It didn't matter if they were uncomfortable sitting on the dock nor did it matter if they caught anything or not. It didn't even matter if they had snacks, like his favorite peanut butter, tomato and mayonnaise sandwich or whether they just had granola bars and potato chips. None of that mattered because *this was about fishing with Dad*. That's all that mattered.

"Gee, that's great," his mother said without the enthusiasm to match the words. "Where is your brother?"

"He's out," Drake answered, knowing that he shouldn't get his brother in trouble by telling her that he never came home last night. He also wasn't going to mention that it wasn't the first time Colin didn't come home, or that he found funny looking cigarettes in their bedroom. He didn't need to experience the wrath of Colin. It just wasn't worth it. Drake had no idea where he was but would bet his life savings that Colin was up to no good.

"So, where is Dad?" Drake repeated his question. "We're going fishing today." He adjusted his hat and stood a little straighter with pride and hopeful anticipation. His mother's expression became sad for she knew there was not going to be a fishing trip today.

"I'm sorry honey, I don't think he's up for it today."

"But he promised!" Drake argued and started slightly rocking back and forth.

"Maybe another time," was all that she could come up, and cringed at the obvious disappointment in his face. She looked away and pretended to be seriously intent on cleaning the kitchen.

"But he said we would go today!" Drake once again protested, trying to continue his logical argument. His mother didn't answer him.

Drake ran upstairs to find his father in bed, wide awake. His father's hair was completely disheveled, with bloodshot eyes and he had several new scratches on his face. The fact that he hadn't slept for days matched exactly how he looked. He was dead tired, but nowhere near being able to fall asleep.

"Dad, it's time to go fishing, are you ready to go?" Drake asked in a way that indicated his hope was combined with fear of what the answer might be. He stood on his tippy toes to get a better look at his father; Drake smiled with all the cuteness and anticipation an eight-year-old could muster. His cheek slightly pulsed from the fear that he was going to get the answer he always got from his father.

"Not today," his father grumbled. "Why don't you just leave me alone?"

"But Dad!" Drake objected.

"Didn't you hear me?" he asked with an annoyed tone, his patience already gone. In reality, it was never there.

"But…" Drake whined.

"Get out!" he screamed, startling Drake and making him flinch and jump back a few steps. He quickly began to leave the bedroom with the tackle box and fishing pole still in his hands, and as he turned around, he heard the quick sounding "snap" as the pole broke against the frame of the door.

"Now look what you've done, you idiot." his father shouted and started to roll over to get out of bed. That was all Drake needed to see when he decided to literally run for his life. He left the broken piece of the fishing rod, and started to cry from the fright and stress, and ran down the hallway to hide in his room.

***

Ten hours later

8:00p.m.

Will Chesterson had barely moved out of his bed since yelling at his son about a fishing trip that would never happen. Once again, he let his younger son down.

His older son, Colin, was already cynical and indifferent about his father. Will could chalk it up to Colin being a rebellious teenager, but Colin had learned to expect all promises to be broken. Colin had been left alone to fend for himself too many times and Will knew it. Will already had given up on Colin; he was a lost cause.

But maybe it could be different with Drake, Will wanted to convince himself. Maybe it wasn't too late for him to be a good father. Maybe it wasn't too late for him not to lose another son.

Will finally dragged his weary body out of bed and headed towards the bathroom. He looked at himself in the mirror and was immediately disgusted. Here was a man 39-years-old but looked more like 59. His hair was greasy, and the lines on his face became more prominent as he recognized his own foul breath. His hand involuntarily twitched, as he tried to place toothpaste on the toothbrush.

That's it, I'm done with this stuff," he declared. He took a deep breath, and said it aloud again, "that's it, I quit." He started to brush his teeth and enjoyed the sudden minty freshness in his mouth. It'd been 30 hours since he experienced such freshness, and it provided some hope in his declaration for new sobriety.

"I'm going to be a good father from now on," he promised. "I'm not going to let Drake down, you can count on it," he said with a little more oomph, pointing at himself in the mirror. He stood up straighter, winked at himself in the mirror with the certainty that he was a changed man. *Better yet, a new man.*

***

Four hours later

Midnight

Will Chesterson gazed at the shard of crystal methamphetamine in between in his fingers. It looked exactly like a shard of glass and he stared at it a few seconds more, and then glanced at the small glass pipe in his left hand. He remembered his promise from just a few hours ago, but he was going to just make a *small alteration* to that promise. He just needed *one more hit*. That's all, *just one more*, and then he would quit for real this time.

He couldn't quite understand why he could take a hit every other day or so, but the *rush* didn't last that long. Sometimes it didn't last at all. It didn't make sense to him that taking more drugs resulted in less of a high.

He knew he'd let down his son once again. When he made that promise four hours ago, *he meant it*. He really did want to be a good father and wanted to be a good husband. But he wanted *something else even more.*

144

He sighed aloud and thought, *who was he fooling?* This stuff had a hold on him that he could not control. He was involuntarily moving his fingers and his left cheek was twitching. His body needed it, and there was *nothing and no one that was going to stop him.* He got out his lighter and lit up the shard and received another disappointing experience.

***

Two hours later

2:00a.m.

He'd already driven to his dealer's house two days ago to buy an 8-ball. But he and Abbey had gone through that 3 ½ grams of drugs way too fast. He was out again to the dealer for *just one more gram.*

He was having a hard time scraping up enough cash to pay for his little shards of joy. He'd already been to the pawn shop twice today. He knew he was running out of money and things to sell, and he was getting frustrated about that. But he'd worry about that later. He'd *have to worry about that later* because at that moment nothing else mattered to Will except lighting up that next shard.

***

2:30a.m.

"Did you hear that?" Will asked his wife while they were in the garage. The single car garage door was always closed because he and his wife Abbey used it as an overflow living area space. But more importantly and frequently, it was their party space. There were only a few more hits left in the meth pipe when Will reluctantly gave it to his wife for the last inhale.

Suddenly, he exclaimed, "That. Didn't you hear that?" he asked again.

"Hear what?" Abbey asked with little concern.

"There's somebody up in the attic!" he complained and continued, "I can hear them walking around and playing music. Don't you hear the thump, thump from the bass?" he asked and started pacing around the garage.

There was a small attic space directly above them and he kept looking up, seeking signs of someone in his attic. What were they doing up there?

How long have they been there? Were they going to attack his family? Will really panicked when he thought that maybe they were there to steal his meth? He was starting to get agitated and stressed, and his wife could feel the tension in the room rise.

"Did you know about this?" he accused his wife. He went over to Abbey, grabbed her by the shoulder and stared down into her sunken eyes and asked again, "why'd you let them in?"

"You're crazy," she replied. This was the wrong answer.

"Liar!" he said in anger and took a long swooping swing and slapped her on the side of the head, catching her ear. It didn't take much force to push her down to the ground.

"I'm not going to let them get away with this. They're not going to steal any of my stuff!" he yelled and went over to the toolbox in the corner of the garage, flipped open the lid and yanked out his handgun. He started pointing it at the ceiling and continued pacing back and forth.

"You come down from there, or I'm going to shoot you," he threatened. He could hear movement above him. And the music was still thumping something awful. Will put his hands to his ears to try to block the noise, and he kept turning in circles.

Abbey tried to move away from him in fear that the gun could go off and shoot her.

"Get out of that attic, right now!" Will once again demanded. "They've probably been up there for weeks. They probably have been stealing our food in the middle of the night," he exclaimed to his wife.

Will remembered losing some of his meth, so it was probably them. "They stole it!" he said convincingly to no one in particular. How dare they live in *his house*. He was getting angrier and more agitated the more he thought about it.

"Come down now, or I'm going to shoot you," he said and pointed the gun from one corner of the attic to another. He constantly kept walking back and forth, and then would stand still trying to listen for exactly where they were in the attic.

"We'll see how smart they are when I call the police," he stated, nodding his head, impressed with the brilliance of his idea. He placed the gun back into the toolbox.

In less than ten minutes, Officers Jamie Murray and George Reinhart were at the Chesterson residence. This was the second time they'd come to this house. Previously they had responded a few months ago on a domestic violence incident where the neighbor had called because Will was screaming at his wife at the top of his lungs in their front yard.

At that time there was no physical evidence of abuse, and Abbey denied that anything had happened. The state of Nebraska, like many other states, mandates that an abuser be charged with a domestic violence assault if there are physical signs of abuse that contradict the victim's denial, such as bruises, a bloody nose or a broken bone.

Tonight, dispatch had informed Officer Murray that the homeowner, Will Chesterson, had called about someone breaking and entering his residence and living in his attic. When the officers arrived, Will seem surprised to see him.

"What are you doing here?" Will asked with defiance. The last thing he wanted was for a police officer to find any remnants of his drug use. Of course, he didn't remember that this same officer had been at his house months earlier, and even to the untrained eye, it would be obvious that Will and Abbey were frequent drug users.

"We received a call about some people living in your attic," Officer Murray stated. He peered through the front door and saw trash on the floor, dishes all over the sink, a cracked window and an ingrained smell of tobacco and marijuana. *Home sweet home.*

"Who told you that?" Will asked and turned to his wife in annoyance.

"You did when you called 9-1-1." Officer Murray stated before Will could think about blaming his wife some more. "Why don't you show me the attic, and I'll check it out for you," he said more as a statement and less as a suggestion. He gestured his hands to motion them towards the garage.

"OK, follow me," Will reluctantly agreed.

"*I've seen this movie before,*" Officer Murray thought to himself.

It didn't look like much had changed since he had been to the house a few months ago. The parents were still regular drug users, and as he went down the short hallway towards the garage, he saw an eight-year-old boy peering around the corner. He remembered there being an older son, a young teenager, who was nowhere to be found.

It was common for meth users to have very vivid hallucinations that they are convinced are real but are completely disconnected from reality. Officer Murray knew that Mr. Chesterson was convinced there was somebody in the attic. Maybe there was, and he had to be cautious in approaching the situation, until it could be proven that it was a hallucination.

They entered the garage, and Officer Murray could see more trash on the floor, ants on the floor near half eaten food and a well-used meth pipe. He immediately saw a rope hanging from the garage ceiling for pull-down attic stairs.

"Is this the only access to the attic?" the officer inquired.

"Yeah, they're up there, don't you hear them?" Will asked, still visibly agitated, and started picking at the sore on his forehead. "They won't turn off that incessant music," Will stated. The room was completely silent to Officer Murray.

"Go back into the house so I can investigate the attic," Officer Murray stated. Neither Will nor his wife Abbey made any attempt to go back into the house, but they did step back from the ladder.

Officer Murray had a heightened sense of awareness as he pulled the rope downward since anything could happen. The ladder stairs folded out and he shined his flashlight up into the attic with his left hand, with his gun drawn towards the darkness in case there truly was a threat.

"This is Officer Murray with the Bellevue Police Department, come out of the attic and down the stairs slowly. Right now," he commanded. Nothing happened.

"They're up there, I'm telling you," Will interjected, "can't you hear them scurrying to the corner of the attic?" Will asked, unable to stand still as if he were a hyperactive child.

Officer Murray took one step on the ladder to test how stable it was, and was pleasantly surprised to determine it was sturdy, and was probably the only remaining thing in the house that was not worn out or destroyed by its occupants. His eyes were completely focused on where his flashlight was shining, then he told the people in the attic to come down the stairs, but he heard no movement or response.

When Officer Murray arrived at the top of the attic stairs he quickly flipped to the left and in a quick sweeping motion did a complete 360 viewing of the attic. Officer Reinhart was right behind him.

At first, they didn't see anything or anyone. They again shone the flashlight in a slower motion, and saw some boxes and a broken crib, but nothing else. They did a third pass just to be sure there was no one hiding behind any of the boxes, and both came back down the stairs.

There wasn't any evidence that someone had been in the attic for months. There were no signs of people, food, trash or anything else that might be left behind by somebody trying to hide out in an attic. There was nothing and no one. It had all been in Will's head.

***

Two Months Later, December 2019

8:56p.m.

"9-1-1, what's your emergency?" "It's my mom."

"OK, tell me what's going on."

"I'm afraid," the boy stated, and started to cry.

"What's happened to your mom?"

"She's bleeding," the boy struggled to reply. "Where is she bleeding from? Did she get hurt?"

"Her nose," Drake responded and continued to cry, "I think my Dad's going to kill her," he wailed.

"I've already got the police headed to your house. I want you to stay on the phone with me until an officer arrives and will make sure you're safe, OK? Do you think you can do that?"

"Yeah, I think so. I just want him to stop," Drake responded in desperation, trying hard to hold back the tears.

***

Eight minutes later

"Don't hit me again! I hate you!" Abbey screamed at her husband, just as Officers Murray and Reinhart got to the front door, and it looked like the dispute was still going on.

Abbey opened the front door, oblivious to Officer Murray, as she tried to get out of the house and away from Will. Will was not far behind, and he stepped out the front door into the crisp Nebraska winter air.

Officer Murray quickly got in front of him to prevent him from continuing after Abbey.

"I'm going to kill that stupid little bitch," Will said in a rage as he pointed at Abbey.

Abbey turned around, pointed her finger at him, and shouted, "I hate you; I hate you!" She put her hand up to her nose to try to stop the blood from flowing. It had completely soaked her sweater and now was dripping onto the snow in the front yard.

Between her physical injury and hearing her tell Will not to hit her was all the evidence needed to make an arrest for a misdemeanor domestic violence assault. Officer Murray said, "Turn around, and get down on your knees." Officer Murray went to retrieve his handcuffs from a pouch attached to his belt.

But Will Chester Chesterson wasn't going to follow his instructions. He was tweaking in a big way, and he was not going to allow anyone to stop him from sending a message about *who's in charge around here*.

"Get on your knees or I'm going to have to taser you," Officer Reinhart commanded. Will completely ignored his command and headed towards his wife at the front of the yard.

"Will, it is up to you how we handle this. It is totally up to you," Officer Murray told him, but Will kept moving towards Abbey.

"Stop right there," Officer Reinhart commanded, waited a split second and hit him with the taser.

Will flinched and looked back at the officer with angry eyes. Officer Reinhart was focused on Will, expecting him to fall to the ground and provide enough time to be handcuffed. But Will kept walking towards his wife, his hands clenched in a tight fist and sweating profusely.

Officer Reinhart stepped closer to Will and shot him with the taser again. Will flinched a second time. A normal person would go down after being tasered just once, but in his drug fueled rage, his hostility and adrenaline were in control of his body. He brushed off the taser wires and took another step forward. Reinhart was out of taser cartridges.

Officer Murray hit him with pepper spray, but it had no effect. His eyes didn't water, his nose didn't run and Will didn't seem bothered by it. The meth had dulled his ability to feel pain. *How does this guy keep going?*

"Just comply!" Murray told him, but there was no reaction.

A third patrol officer arrived on the scene. A frustrated Officer Reinhart told him to taser Will a third time. He slowed his step, and then finally fell to his knees. Officer Murray quickly tackled him, put his left hand on Will's shoulder and pushed him down to the snow.

Finally, Will was starting to run out of energy and it took all three officers to handcuff Will. Officers Murray and Reinhart helped Will to his feet and started to walk him to the back of the patrol car.

"No, don't arrest him," Abbey pleaded.

"Please ma'am, step back," Officer Murray told her.

"Leave him alone, he didn't mean it. I'm OK. I don't want to press charges," Abbey replied, hoping that was enough to get her husband out of handcuffs. It wasn't.

"I hate you!" Abbey screamed to the officers as they escorted Will to the police car. "You're ruining my life. Why don't you just mind your own business and leave us alone!" she continued. Officer Murray ignored her request, and they put Will in the patrol car to wait for the ambulance.

Standard procedure is that anyone tasered or sprayed with pepper need to be checked out by medical professionals.

Abbey didn't say a word and stared at her husband through the window of the police car. She was still standing in the front yard, and she looked down and realized her sneakers were wet from the snow, suddenly noticing that she felt cold.

Abbey's blood had stopped dripping and Officer Murray asked if she wanted him to call an ambulance. She declined. He handed her a card and said, "This is the local battered women's shelter; you need to give them a call; they can help."

She looked at the card, didn't say a word, and headed back into the house and saw the third officer checking on Drake.

"I'm Officer Swanson, and you can call me if you are in trouble," he stated and handed his business card to Drake and then to Abbey. She took the card from him without making eye contact and walked into the kitchen. She threw the card into the trash can, shook her head in disgust, and muttered under her breath, "why did that kid have to start trouble?"

The three officers searched the house and found Will's gun and confiscated it, adding to his criminal charges since he was a felon in possession of a firearm.

Mr. Chesterson was released from the hospital 90 minutes later and was taken into custody and brought to jail. He still had an above normal resting heart rate of 125 beats per minute, still affected by the drugs he took hours earlier.

***

"For the night is far from over And the storm is coming on.
And the wind is blowing colder. And he's very far from home.
When hell falls cold and wet. His heart soon forgets.
That ever he was loved or wanted to be loved."
-- **Big Head Todd and the Monsters**, *Soul For Every Cowboy*,

***

Eight days later

11:18a.m.

"We need to get a gun," Will told his wife as they got into their car. Will was given a summons to later appear in court and was let out after making bail of $15,000, 10% of which was from Abbey who was able to scrounge up some cash by selling the television, phone and several other possessions. The remaining was covered by a bail bondsman.

"OK," was all that Abbey could respond with.

"Head over to the pawn shop," he stated flatly, as Abbey turned onto Galvin Road.

Ten minutes later, they were parked in front of the pawn shop. Will had had a previous felony conviction, so he would not be able to legally purchase a handgun. After being let out of jail that morning, Will searched the house for his gun but couldn't find it. He was convinced that the people had come back into his attic and had stolen his gun. It was imperative for him to get a replacement.

"What kind do you want me to get?" Abbey asked.

"I don't care, whatever is the cheapest."

"I don't have any money," Abbey stated without emotion. Will looked at her with an annoyed expression and then nonchalantly told her, "Use your wedding ring." Abbey shrugged her shoulders without saying anything and went into the pawn shop.

Fifteen minutes later she came out with a .22 caliber Ruger handgun and she was ringless. She handed him the gun, briefly looking down at her finger, shrugged her shoulders with indifference and started the car.

"Go to Walmart for ammo," Will told her. She nodded her head and headed in that direction; her face was expressionless.

11 hours later

10:09p.m.

"You ain't no prize," Will said, scoffing at his wife and lighting up another shard in his pipe. "You ain't getting better looking," he said with intended cruelty and disdain.

"Yeah, well, just give me another hit," she replied, brushing off his insults. Her face was tired and worn, and it had been a different decade since she used make-up. Why bother? Who was she going to impress?

Abbey expected this treatment and was way beyond the point of caring for the man she was married to. He reluctantly handed her the pipe.

Will suddenly stood up, tipping over the kitchen chair and surprising Abbey with his sudden motion. "Damn it! They're back!" he exclaimed and headed out towards the garage.

Abbey grudgingly followed him only because he still had the meth pipe. Drake was in his room and came out to see the commotion.

"Those people in the attic, they are so damn noisy. Did they think I wouldn't hear them?" Will asked defiantly. He rubbed his eyes and ran his fingers through his greasy hair, stopping at his cheek to pick at another sore.

"Yeah, I hear them too," Abbey said, figuring it was best to agree with Will rather than start an argument.

Will immediately went to his toolbox where he'd stashed the Ruger just a few hours ago. He grabbed the gun and stared at the rope hanging from the ceiling and told Abbey, "I'm going to get them."

"Mom, what's going on?" Drake asked in a panicked tone and clutched her leg for comfort.

"He's getting the people living in the attic," she stated with little emotion or interest. She simply wanted Will to finish his investigation so she could get that next high. Maybe there were people upstairs, or maybe not, and it didn't really matter to her. *She just wanted to smoke that next piece of glass.*

"What people?" Drake asked, looking around and trying to figure out what his parents were talking about. Both Abbey and Will ignored his question.

Will took aim at the imaginary spot that he thought the intruders were hiding and pulled the trigger. Boom! The sound was deafening in the small garage and there was a hole near the corner of the garage ceiling.

"I got him," Will declared. Drake was shaking in fright from the noise and tension from the uncertainty of what would happen next.

Will managed to pull down the attic stairs and started up. As he lifted his leg for the next step, he bumped his toe into the edge of the stair, and he lost his balance and fell forward. He bounced off the attic stairs and landed onto the garage floor, dropping his gun.

Will groaned on the floor, and a small trickle of blood ran down his forehead. In his drug-fueled delirium, he was convinced that the intruders came down the stairs and pushed him off while they tried to escape. Abbey didn't react and had no intention of helping her husband.

As he laid on the ground moaning, Abbey noticed that Will left the meth pipe next to the toolbox. She went over to inspect it, to see if just by chance anything was left. She lifted the glass pipe up towards the garage light, trying to see if maybe, just maybe, she could light more.

Will rolled over onto his hands and knees and slowly got to his feet. He took a few steps over to grab the gun and then noticed Abbey with the meth pipe.

"You give me that back," Will yelled, pointing the gun at Abbey. "How dare you push me down the stairs and then try to steal my pipe! I told you people to get out of my attic."

"Dad what are you doing?" Drake screamed, "Don't hurt us! Please!" he said, still hugging at her hips.

Will just ignored him. The only thing he saw was an intruder trying to steal his stuff. He didn't care about whether the intruder was going to hurt his family, he only cared about one thing, *protecting his stash.*

He stared at Abbey with his bloodshot eyes, focused on what she had in her hand. His anger was building up at the intruders that had been bothering him for months. He had finally been proven correct and now he had the thief trapped.

Abbey started to put the pipe down on the workbench next to the toolbox, but that motion caused Will to involuntarily flinch, and the gun went off.

***

The next day

Jamey Murray stared into the dancing flames coming out of his fireplace. He enjoyed the warmth and comfort it provided to the room. He took a sip of his *Buffalo Trace* bourbon, noticing its soulful amber color and smooth finish. It also warmed his body on this cold December evening.

The department issued its usual twice daily special report of significant police activities and he learned what happened to Abbey Chesterson the night before. It could have been predicted, and he let out a sigh as this was a common outcome.

Unfortunately, he'd seen it more times than he'd like to think about. He pushed the negative thoughts from his mind. He had no idea who Will and Abbey Chesterson really were.

He only knew what he'd observed on the multiple calls to their residence. If he's been called to a residence several times, there was usually a bad outcome.

Tiffany walked into the room, and he gave her a broad smile and raised his glass. That's what he really needed, to see his wife's pretty face. She smiled back and sat in the chair next to him, and briefly looked at the fire

"Do you remember the domestic case I was telling you about a few weeks ago?" Jamey asked. "The one with two boys in the household."

"The one you've been to several times?" Tiffany asked.

"Yes. The husband was high on drugs, as usual, and was out of control. He was hallucinating and shot his wife in the neck last night. She didn't make it," he said solemnly.

"How awful," Tiffany exclaimed.

"And the worst part, is that he did it in front of their eight-year-old son."

"That poor kid, he must be traumatized," Tiffany replied.

"I'm sure he is, how could he not be?" Jamey asked. "They had another son, a fourteen-year-old who was not home at the time. Those kids have seen their father beat up their mother multiple times."

"And now those kids have to live with the fact that their father murdered their mother," she stated. "I'm glad you don't take all the crap you have to deal with and make it personal," she told him.

"Yeah, that's the tough part of this job, you really see the worst in people. Domestic violence situations are so unpredictable. Maybe at one time they had a happy marriage, but that was long gone before I ever arrived."

"I hope those kids can get some counseling," she said.

"They should be able to, but the question is what will the lasting effect be on those boys? Their mother is dead, and their father will most likely be in jail at least until they are into middle age."

"This kind of traumatic incident will be a crossroads in their life, I just hope that they can make it through it all," Tiffany expressed.

"That's the real tragedy, the combination of drugs and domestic violence and how it makes everything worse. It's one thing to have anger management issues, but then you throw in drugs and an enabling spouse and these events are inevitable," Jamey stated. "You have two kids who have been raised in this household and this is what they know, that's *all they know*."

"That's what they think is normal."

"That's the other tragedy about this," she exclaimed. "They've seen dad assaulting mom and maybe once in a while fighting back, with it culminating in their father killing their mother," she said.

"So that's the $1 million dollar question. What happens to these two young men? As they grow up, which side of the coin are they going to end up on? Are they going to stay completely away from drugs and understand that you don't treat women that way and maybe try to protect other moms like that? Or do they grow up seeing that it's normal to abuse your spouse?" Jamey asked.

"And all of society suffers for it. Does the cycle continue with them or was this a shock and they go the complete opposite way and become fantastic husbands and fathers? Maybe they will resolve not to be like him," Tiffany said in a hopeful manner.

"Maybe. But maybe not," Jamey concluded, and returned his gaze to the fireplace. There wasn't anything left to say.

***

Five Fun Facts About Jamey Murray

1. He writes left-handed and shoots and plays golf right-handed.

2. He has never hit a homerun in baseball, from Little League through the Junior College World Series.

3. He has never smoked anything.

4. After numerous hunting trips, he never had an opportunity to take a shot at an elk.

5. His second-grade teacher said he was worst singer she'd ever heard.

In the Batter's Box

IV.

Firsthand Knowledge

December 2012

> "Who is gonna make it?
> We'll find out in the long run"
> —**The Eagles**, *The Long Run*

It was almost time. But before getting into the car, he paused to look at Colorado's most famous and majestic mountain, Pikes Peak. Its beauty viewed from the relatively flat city of Colorado Springs can hide its ability to intimidate.

No one will tell you that getting to its peak at 14,115 feet above sea level is ever routine. Hiking it is difficult even for those with experience. Or you could take the effortless way up there, as many tourists do, by riding the cog railway to the very top and stroll into the highest elevation donut shop in the world.

Life may be a journey, but rarely do people sit back and relax their way to the top of the world. Most times you need a goal in mind and must pursue it relentlessly. Sometimes you need to forget what others say if they're negative and pessimistic.

Most times you should follow your own path, but that is achievable only when you can clearly see your path. Only if and when you know your objective. When you finally understand your path there's a sense of peace and understanding, but there's also a sense of urgency to complete and achieve the goal.

People who hike up Pikes Peak prepare for the long and difficult route. But there's an incredible feeling when you reach the summit, a moment of real accomplishment, something to be proud of, and something that you'll remember for the rest of your life. He was going to feel that way in less than an hour when his name was called.

To say that his chosen path was difficult or unlikely would be too simplistic, a too neat and tidy explanation. His path was much more complicated and like many people, the road to his career was not straight, and included curves and plenty of ups and downs.

But it did not bother the man that his road wasn't short and direct. It wasn't a straight line. He realized that all his life events eventually got him to where he was right now, driving to a nondescript building in Colorado's second largest city, soon to be the most recent graduate of the Pikes Peak Police Academy.

He wasn't the youngest graduate at twenty-eight years old, but he was bursting with youthful enthusiasm and very ready to start his adventure as a police officer. That's how he viewed it, an adventure of a lifetime and a career that he could wear with pride.

Perhaps no one would have guessed this career path, including himself, when at fifteen he was caught trying to steal a magazine from a 7-11. It seemed like a fun thing to do at the time, demonstrating to a girl that he had the guts and the wherewithal to steal from a store. Looking back at it now, it was a stupid idea, but more importantly, it begs the question of what kind of girl would be impressed by a young thief?

And almost certainly no one would have guessed this career choice when he was seventeen years old and was arrested for driving under the influence of alcohol. Bad teenage choices for sure, but luckily it did not disqualify him from pursuing a career in law enforcement.

Becoming a police officer might have been the last career choice in his mind. His high school interactions with law enforcement were negative and frustrating.

The local police seemed to be tougher on him than his other high school friends. Yes, he was making mistakes that warranted police interaction, but a couple of the local officers seemed to have it in for him.

He'd been living in the town of Buena Vista since the age of twelve, with his father being a native from Colorado and his mother from West Africa, which is also where he was born. He viewed himself as a *genuine African American*.

He wondered many times if he was targeted by certain officers because of his skin color. They never used racial slurs, but their actions made him question their motives. His interactions with the police led to disdain and hatred for certain officers and a general dislike of law enforcement. He didn't trust them.

None of his offenses rose to the level of a serious crime, but people that knew him would not have guessed that law enforcement was in his future. He was never physically targeted by the local police, but his perception of their demeanor and intensity communicated their dislike of the young man. Certain officers acted that way with everyone, *but it was amped up with him.*

After high school graduation, he became a productive member of society with a series of restaurant and construction jobs. He had always learned a good work ethic from his father, so it seemed natural to be employed and self-sufficient as an adult.

He still enjoyed hanging out and partying with his many high school friends. Those were good times filled with camaraderie and lots of laughs. But in his mid-20s, his mindset began to change. He was entering a new age of maturity.

He was a part owner in a local landscaping company, and it was paying the bills, but it wasn't hitting its mark for long term fulfillment. He thought about working at the local prison as a corrections officer, but it didn't seem quite right. His friends were going in all different directions and some of them had no direction.

The idea of law enforcement was beginning to appeal to him. He was starting to think of his high school experience with police officers, and concluded that their actions were not merely unwarranted, but were deficient. That's not how a police officer should behave and interact with the citizens.

He was convinced there was a better way and wanted to be part of a better policing society. He'd been on the other end of policing and believed he'd have a unique insight when the experience came full circle. He could relate and understand the human element of why people do what they do.

It was only six months ago that he enrolled in the police academy. He'd done his research, and the more he found out about what he'd learn at the police academy, and the career opportunities available, the more he found it interesting and exciting.

There was a side benefit to enrolling, and that was once the commitment was made, it was harder to turn back or be talked out of the decision. Also, he knew he needed some distance and independence from his life in Buena Vista.

He remembered telling some of his friends that he wanted to become an officer and they were flabbergasted and tried to get him to stop the pursuit of becoming a police officer. There were no family members in law enforcement that he could talk to; he made the decision solely on his own.

Instead of listening to the naysayers, something in his gut told him that this was the path he should follow. The more he thought about his future, and the more he thought about the doubters, the more resolved he felt to prove them all wrong, see it through and be successful.

As the oldest child, he felt some pressure to be successful and become a role model for the family. He had something to prove to unsupportive friends and family, the town of Buena Vista, and most importantly to himself. He wanted to make it in the long run. When it came to a career, he finally had that fire in his belly. Graduation from the academy was to be his first accomplishment in his law enforcement career.

It wasn't easy to temporarily move himself to Colorado Springs, a town where he knew no one, and attend the academy. Now he was truly on his own, after breaking up with his girlfriend just a few weeks before classes started in the summer. He honestly thought she was the one, and it was disappointing when the hard truth hit him that they were no longer together.

And there wasn't going to be a Hollywood-style romantic reunion. Maybe that breakup could have been the excuse to forgo the academy, but he held on strong and focused on his classwork and training. It wasn't easy to push out the pain of a relationship that was not meant to be. But sometimes *pushing through* it can build more strength.

In sports, people sometimes call it having *heart*. In life, it is mind over matter, it was something to prove with pure perseverance. Focused determination usually wins in the end.

He and his classmates were seated on the small stage. The leader of the academy was calling up everyone in alphabetical order. The man felt a pang of nervousness and excitement in his stomach; this was it; this part of the journey is completed. This part of the goal is done. But it was only the first part. The adventure would soon begin for real. He waited another moment, stood up and walked forward as his name was called.

Meet Mohamed Lamine Mullenax, age 36

Christian

Man

Son

Brother

Husband

Father

Daddy

Uncle

Patriot

American

High School Wrestler

Family Grill master

Arrest Control Instructor

Deputy Sergeant, Chaffee County Colorado Sheriff's Office

SWAT team member

March 2016

In 1989, the four-door Cadillac in the Fleetwood model rolled off the manufacturing line at a whopping 17 feet in length. This luxury vehicle is not to be confused with the Fleetwood brand which made a 17-foot camper that was great for a long weekend. Not so great as a permanent residence 27 years later.

It was getting close to sunset when Deputy Lamine Mullenax slowly drove down the dirt driveway and saw the Fleetwood trailer parked on the side of a small rundown house. That camper was the current residence of Kim and Bree Bertrand, where he was about to perform a welfare check.

A welfare check is when an officer visits the home of an individual or their child to assess whether a person is harming someone or themself. It can cover a wide variety of situations, such as threats of violence, or when a person has talked about suicide. It also can be performed to check on whether a child has been neglected. Most times the calls are initiated by the individual's social media post, a concerned friend, neighbor, family member or teacher.

Buena Vista second grade teacher, Mrs. Thompson, noticed that her student Bree was wearing the same clothes the entire week and had only brought her lunch once. Bree told the teacher that she'd "forgotten" her lunch, but Mrs. Thompson overheard Bree tell a friend that she didn't have any lunch to bring. Bree seemed a little down and unresponsive during class, which was unusual for her.

Bree was distracted and although second graders aren't known for their long attention span, this was out of character for Bree. She was usually a rather good student, but this had been a bad week for her and continued when Bree failed her spelling quiz. Vocabulary words were an area where Bree excelled, and Mrs. Thompson became concerned.

Thinking back several weeks, Mrs. Thompson concluded that today was another indicator of Bree's steady decline. Something was wrong and Bree's situation was getting worse.

Deputy Mullenax turned off his patrol car, stepped out and headed towards the trailer. He noticed an extension cord coming from a window in the house that was plugged into the trailer.

He observed a skinny black Labrador mix come out from under the camper and was chained to the trailer's hitch. It looked like the dog continuously stayed outside since its hair was mangled and dirty. Maybe that wasn't such a big deal in the summer, but since it was March the dog would be exposed to snow, rain and mud.

The fifteen-foot chain for the dog created a densely populated circumference of dog poop. The area left little room for a clean area which also meant that the dog was frequently sitting in it. It barely raised an eyebrow as the deputy approached the trailer. Apparently, its days of protecting the home front were over.

The deputy knocked on the door and a few seconds later Kim opened it, surprised that she had a visitor. The first thing that Deputy Mullenax spotted were her eyes. Not the color, but the way they drooped, were bloodshot and looked very tired for someone who was only 24 years old.

"Yeah?" was all that Kim managed to say. Being exhausted at that moment was the cumulative effect of multiple events and life choices, many of which had not been in her best interest.

***

Kim remembers *that* day like it was yesterday. It was the day that her life forever changed. She was sixteen years old that warm summer afternoon, lazily watching the *Jerry Springer Show* when her mother came home from work. She immediately hassled Kim for watching trashy television. She was tired of her mother constantly pestering her about wasting time, only working a few hours a week and hanging out with people her mother considered to be the *wrong crowd*.

But was there a *right crowd* to be found in Trinidad, Colorado? Kim didn't think so. What did it matter if her mother didn't approve of her friends? Who is *she* to be telling her what to do? This woman gave birth to Kim when she was only 18 years old and whose greatest career claim to fame was receiving a $100 tip at the diner on Christmas Eve in 2009?

As her mother continued to complain about Kim relaxing on the couch, she received a text from Lance, her boyfriend. His neighbor had just returned from the liquor store and Lance was able to buy from him a liter of blackberry brandy, Kim's favorite. That was all she needed for an excuse to get out of the house. Ten minutes later Lance showed up on his motorcycle.

Lance tried hard to be the stereotypical bad boy, riding his motorcycle as his long hair flapped in the wind. He had horrible grades and should have repeated his senior year if he hadn't been expelled for fighting and coming to school drunk. The last straw was when he exposed himself to the school principal.

He considered being expelled a badge of honor. Seventeen-year-old Lance didn't care, and he soon started working in his uncle's automotive shop making surprisingly good money for a kid his age. That was six months ago, and the extra cash enabled him to have the loudest motorcycle in the county, purchase a leather jacket and studded boots to complete the "Hell's Angels" wannabe look.

Kim liked being around the rebellious Lance and his "I don't care what the world thinks" attitude, but she didn't realize that she was going to soon join that category. He was sweet-talking her about getting married someday and moving out of their one-horse-town and starting a new life.

Lance dreamed of moving to San Antonio, Texas where he had an older cousin that worked in a sheet metal shop who was promising Lance $25 per hour to be a welder's apprentice. That sounded like a pot of gold to Lance. The only question for him was how long was he going to wait for Kim?

They headed to an old broken-down homestead cabin on the edge of town. It wasn't the *Ritz-Carlton*, or even a *Motel 6* for that matter, but it had privacy. It was quiet and it was a great place to drink and convince Kim to lose her inhibitions. Kim loved being the rebel's girlfriend and he looked even more attractive after she finished half a bottle of the brandy. She knew what he wanted next. And she was prepared to give it to him.

Kim was going to be a junior in high school in the fall and had two more years left, which when you are a teenager seems like an eternity. It was a long time to wait to leave town and run away together. Two months after the blackberry brandy afternoon, Kim told Lance that she was pregnant.

They fought for several days; he was pressuring her to "take care of the problem." The rebel duo's relationship started to fall apart. *How could she give up this baby? What if her own mother had made that kind of decision?*

It was not something that Lance could comprehend, and he wanted no part of "responsibility," so exactly one week after she told him, he left for Texas. Kim was crushed. Kim tried to get his wages garnished for child support, but the weasel only lasted six months at the welding job and she wasn't able to track him down again.

When Bree was four years old, she was convinced by a high school friend to move to Buena Vista and be her roommate. She had a chance to start her life over. Her relationship with her mother was strained, so she figured she didn't have much to lose. Unfortunately, she didn't have much to gain either.

But when her friend got fired from her job and returned to Trinidad, that left Kim and Bree on their own. Kim was employed as a cashier at the *True Value* hardware store, but she didn't have enough money or desire to move back to Trinidad. Kim didn't see much point in leaving, so she stayed right where she was.

But with no family or friends, it made being a single mother even harder than it already was. Sometimes she resented her life, and it was hard to remember the carefree days of high school. But she didn't have a choice. Luckily, Bree was a well-behaved child and was a good student. Kim couldn't figure out where Bree got her smarts from, but she was sure glad that she had them.

Most of the time she thought about Bree's future and dreamed about what she might do someday, and what she might accomplish. Kim was sure that Bree's future was bright and hoped she'd do something special with her life. Kim wanted Bree to avoid the mistakes she made and was proud of her little girl. She truly loved Bree more than life itself.

Kim didn't think much about her own future, that is, until she met Joe about a year ago. They quickly hit it off and he even enjoyed being a father figure to Bree. Kim allowed herself to dream about the three of them being a family. Kim desperately wanted to have a real father for Bree who could be a good role model and live in a stable household.

When she told Joe a few months later that she was pregnant with his child, she was terrified of what his reaction would be. She was a little surprised and thrilled that he was happy and excited about it. She couldn't have asked for a better reaction. He talked about the future, *their* future.

173

Joe told her that he was a long-haul trucker, which conveniently explained why he would be with her for several days in a row, and then be gone for a couple of weeks. A few weeks after revealing her pregnancy, she found a picture of Joe tagged in a Facebook picture with his actual wife and child. He was already married to someone else in the next county over.

When Joe was caught, he didn't try to apologize, he didn't try to make excuses and he didn't make any promises to leave his wife for Kim. He just told her that it was over. When Kim reminded him of the baby, he told her that he'd find a way to provide support. *What did that mean?* She so wanted more than financial support; she wanted a family.

Kim was left with more questions and less certainty. Joe came around less and less. And that's when her world spiraled downward, and she became depressed. It was harder to drag herself out to work, let alone pay attention to Bree's needs, help with her homework or anything else. She felt a sense of loss and didn't know where her life was going. She became apathetic about everything including taking care of her house trailer and daughter.

Kim had no energy, as if the world had sapped both her mental and physical strength. She was mad at herself for getting burned by Joe. Her negative attitude didn't help at work either, and it was noticed by her employer. She was let go just six weeks ago. She lost her appetite and was losing weight. She was able to file for unemployment, but it didn't provide much money, and for the last week other than getting Bree off to school, she just sat in her trailer and watched TV. *And cried.*

She hardly ate anything all week and was literally running on empty. Unmotivated to get off the couch, she didn't cook, she didn't clean, she didn't go grocery shopping, she didn't tend to Bree and forget about caring for the mutt outside. She was *tired of everything*. She was at her lowest, and when she thought it couldn't get any worse, Deputy Mullenax showed up at her door.

"I'm here to check on you and Bree," the deputy said after introducing himself.

"Why? We are fine," Kim said without much enthusiasm and she automatically rubbed her seven-month pregnant belly.

"Do you mind if I come in?"

"Suit yourself, although there isn't much room," she said and took a step backwards.

"You have a daughter Bree, right?" Deputy Mullenax asked.

"Yeah, she's right over here." Bree was sitting at a small table and looked up at the deputy although she didn't say anything.

"How are you doing Bree?"

"OK," she whispered, appearing timid and scared. She was not the outgoing child that Mrs. Thompson had described.

Underneath the table the deputy noticed a large boot. "Is there anyone else living here?"

"That's Joe's, although he hasn't been around much lately. Maybe he doesn't like my decorating tastes," she said in a sarcastic tone. It was then that Deputy Mullenax took in the full view of Kim's decorating tastes. Or lack thereof.

The place was a mess. There was trash on the floor, along with discarded mail, empty boxes of cereal, wrappers from fast-food joints as well as leftover French fries. There were multiple dishes, glassware, a frying pan and a pot in the sink. All of it was dirty and whatever she cooked was burnt on.

And don't forget about the littered empty beer cans. Were all of these from Kim or her infrequent guest? He slightly shifted his stance, turning his 6 foot and 205-pound frame to soak in the contents of the camper, which felt cramped. When his brown steely eyes moved back to Kim, she got defensive.

"I haven't had a chance to clean up this afternoon," she stated. She hadn't had a chance to clean up this month would be a more accurate statement. Just looking at the chaos would increase someone's stress level.

The deputy's gaze redirected toward Bree and she was wearing blue jeans and a long sleeve white top that was soiled in multiple places. The stains on her shirt did not look recent, and it appeared that either the shirt hadn't been washed in a long time, or Bree just didn't have enough clothes to wear.

Bree's hair was matted and unkept because it hadn't had a comb through it for days. She had some sort of food stain in the corner of her mouth and her nails were dirty. She looked as if she was living on the streets. *It's sad that this innocent child was living in this squalor*, the deputy thought to himself. This child didn't know that it could be better than this.

"Are you and your daughter doing OK?" Deputy Mullenax asked. It was an open-ended type of question where he was hoping to receive a detailed response about their living situation. But Kim was not in the mood to talk.

"We're doing fine, but we are not living in a mansion as you can tell," she stated with more sarcasm. "Why, did somebody complain? What are you going to do, arrest me for being a messy mom?" she asked with a bit of aggression.

He ignored her attitude and stated, "I am primarily here to assess the welfare of the child. It's cold in here, does your heater work?"

"Sure, when the tank has propane in it."

"Are you out? It's supposed to get near freezing tonight," he replied as he looked out of the window at the darkening sky.

"Yeah, I just need to get a ride so I can get some more propane. It's no big deal," Kim stated, suddenly realizing that not having heat in the camper *was* actually a problem. It also struck her that her flippant attitude wasn't going to help the situation.

"What about food, do you have things in the house for Bree to eat?"

"I need to go to the store, I guess," Kim stated and cringed knowing that was her second bad answer.

There were only a few cabinets near the kitchen that were designed for food storage, and the deputy opened it up to find one can of chicken noodle soup, and an open box of Cheez-Its that was lying on its side and appeared empty. They had a small refrigerator in the camper and when he opened the door the situation was even worse. Inside the refrigerator was an open moldy container of yogurt and two cans of beer. That's it. He was close enough to the refrigerator to realize that it wasn't cold.

"We have to eat out a lot, that thing is busted," Kim commented and squirmed on the inside. *Another wrong answer.*

"You need to have adequate food for your child," Deputy Mullenax stated flatly. "How could you be wiped out of food?" He was starting to get frustrated and felt a tinge of anger as Bree's neglect was obvious. How could a mother be so irresponsible? *What was she thinking and what would be the long-term effects on Bree?*

"Yeah, I know that. We'll get some food; I don't need you coming in here to tell me how to take care of my own kid," Kim countered.

"I'm not trying to tell you what to do, but there's concern that Bree is not taken care of as well as she should."

Deputy Lamine Mullenax thought to himself, *I'm only seeing this today, I can only imagine what is going on at other times. Actually, I can imagine; it's probably worse.* He got the impression that Bree was somewhat isolated and there wasn't a visible toy in the place.

"She's just fine, she just needs a bath," Kim stated defensively. "We were about to go out and get some dinner," she said trying to muster up some confidence.

The deputy took another step towards the back of the camper where the sleeping area was and spotted one of the frosted plastic windows had a hole in it the size of a softball. "That hole is right above the sleeping area, it's got to be cold in here at night."

"We have blankets," Kim said softly in a dejected manner and then started to visibly get upset. Everything the deputy was pointing out she had an excuse for, but it was a bad excuse, *and she knew it.*

Her situation looked bad and she started to tremble when she realized what must be going through the deputy's mind. *This home was not adequate for raising a child. It's as if the kid was a prisoner. And what about the baby that was on the way? It opened a pandora's box of questions, none of which Kim would have a good answer.*

"I can get some duct tape and cover the hole. It will be good enough until I get it fixed," Kim tried to argue. The guilt that she had been suppressing for weeks was now manifesting itself, and then she lost it.

"I've been having a rough time lately. I'm sorry," she stated and started to cry. She appeared broken and emotionally trampled. It wasn't the deputy's place to judge Kim, for he didn't know what she'd been through, but he had a job to do.

"I'm going to have to call the Department of Human Services, they are going to have to make the decision on this one." The deputy felt a variety of emotions from frustration and sadness to concern about Bree's future. How would she develop into a teenager and beyond if she didn't have a stable household? The situation was lowering her odds for long term happiness.

"Do you really have to do that? I can't let you take my child away from me!" Kim argued as tears streamed down her face and she was trembling. "I promise to fix all of this," she said in desperation.

"Unfortunately, we need to get DHS out here based upon what I have observed here this afternoon. It's probably only going to be temporary. Do you think you can get some propane, have someone look at that refrigerator and patch up that hole in the next couple of days?" he asked. Deputy Mullenax needed to thoroughly document the current conditions because if the situation worsened, and more drastic action needed to be taken, there would be a detailed historical context in her file.

"I think so," Kim said in a defeated tone and rubbed her belly out of nervousness.

"And get some real food and maybe do some laundry?"

"OK," she stated, and the tears continued to flow, her eyes even more bloodshot. This was Kim's wake up call. She felt an overwhelming sense of shame. *What have I done to Bree?* She knew that the last few months had been tough for her and she was doing a lousy job taking care of Bree. When Bree was born, she promised herself that she would be a good mother, and looking around, she knew that she'd let her down. It was hard to face reality and the deputy staring at her.

She couldn't fool herself anymore. "I know I can do better. Bree deserves better," she admitted and nodded her head in acknowledgement.

"That's good to hear. When the social worker gets here let's have that conversation. I don't think Bree can stay here tonight, but if you make a plan and get these issues taken care of, you can file a petition to have Bree return home. You have a chance to make this right," Deputy Lamine Mullenax said in a calm and sympathetic tone.

"I can promise you that deputy," Kim stated. "I won't let Bree down again. Thanks for the advice."

The deputy was hopeful, but he had his doubts. He'd seen many people make lots of promises throughout his career, and most of them never followed through. Would Kim? *He was optimistic, and that was as good as he could expect.*

February 2018

It was the most difficult phone call Ralph Murphy would ever have to make. He stared at his phone and pointed his finger but couldn't quite touch the screen to initiate the call. His hand started shaking. *How do I make this call,* he thought to himself? *How can I possibly get the words out?* He looked at his phone again; it wasn't going to dial by itself.

He involuntarily shook his head and wiped a few tears from his eyes. Her name was already on the screen and all he had to do was push the button. He walked a few steps forward, sensing the need to be physically moving and then pushed the button to call his wife.

"I'm at the end of County Road 301, where it dead ends," he stated and then froze when he realized how he described *that* part of the road. The pit of his stomach was tight, and he felt like he was going to throw up. His head hurt and he felt a little dizzy. None of this seemed real, but there was no way to avoid it.

"What? Why?" Barbara Murphy asked. "Where's Lyle?" Their son had left to check their post office box but never returned. And that was two hours ago.

"He's here, but…" Ralph answered as his voice trailed off.

"What's going on? What's happened to my Lyle?" she asked, with her voice breaking from nervousness. "Tell me what happened!"

Lyle had been acting strangely for the past few months but neither parent could pinpoint the change in his behavior. It wasn't a radical change, but rather a subtle shift becoming more withdrawn and detached from the family. He would explain his behavior by saying he was "bummed out" but he couldn't fully explain what he was "bummed out" about.

When asked to further elaborate, he'd simply hide out in his room. It wasn't unusual behavior for a teenager, but it was unusual for Lyle.

"It's Lyle. He has…" Ralph said but couldn't make himself finish the sentence.

"He's what?" Barbara asked. "Don't tell me something's happened to him. Please don't tell me that Ralph," she screamed into the phone in desperation and panic. "Tell me that he's going to be OK," she pleaded emphatically.

"You should stay at the house. The police will be here soon. I just don't believe it, I can't believe that he would do that to himself," Ralph replied, his heart beating faster from duress.

Ralph recognized that Lyle seemed to be lacking energy, didn't seem to care about anything in his life, and was genuinely sad. Maybe he was even a little depressed, but he couldn't have been *that* depressed, he couldn't have been depressed enough to do what he'd done. *Why didn't Lyle come to him?*

"Noooo," Barbara wailed and could no longer hold back any tears. A thousand thoughts rippled through Barbara's brain, and none of them were good, none of them had a happy outcome and all of them involved something awful happening to Lyle. How bad, she wasn't sure, and she couldn't bring herself to ask for specifics or contemplate the *unthinkable*.

"Somehow we'll get through this," he said in an unconvincing manner. He tried to come across as strong, but he just couldn't do it. He couldn't muster the energy required to pull off the confidence for this insurmountable task, especially when he didn't believe it himself. He didn't know how they were going to get through this.

"How can you say that? I just want my Lyle back," she countered.

"Someone from the county police just pulled up, so I gotta go. Remember, just stay there in the house," he replied and looked up at the afternoon sky and felt the cold breeze hit his face.

Deputy Lamine Mullenax parked off to the side of the road and approached Ralph Murphy. Lyle Murphy was in the Jeep. The motor was off, and it looked like Ralph didn't touch anything else. There still was a hose duct-taped tightly to the tailpipe which was wrapped around to the passenger side of the vehicle and held in place by the window and strips of more duct tape. Lyle's face had a purplish-blue tint as he'd asphyxiated himself less than an hour ago.

Deputy Mullenax saw the look on Ralph's face. It was the look of a father who'd seen the end of the world, which was accurate because it was the end of *his* world. His and Barbara's life would never be the same. And of course, Lyle's sixteen-year-old life was cut short by his own doing. The deputy opened his mouth to say something, but no words came out. What words could be said at this moment that would be meaningful, or make a difference?

Deputy Mullenax knew Ralph and his family for years since Ralph was the family's dentist. *How do you explain what happened to your wife*, the Deputy pondered? *How do you explain it to anybody? How do you start the explanation at all?*

Thoughts were racing through the deputy's head. The intensity of emotions that this man must be going through is hard to fathom. Dealing with criminals is one thing, when someone has made the decision to break the law, it's usually part of a series of bad life decisions. Criminals frequently hurt other people and seeing the unnecessary pain was difficult, but this was different. *What words have value to describe the situation?*

Ralph continued to walk around the Jeep as if somehow the situation would look better from a different angle, hoping by some means that he'd made a mistake in his assessment and maybe from a different position he'd perhaps see something different.

Ralph put his hands on the window and peered in one more time, tears streaming down his face in anguish, sadness and raw pain. Seeing his son in the car, lifeless, consumed his whole body in pain.

Deputy Mullenax knew that the scene did not need further disturbance or contamination, but more importantly he wanted to help Ralph. He pulled him away from the Jeep, grabbed the back of his neck, pulled him closer and gave him a tight hug.

Ralph was startled at first, but then hugged him back and the flow of emotions came out of Ralph. After several seconds, Ralph regained control and was grateful for the embrace, and he stared at Deputy Mullenax and then noticed two other police cars arriving at the scene.

***

Five hours later

The setting had an eerie and almost Halloween feel to it. The fire was out but the air was thick with smoke which partially blocked the moonlight, adding to the spooky and haunting feel.

The small house was completely destroyed by the fire and there were a few neighbors gathering to observe what had happened. The fire started quickly and spread from the bathroom to the entire house, and by the time the fire department got there, it was completely ablaze.

The County Sheriff had been called in to assist the fire department, and luckily the fire did not spread to any other neighbors. Deputy Mullenax was the first officer to arrive at the scene, even before the fire department. There was a propane tank on the property, so both the first responders and bystanders needed to move away from the house. There was nothing more they could do.

A neighbor and friend of the family was crying as she described the suddenness of the blaze and told them that a woman and her ten-year-old daughter lived in the house. She was visibly shaking from the fear and worry that they did not make it out alive.

"I heard them screaming!" she sobbed, and a chill went through those who heard her. Eventually, it was determined that the heat had dissipated enough, and it was safe to examine the inside of the house.

Soon two firefighters brought out what appeared to be an adult sized body. It brought a stark reality to the situation and the tense feeling in the air got worse when a few minutes later, a child sized body was taken out of the house. Everyone's fear and concern were realized.

The charred remains were of the woman and her child. It was gruesome to *see and smell* the burnt flesh. There was no hair remaining on the bodies and most of the clothes were indistinguishable, and black burnt pieces of flesh covered the remains.

People become numb to death scenes on television because they are prevalent, but seeing it firsthand was another matter. Deputy Mullenax, another officer and a firefighter knelt on the ground to say a prayer for the souls of the deceased. "I'm sorry I couldn't get here quicker," someone said aloud, and the other two men nodded in solemn agreement.

It took them a few minutes to put the remains in the body bags to be transferred to the coroner. The charred corpses of people who were going about their normal lives just a few hours ago brought home the finality of it. This was a mother and child, but they also meant something to the remaining family and friends that would never see them again. It was hard to look at and Deputy Mullenax shifted his gaze away from the bodies but was unable to push it out of his mind.

Seeing those bodies cemented the fact that in this life, nothing is guaranteed, and life could be altered or ended in an instant. In one shift at work, he'd seen three dead bodies. The reality of that sunk in, with no direction or guidance of how to react to it, and no direction or guidance on how to process the situation or how to deal with it.

He had no choice, and he had deal with it. Sometimes there aren't any good answers or explanations to be found. What the scene did reinforce with acute clarity is that you must hold on to what's precious. *Why does it take a tragedy for us to be reminded of that?*

"I've got some bad news," Lamine said into the phone as he walked away from the house.

"Oh no, what is it?" Averi, his wife answered.

"Doctor Murphy, our dentist, his teenage son committed suicide a few hours ago."

"Ugh, that's terrible."

"Yeah, I was called out there just after he found him."

"Where are you now?" Averi asked.

"I'm at the south end of the county and they just put out a fire. Two people were burned to death, a mother and her daughter," Lamine replied. He had a strong tug to be at home with his wife and child, a physical need to be closer to them.

"Oh my gosh, that's awful."

"I know, I don't think I'll ever get that image out of my mind. It's just a tragic end and loss of life. This was somebody's sister and daughter, and cousin and friend and now they are just gone."

"Is there anything that I can do?"

"No, it's made me think about what's really important in my life, which is you and the family we've built. And are building. That is what really matters. I love you," Lamine told her.

"I love you too honey."

"I'm sorry when I get grumpy about petty stuff. Things that really don't matter," Lamine added.

"Well, you are not the only one, I can lose perspective too," Averi stated.

"Seeing all this is just a kick in the gut. But I can't change what's happened to any of these people today. I'm at a loss of what to do or say."

"Unfortunately, there's nothing you can do to make it better and this is something that will change you forever," she replied.

"No, all I can do is hold on tight to what's important to me, what's important to us," Lamine concluded.

***

Late October 2018

"Now just calm down Rudy," Eli said to him.

"I don't want to *calm* down, I want you to get out of this house!"

"I'm checking in on your parents. What's going on here?"

"It's none of your business!" Rudy suddenly screamed at him, changing his demeanor from calm to incredibly angry in just a few seconds. It was then that Rudy pulled out a 15-inch metal pipe from his back pocket. He slapped it into his palm in a menacing manner and said, "You need to go back home before you get hurt, old man."

Eli stared into Rudy's eyes and didn't like what he saw. Rudy was serious and his facial expression conveyed both unemotional and threatening nuances. It told Eli that Rudy didn't value life, anyone's life, and would have no problem pummeling Eli with the metal pipe.

Rudy had been on and off drugs for much of his 44-year-old life, and Eli had firsthand knowledge of Rudy being out of control, but this was the first time that he was threatened. And with Rudy being a large man at 6' 3" tall and 270 pounds, it wasn't someone that 62-year-old Eli could take on.

Eli hesitated and wasn't sure what to do. Rudy was supposed to be taking care of his aging parents, but lately he'd spent most of his time pawning their household items to fuel his drug use. What was going to be next? A life insurance policy?

He hesitated to leave, trying to figure out if he should attempt to calm Rudy down or call the police. What Rudy did next made it an easy decision.

"OK, I'll leave, but you need to take care of your parents," Eli replied cautiously.

"They've gotta go," Rudy said in a calm, cold and calculating manner.

"What does that mean?" Eli asked.

"If you don't get out of here right now, I'm going to kill you along with them. I've got enough acreage in the backyard to bury all three of you," Rudy commented in a 'matter of fact tone.'

Eli believed every word Rudy was telling him. That was all that Eli needed to hear and he stepped out of the living room where his neighbors, 84-year-old Jonah and 81-year old Lisa were quietly watching television, oblivious to what was going on and barely functioning.

Rudy continued to give him a dark look, and Eli walked sideways towards the front door, with one eye back towards Rudy. As soon as he got to the front door, he quickened his pace, looked back once again to make sure Rudy wasn't following him, and headed straight towards his house.

As soon as Eli reached his house, he locked the door and called the police.

Rudy watched his sickly parents glued to the television, almost lifeless, and it wouldn't take much to put them out of their misery. And if they were out of their misery, Rudy figured he'd be out of his misery as well. He was tired of taking care of them, not that he made much of an effort to do that, which also attributed to their deterioration. They had medication that Rudy typically forgot to give them. He barely provided any food and forget about personal hygiene.

Rudy was more interested in getting his next high rather than caretaking. The only thing he wanted to take care of was selling the house after their death. *But how to explain their disappearance? What to do with the bodies?* That was the real question he was now fixated on.

He slammed the pipe against his palm again, thinking about how to get away with it and what to do next. He could easily forge their signature and sell their car, and that would be a lot easier than trying to permanently get rid of them and disposing of the bodies. He wouldn't get much for their car, but it was a start.

Then he heard the sirens from half a mile away, and when they got closer, it registered that they were coming for him. He decided to hide out in the backyard shed. But it wasn't a great plan.

As he was turning into the long dirt driveway, Deputy Mullenax observed Rudy exit the house and walk the fifty yards towards the shed. The deputy checked inside the house and found the parents to be alright, so he left the house and took the long and lonely walk from relative safety of the house to see what was waiting for him in the shed.

"Rudy, I know you're in there. Come out of the shed slowly," Deputy Mullenax instructed. He was familiar with Rudy. He knew Rudy's parents Jonah and Lisa because they lived on the same road as Lamine's parents.

He also knew that Rudy was a regular drug user and hadn't been able to hold down a job in years, usually just long enough to get unemployment benefits. Rudy spent most of his time in scrapyards trying to find valuable parts to sell on eBay. Deputy Mullenax waited a few more seconds, but Rudy didn't come out.

"Come on Rudy, I saw you go into the shed. Don't make me come in there and get you."

"Go away! I've got a gun and I'm not afraid to use it," Rudy lied, hoping that the proclamation of his weapon would scare off the deputy. It didn't.

Deputy Mullenax stepped a few feet back from the shed door and moved to the right, a safer spot than in front of the shed door. Rudy's actions now warranted calling in the Chaffee County SWAT team.

Rudy was being stubborn and wouldn't come out of the shed, even though he knew he was surrounded by the SWAT team. He was still feeling the effects of methamphetamines and heroin, which contributed to his delusional state and the false hope that the police would simply vanish. But of course, they wouldn't. The officers could hear Rudy move items inside the shed and bang against the door. He was barricading himself in.

The SWAT team attempted to coax Rudy out of the shed and negotiate a peaceful ending to the standoff. After that didn't work for several hours, the SWAT team decided the safest way to get him out of the shed was to use tear gas. The officers took a few minutes to remove some of the barricades Rudy had placed by the entrance. Then the gas canisters were thrown inside. In less than a minute Rudy had exited the shed and was giving himself up.

It would be left up to Deputy Mullenax to take him to the county jail in Salida. Deputy Mullenax guided Rudy into the back of the patrol car and he began the thirty-minute ride towards Salida, keenly aware that it was past 2:00 a.m. and he was tired.

"Why are you doing this to me?" Rudy asked. If it weren't obvious why Rudy was being taken to jail, there was nothing the deputy could say to better explain it to him. "You're ruining my life, I don't know why you have to do this to me," Rudy continued. The deputy ignored him.

"You know Lamine, I know who you are. I know where your parents live," Rudy said in a threatening manner. Deputy Mullenax did not respond.

"When I get outta here, I'm going to come and get you," Rudy continued and said, "I am going to pay you a visit."

Still, Deputy Mullenax did not respond. There was no benefit to having a conversation with Rudy. The deputy had heard all the talk before. Most of the time, he'd ignore it and let it roll off his back.

It wasn't too concerning because Deputy Mullenax knew he could take care of himself. But now he has a wife and child. It made him wonder. *Is it just big talk and bluster? What if he follows through with his threat?*

The deputy had to take it seriously, especially working in a small town where you know the criminals and the criminals know you. It is not anonymous policing like you would have in Denver or another large city.

"I bet you don't do this to your brother, do you?" Rudy said, continuing his attempt to get under the deputy's skin. "You let *him* get away with everything, but I get arrested, get exposed to tear gas and get taken to jail. It's not right. This is all your fault."

"Don't think I don't know what you're up to Lamine," Rudy whined and continued, "You make sure only certain people around here get caught with drugs and get hassled by the police. You're in control of it all. I'm not part of your inner circle so you protect your brother and leave guys like me hanging out to dry."

The deputy was getting agitated but didn't let it show on his face. Unfortunately, his younger brother had gotten into drugs and was known to be in that lifestyle by both law enforcement and the drug user community. Lamine always felt a twinge of embarrassment when his brother's drug dependence came up. It was frustrating that people he arrested would try to use it against him.

"Why are you doing this to me?" Rudy growled.

Criminals just don't get it, thought Deputy Mullenax. He has a job to do and making an arrest is not personal. Rudy chose to take drugs, Rudy chose to threaten his parents and a neighbor, Rudy chose to not leave the shed, and *he is blaming the deputy?*

"Answer me! You're going to be one sorry nigger if you don't let me go," Rudy exclaimed in a last dich effort to be released.

Is that best insult you have? The deputy thought to himself, *can't you come up with something new?*

Deputy Mullenax had heard it all before, the complaints, the blaming, the racial slurs and baiting insults, the constant bad attitude and destructive behavior from criminals, especially in the back of his patrol car. He mentally rolled his eyes and was solely interested in getting to his destination so he wouldn't have to listen to this idiot anymore. He was tired of being patient.

Finally, he pulled behind the wall of the Salida jail's sally port, which is an area designed to securely facilitate the transport of the prisoner from the patrol car into the building.

The jailer was there to prepare Rudy to enter the facility. He first inspected him for any visible injuries and asked, "Are you hurt? Do you need any medical attention?" Rudy just stared at him, still upset that he had been taken to jail.

"Do you need to see a doctor?" the jailer asked again and waited for a response.

"I'm fine," Rudy answered sarcastically.

"I need to ask you several questions before you're transferred inside. "Have you ever had HIV or AIDS?"

"No," Rudy responded.

"What about Chickenpox?"

"I had that as a kid, I think."

"Have you recently had suicidal thoughts?"

"No, why do you keep asking me these *stupid* questions?" Rudy asked with an annoyed and contemptuous tone.

"We also need you to take a portable breathalyzer test," the jailer stated.

"I haven't been drinking."

"It doesn't matter. We do this for everyone, it's for your own safety so we know whether you need to be placed in a temporary holding cell or with the general population." Rudy reluctantly breathed into the unit.

"I don't remember drinking today," Rudy replied after the jailer told him that his results showed he had .12 blood alcohol content in his system. He was legally drunk, but the test didn't check the level of illegal drugs.

The jailer didn't respond because he didn't care and there was really no point to having a conversation. The jailer then took him into a small secure room and handed him an orange jumpsuit and simply told him to strip. Rudy stared at him in disbelief and was getting angrier by the minute.

"Here!" Rudy shouted and threw his T shirt at the jailer. Being inside the jail forced Rudy to recognize his situation, which triggered his emotions. "Here's another one," Rudy said in anger and threw his jeans at him.

"Here you go, why don't you check this out!" Rudy shouted and threw his underwear at the jailer. The jailer was unemotional and blasé because he'd seen an angry strip search many times before.

Nothing Rudy could say or do would be anything new or surprising to the jailer, for he just wanted to get it over with as quickly and efficiently as possible. Rudy was being difficult simply because he *could*. And because he had no control over anything else.

"Raise your arms and point to the ceiling," the jailer instructed. Rudy decided to ignore the instruction.

"Do you want to be placed in the restraint chair? Do I need to get a few other guys in here to help me? That's not going to be a fun time for you buddy, let me tell you," the jailer said sternly with a tinge of irritation. The look on the jailer's face told Rudy that what he said was true; it would not be a good time for Rudy if he was physically forced to comply.

"Fine," Rudy replied and raised his arms as he was previously instructed. The jailer then took account of any scars or tattoos and checked his personal belongings for any weapons or drug paraphernalia.

Lastly, Rudy was instructed to put on his orange jumpsuit. He was then moved into the jail administration area to be officially booked and fingerprinted and lastly was led into a holding cell to ensure the effects of his drug and alcohol would wear off. He was transferred to general population the next morning and would later be arraigned in court.

***

"A man travels the world over in search of what he needs, and returns home to find it."
—**George A. Moore**

One Year Later

Frosted flakes or granola cereal? Fun versus boring? Which to choose? Healthy versus tasty? Those were the decisions of the moment for Lamine as he was walking down the grocery aisle pushing his cart, trying to quickly get the long list of items on his list.

He placed the cereal box in his cart, and when he looked up, he saw Rudy headed his way. Lamine was a little surprised to see him and wondered, *was he going to recognize me out of uniform?*

The last time Lamine saw him, Rudy made threatening remarks. *Was he going to cause a scene?* Lamine was in no mood for an altercation with a meth user in the grocery store on his day off.

He hoped Rudy would not pay attention to him and simply walk on by. A few seconds later their eyes locked, and Rudy's face indicated that he'd recognized him. *Here it comes,* Lamine braced himself.

"Hey, I wanna thank you Deputy Mullenax," Rudy said as he approached the officer.

"You do?" Lamine responded. That was the last thing Lamine expected Rudy to say. He probed Rudy's facial expression for authenticity.

"Yes, you saved my life," Rudy replied sincerely. He appeared relaxed and at peace.

Lamine could tell he was different. "That's not how you felt the last time I saw you in the back of my patrol car," he said with a smile.

"Well, I'm sorry about that," Rudy replied, and he also smiled and then continued, "I was using a lot of drugs back then. That night was the worst reaction to the drugs that I ever had. I never realized how bad it was until that night."

194

"You made it tough on everyone that night," Deputy Mullenax replied. "Do you remember that we had to call the SWAT team to get you out of that shed?"

"Sort of. Sorry for that. I sat in jail for six months and sobered up. I had a lot of time to think about my life, and how much of it I've wasted," he said in a calm and somber manner and continued, "I'm home now, in a spiritual sense."

"It sounds like you made some real changes to your life," Lamine gently replied after surmising that Rudy didn't appear to be an active drug user.

"If it wasn't for that day and you arresting me, I was headed for an overdose, I'm sure of it."

"You look much more together now."

"I am thinking clearly these days, what a difference!" Rudy said heartily.

"That is good news; I am happy for you," Lamine said and smiled again. "I really am."

"Yes, I didn't have any drugs while in jail, and luckily I was able to get some counseling. It's been a tough road, but I definitely feel like I'm on the right track."

"Wow, that is so great for you," Lamine replied with genuine delight.

"Well, I'm glad I ran into you today, and wanted you to know that I wouldn't be standing here today if it wasn't for you," replied a contrite Rudy.

"Hey, I was just doing my job, but you're the other end of that equation. Only when you had a desire to make things right in your life was it actually going to happen, and now you've got your life back."

"If I run into you again, I hope it's only when you're off duty," Rudy said with jest and headed down the grocery aisle.

"Me too," Lamine responded, a little more hopeful about society than he was five minutes ago.

October 2019

"How's it going grill master?" Averi playfully said with a smile and placed her affectionate hand on Lamine's back.

"It's coming along just fine," Lamine answered and flipped over a piece of steak. He admired his work in process, grilled steak and chicken. He loved to cook and especially grill meat. There was something instinctually human about a man cooking with fire.

Food brought people together and this was going to be a fantastic meal for a fantastic day. The journey was finally complete and after years of emotional ups and downs it was finally over.

But the celebration wasn't because it was an ending, it was because the day marked a beginning. This was the first day that Javon would be his officially adopted son.

The emotional rollercoaster started four years ago when Javon was just a baby. Lamine remembers when the decision was solidified, when he knew that he had to get Javon out of *that* situation. Lamine's sister Laila was not taking proper care of Javon, as she relied on a combination of Javon's older teenage brother, Lamine and their mother to pick up the slack.

Laila was disinterested in taking care of an infant and preferred to instead hang out with her friends all night, feed her drug habit and let go of her responsibilities. She'd sleep in until noon after frequent partying, which wasn't a good match with her baby's schedule.

It was three in the morning and Javon's mother wasn't at home. No one knew where she was, and it became clear to Lamine on that early morning that he needed to intervene on Javon's behalf.

Lamine and Laila already had a contentious sibling relationship. He was nine years older than Laila and she perceived him as an authority figure, which she resented. Her view of Lamine was hardened when he became a deputy, where she viewed him not only as a family authority figure but also a public one as well.

Laila didn't have a long-term place to live and was couch surfing all over the county. Her life choices of drug use, abusive boyfriends and ending up in jail several times put her at odds with Lamine's profession.

His irritation and disappointment with her ran deep. She was in no position to properly take care of this child, but that didn't mean that she was going to easily let Javon go.

Luckily, the court could see that Laila was not capable of raising Javon. His father had already signed away his rights, thus paving the way for Lamine and Averi to adopt Javon.

Initially Lamine's parents had thought about adopting Javon, but given their age it didn't make sense. Lamine convinced them that his household would provide an excellent home for Javon. The adoption process started before he married Averi and she accepted and loved Javon as her own child.

"There were times that I wasn't sure that this day was actually going to happen," Lamine reflected.

"It's really here," Averi stated and smiled. "Javon has been living with us for so long that tomorrow won't really seem any different than yesterday. Yet, this is definitely a milestone in all of our lives. Look around us, this is really what it's all about," she said and soaked in what was happening in their backyard.

Lamine was grilling up the food, Javon was sitting at the picnic table laughing with his grandparents, along with several friends and coworkers who joined them to celebrate the occasion. An outside observer might think it was just another afternoon barbecue, but she and Lamine knew better, this was truly a turning point.

"The bottom line is that Javon deserves a future, despite the fact that his biological parents don't know what they're doing from one day to the next," Lamine commented. "That didn't have to be Javon's life too. He deserves a better chance than that."

"We'll provide that for both him and Cathryn. I can't believe that our daughter is already a month old. We have such a great family and it's so nice that the uncertainty of Javon's future has been lifted." Averi stated.

"Boy is that the truth," he said. "There were many sleepless nights where I thought we might lose our bond with him. Now we don't have to worry about that, and we don't have to worry about my sister showing up out of nowhere demanding to see Javon or trying to take him for the holidays. She won't be able to ruin any more Christmas plans in the future or guilt us into changing our plans and jumping through hoops for her."

"I know, and half the time she would flake out on whatever plans that were made anyway. She didn't even show up for her last court appearance."

"Yes, sometimes my siblings make me crazy. It's frustrating to watch your siblings ruin their lives. I still can't figure out why both my brother and sister ended up on drugs and making bad life choices. I just don't have an answer as to how or why that happened."

"Yes, I know that has been really tough," Averi replied.

"I guess I am still upset for what they put my parents through, especially my mom," Lamine said and slightly shook his head.

"She was naive about how kids could get into drugs, and I know that she was depressed about all the things that they were doing. In some ways my mom was never the same, and I guess deep down I blame them for taking my mom away from me. Maybe my relationship with my sister and brother will never be that great, but I hope that someday they get on the right path and find a relationship with God."

"It's been going on for a long time, I guess sometimes you just need to let some of those emotions go," Averi said and continued, "You've tried to help them before, and they still refuse your help. You know you are not responsible for them and the life choices they've made."

"In my head, I know you're right, yet in my heart, there is still a part of me that wants to protect them."

"That's because you have a big heart and regardless of everything that's happened, you still love your brother and sister."

"I do, but it's in God's hands now. Just like this adoption, I prayed many times to understand God's will for Javon's future," Lamine stated. "I honestly believe that God has spoken, and that's why we're celebrating his adoption today."

"Yes, he's truly *our* little boy. And with our daughter, everything is perfect," Averi replied.

"Javon knows that this is a special day too. He's only four years old so he doesn't fully comprehend what's going on, and I'm sure we'll have conversations with him as he gets older," Lamine replied.

"I'm sure he feels more secure knowing that this is going to be his permanent home," Averi commented.

"Today is a celebration of the soul. You're a great mom, and both kids are lucky to have you. I'm lucky too," he stated and smiled at his wife.

***

"Your greatest contribution to the kingdom of God may not be something you do but someone you raise."
— **Andy Stanley**

Five Fun Facts About Lamine Mullenax

1. Passionate prankster.

2. Avid mountain biker.

3. Frequently breaks out into song.

4. Fluent in the French language.

5. Enjoys jumping into cold water (i.e., polar plunge).

V.

Channeling Olivia

July 21, 2020

"And now for you nice ladies and gentlemen out there
Who don't understand the Italian language,
I'd like to do two choruses in British"
--**Louis Prima**, *Lazy Mary*

She smiled to herself as she listened to the first song from her Italian cooking playlist. It was going to be a good day. Anytime you are making a pot of tomato sauce, meatballs, sausage and pork in the old-world tradition, you just can't help but feel good. It brought back memories of family dinners, especially around the holidays.

There was something soul warming about nostalgic food and keeping the traditions alive mattered. She had made the meatballs earlier, by hand, the only way she knew how to make them, and they started to sizzle in the frying pan. She would cook them about 3/4 of the way, later adding them to the big pot of tomato sauce. In a large pot, the onions sautéed in extra virgin olive oil and were starting to become translucent. Perfect.

She added the crushed garlic, salt and pepper, which would initiate several hours' worth of incredible smells. The recipe she used was from a cookbook that was only four months old, given to her by her parents, celebrating their 30th wedding anniversary. She mused to herself that it was nice to get a gift from her parents on *their* anniversary.

She was starting to get a reputation with her coworkers for being quite the young chef, so a month earlier she had made a triple recipe and sold containers of tomato sauce. She had been paid to cook, so technically you could call her a professional chef. She liked the thought of that. She added some fresh basil and then the tomatoes. She scanned the recipe to see what was coming up next.

Traditional Style Italian Tomato Sauce (Gravy)

- o 1/2 cup olive oil
- o 2 cups onion, chopped
- o 3/4 cup basil, fresh (about 30 leaves)
- o 5 teaspoons garlic, crushed
- o 168 ounces tomato sauce, (6 large cans)
- o 1 tablespoon sugar
- o 1 tablespoon salt
- o 1 teaspoon black pepper
- o 18 ounces red wine
- o 28 meatballs (see recipe)
- o 2 packages sausage, 10-12 links
- o 1 pound pork chops or another sausage package

1) Cook the meat and meatballs and set aside. (Scrape the meat from the frying pan and add it to the pot of sauce in step 6.)

2) Add olive oil in a large pot, enough to generously cover the bottom and heat on medium.

3) Add the onions and sauté for about 5 minutes. Add garlic and gently sauté for another 5 minutes, careful not to burn. Add salt, pepper and chopped basil. Don't be stingy with the basil and add an extra whole leaf just for fun. Whomever gets the whole leaf basil receives good luck.

4) Before the onions are turning a golden brown, add the tomato sauce. Get remaining tomato sauce from the can by swishing a little water and add.

5) Turn heat to medium-low, cover pot and bring to a gentle boil.

6) Add meat and the oil and scrapings from the frying pan.

7) Turn heat to low and gently boil for 30 minutes, stirring occasionally.

8) Add the sugar and wine and cook for another 90 minutes, stirring occasionally.

9) Allow gravy to cool and skim accumulated fat from the top of the pot.

After adding the tomatoes, it would take a while for it to reach a slow boil, which gave her time to finish cooking the meat. She checked her meatballs and they looked great. She had the rolling technique down to a perfect science. In another frying pan, she started to cook the sausage and pork.

An hour later, she added the meat to the tomato sauce and decided to take a little walk with Trevor, her pit bull mix.

Traditional Style Italian Meatballs

- o 2 pounds ground beef, 80% lean
- o 1 cup Italian-style breadcrumbs
- o 3/4 cup Romano cheese
- o 2 eggs
- o 1/2 cup Italian parsley, fresh and chopped
- o 1/2 teaspoon salt
- o 1/4 teaspoon black pepper
- o 1/4 teaspoon garlic powder

1) Combine all ingredients in a large bowl. Use your hands and squeeze the ingredients to mix, about 2 minutes. Mixture should be somewhat moist and when you press the mixture to the bottom of the bowl, it will lift up the bowl.

2) Place mixture into your hands and roll into tightly formed meatballs slightly larger than a golf ball.

3) Place in a refrigerator for an hour before cooking to bind the meat together.

4) Sauté in a pan on medium (low) heat until well browned on all sides. Scrape the flakes of meat leftover from frying pan and add them to the tomato sauce (gravy). This is where the flavor is!

5) Add to already simmering tomato sauce for the remainder of cooking (at least 45 minutes).

Around noon, she got back from her 45-minute walk, but before she could even get inside, the aroma permeated the front porch. She opened the door, involuntarily smiled, and took in a deep whiff. There is nothing quite as comforting as returning to a house filled with the smell of simmering tomato sauce. Her mouth watered and suddenly she became a little hungry. She hoped that's what heaven smells like. She walked into the kitchen, stirred the pot and put her cooking playlist back on and Frank Sinatra was telling her about the *Summer Wind*.

There were only two ingredients left to add, a little bit of sugar and some red wine. This was the best part, because now she could open a bottle of red wine and pour a taste for herself and try one of the meatballs. Quality control is essential. Trevor sat obediently, hoping that he might get a little bite.

She sipped the wine, slightly raised her glass, noting that the bottle from her father was pretty good. She put a meatball in a small bowl with a little bit of the sauce and cut it into several pieces. Oh, this was fabulous. This is going to be a great retirement gift. She put the last piece on her fork and let Trevor eat it; he wholeheartedly approved.

***

She started work at 7:00a.m. the next day and brought several containers into the building. He was already at work, coming in early even on his last day. He could already tell what she brought before she put the bag of containers on his desk and then smiled at her.

"You had a long and great career and I'm glad that I've gotten to know you over these past three years," she told him.

"I can't believe after all this time, it's really my last day. I've been thinking and talking about this for years, but now that it's really here, it doesn't seem real. I'm looking forward to retirement, but I sure will miss the work and all the great people in this building. You've been a great addition to the team."

"You and your wife deserve a great retirement and I'm really happy for you."

"Thanks. We're having a little retirement party with my family this evening, and your sauce is going to be what we have for dinner."

"Real Italians call it 'gravy'."

"Well, I'm not the real Italian here, you are," he said and they both laughed.

"I've got to get to work, I don't want the new boss thinking I'm a slacker," she replied and did just that.

***

13 hours later

"Our dinner was absolutely fantastic. What an ending to my 40-year career. It was so good, my wife cried, saying the sauce, oh I mean the 'gravy' and meatballs, were fantastic. You're the best, take care," she heard on the voicemail.

"Well, here's to you, Jimmy and Laura Tidwell, as you ride off into the sunset," she said aloud, although no one was in the house. "I'm going to miss you Chief."

Meet Megan DiGirolamo, age 24

Child of God
Woman
Daughter
Sister
Soon to be a wife
Patriot
American
Volleyball Player
Fan of *Doctor Who*
Chef of all things Italian
Heterochromian
School Resource Officer
Basic Crisis Negotiator
Police Officer, Town of Buena Vista, CO

1,175 days earlier

April 2017

"Now I know what's wrong with your face!" stated Sergeant Dean Morgan with an expression of sudden understanding and realization.

Megan didn't quite know what to make of that comment. This was the final interview at the Buena Vista Police Department, and potentially being hired as the second female officer and the 10th police officer overall. She wasn't a human resources expert, but she was quite sure that wasn't an approved statement as prescribed in a *Best Interviewing Techniques* manual. Luckily, he clarified what he meant.

"I didn't realize it before, but you have two different colored eyes."

"Yes, well it's been like that since I was about two years old," she said smiling, glad that she didn't suddenly grow a giant wart on the tip of her nose. Over the years, she had lots of people wonder if it was something wrong with one of her eyes. There wasn't anything wrong with her vision, and she didn't see the world differently if she closed one eye versus the other.

It was called heterochromia, and every July 12, the world celebrated *National Two Different Colored Eyes Day*. Well, at least she did. It was always funny when a friend would notice a year after they met and would blurt out, 'you have one green eye and one brown eye!'

It had been a long and somewhat bumpy road to get into this interview chair. In autumn of 2016, she drove through Buena Vista on her way to Gunnison, where she attended Western State Colorado University, majoring in criminal justice. She'd been through Buena Vista before, but never took much notice. But on this trip, she saw the town in a new light. It looked like a great place to work, and an even better place to live.

After thinking long and hard, she decided that college wasn't for her and decided to forgo the final two years and instead enroll directly into the police academy in January 2017. After the first week in the academy, she knew it was the right decision.

She was the youngest person in the academy at 20 years old and was one of the few academy graduates that had a job offer before graduating in May of that year. They say timing is everything, and as luck would have it, Buena Vista was looking to hire a new police academy graduate.

She quickly applied and went through a series of written tests, psychological and personality questionnaires, phone interviews, as well as oral boards, where a member of the police department and the Town Administrator would pepper her with questions. It was coming down to just a few candidates, and this last interview would determine whom the town would decide to hire.

"Okay, well let's continue," Sergeant Morgan replied. "We want our newest officer to fit into our team really well. We'd also like somebody who wants to stay in Buena Vista a long time. Do you think that you'd like to live in a small mountain town, and not be back in the suburbs?" he asked.

"I definitely want to live in a mountain town. After all, my email address has '*mountaingirl*' in it."

"Ah, yes it does. Let me show you some body camera footage and tell me how you would react," he stated and set up a video on the monitor. The interview consisted of questions about the law, but they also wanted to see the candidate's personality and temperament.

He turned on the body camera footage and it showed somebody screaming profanities at the officer. Sergeant Morgan didn't explain the reason the person was verbally abusing the officer.

"Well, you just can't take it personally," began Megan. "You have to ignore what they're saying, because if someone is being questioned, detained or arrested, they're not going to be happy about it. I'm assuming that this happens all the time."

"Yes, just about every day!" he said and chuckled. "You have to be pretty thick skinned around here."

"I don't think I'll have any problem with that," she stated with confidence. She'd seen similar footage at the academy, and although she hadn't yet experienced it firsthand, she was mentally prepared to do her job in a professional manner. They stress that at the academy, you have to be professional 100% of the time.

It was only a few weeks later, when she got the good news, they were making her an offer and she would start right after graduation.

May 24, 2017

She parked her car, turned off the engine and took in a deep breath. This was it. This wasn't just her first day on the job, it was the start of her career. She only arrived in town a few days ago, luckily finding a place to rent just as the town was going to see an influx of summer workers.

Her apartment seemed especially quiet since she knew exactly zero people in town before moving to Buena Vista. She was really on her own. She was "adulting" while the rest of her college friends were heading home for their summer break.

She was starting her real life. She gave herself a mental pat on the back for getting a good job lined up before graduation and proving all the doubters and naysayers wrong. She was going to be a success.

She was now an official police officer, and after watching hundreds of episodes of *Law & Order* since high school, she was going to proudly wear the badge. Not only that, but she'd also be starting on the earliest legally available day to work as a police officer: her 21st birthday. She was simultaneously nervous and excited. It was time to get to work.

After filling out the new-hire paperwork, she received her badge, and qualified at the gun range. That afternoon she would begin field training. This would consist of riding along with one of the sergeants for three months. In a small town, once training is completed, you patrol alone.

That afternoon, Officer Megan DiGirolamo and Sergeant Dean Morgan went out on patrol. A complaint came in about a guy trying to sell magazine subscriptions. The caller thought it sounded like a scam, so they were dispatched to the neighborhood to investigate.

They saw a man in a green plaid shirt two blocks from Main Street holding a clipboard, pen, papers and brochures. The officers got out of the patrol car to talk to the man. He looked to be in his late 30's and told the officers that he was selling comic book magazine subscriptions.

"It's for a charity," he told the officers, and handed them a brochure. Sergeant Morgan looked at the brochure, but it didn't seem legitimate, as it looked amateurish. It was an unusual call, but it wasn't yet clear if he was breaking the law or not. Running a business would require a permit and business license and this guy didn't have one. He also didn't seem to know much about the nonprofit that he was supposedly representing but taking people's money for a phony subscription would definitely be illegal.

Sergeant Morgan told him where the town office was located and where he could get the proper registration. He instructed him to show everyone such paperwork when he tried to sell them the subscription. The man nodded his head and started walking towards downtown.

"I know my kind is not welcome in this town," the man muttered as he walked away, but loud enough for the officers to hear him.

"Did he just call us racist?" Officer DiGirolamo asked as they walked back towards the patrol car. "On my first day?" The man soliciting magazine subscriptions was black.

"That's what he was trying to imply. I would have asked the same questions and given him the same instructions regardless of what color he was," Sergeant Morgan told her. "You better get used to it. Nowadays it doesn't matter what the situation is, almost every person you question, or arrest will proclaim that you are racist or that they're a victim of some sort of police brutality."

"I'm glad that we have body cameras. It will show what really happened."

"True. There was nothing wrong with our interaction with that man. We asked him a few questions and the conversation was respectful on both sides, except for that last snide comment," the sergeant stated. "Chief Tidwell gets complaints all the time and when he shows the body camera footage to the "victim", the person almost always drops the complaint."

"You'll be fine," he continued. "I'll tell you one thing about this job; you won't be bored."

***

September 2017

The Central Colorado Regional Airport in Buena Vista sits at an altitude of 7,950 feet above sea level, which is almost as long as its runway of 8,300 feet. It beats out Aspen as the longest high-altitude runway in the state.

But that length of asphalt was still too short for the Dodge Charger Hellcat which careened off the runway and into a ditch. Officer Megan DiGirolamo was called to assist on the scene just before lunch. It took her five minutes to arrive at the airport, about the same time as the ambulance.

Just past the end of the runway, on the far side of the ditch sat the mangled sports car, facing back towards the runway. Inside the vehicle were two men in their 70s, still buckled in their seatbelts. The car looked visibly wrecked, so even though belted, it was obvious the two men were severely and violently jostled when they drove off the runway.

"What do you want me to do?" asked Officer DiGirolamo.

"Can you help carry one of these guys up to the runway?" the EMT answered with more of a directive than a request. The driver had already been placed on a backboard and she helped carry him to the runway where all the vehicles were parked.

"I'm going to perform CPR, and I need you to run the oxygen bag," the EMT replied. Officer DiGirolamo noticed another EMT and Sergeant Plackner from the Sheriff's Office helping the passenger.

She looked at the unconscious man and could visibly see his contusions, a broken leg and a broken arm, maybe two. Even though both the driver and passenger were wearing their seatbelts, since the car took a hard landing on the ditch it was surprising that the guy was still alive. The EMT placed the oxygen mask over the man and instructed the officer to squeeze the bag every three seconds.

Officer DiGirolamo intensely focused on squeezing the bag at the correct interval. One, two, three and squeeze. "Not too fast and not too slow," she told herself.

It sounds like a straightforward task except when there's a human being lying on the ground less than a foot away from you and whose life was literally in her hands. At that moment, this easy task was a challenge.

Am I going too fast, am I going too slow? Squeeze. Her eyes momentarily locked with the EMT as he was performing CPR, and since he didn't say anything, she surmised that she was doing it correctly and continued.

"I need to be steady and squeeze this bag consistently. This man's life could depend on it," she silently said to herself. *I've got this one single task and I need to do it well.*

She continued to squeeze the oxygen bag, but even perfect pulses of air weren't going to be enough. The EMT was making a desperate attempt and stopped eight minutes later. The officer dared not stop the three second rhythm of air flow.

"OK, that's enough, he's gone," the EMT told the officer and let out a long sigh.

Officer DiGirolamo stopped and then stood up and thought to herself, "How could he be dead, he has several broken bones but there's hardly any blood." She later found out that the crash caused severe internal bleeding and both men died on the scene.

The two men in the Charger were driving up and down the airstrip, testing the capabilities of the sports car. They were pushing the limit of its reputed 199 mile-per-hour top speed.

Why they were allowed to "test" the car unsupervised was going be investigated. And Officer DiGirolamo noticed the lack of skid marks at the end of the runway, which indicated that the brakes were not applied prior to the end of the concrete.

It was unclear whether the crash was intentional or accidental. They ran out of pavement and were going so fast that they flew over the ditch and when the car finally impacted the ground, it flipped it over and it turned completely around, facing back towards the airstrip.

After only four months on the job, Officer DiGirolamo witnessed two lives ending. The officer was trying to process the experience of watching a life slip away and die right in front of her. Death is a natural conclusion to life, but it was surreal how much had changed for those two men in the previous 30 minutes. When she woke up that morning, she could not have anticipated what would occur on what started out as a routine work shift.

Unfortunately, over the next three years Officer DiGirolamo would see another eight dead bodies. In television shows, dead bodies are usually depicted as a headline grabbing murder, with a crime scene of detectives and forensic investigators.

Small towns like Buena Vista rarely had a murder but frequently need to investigate dead bodies for other reasons. The police are always called in for cases of suicide, drug overdoses and automobile accidents.

But how to process witnessing someone's death? Officer DiGirolamo had to be professional and unemotional enough to perform her job duties, but sometime later it eventually takes a toll on the psyche. Dealing with dead bodies is part of the job, something that you don't want to get used to, but you don't have a choice.

It isn't like working in an office. Sometimes the personal impact doesn't register with an officer until days or months later. Although counseling is available, no one is going to hold your hand through tough policing circumstances, and a certain amount of mental toughness is required. It is a constant reminder of their own mortality.

A police officer willingly puts themself in dangerous situations where a loss of life is possible and there is little certainty how each incident will play out. In law enforcement, there is no way to avoid dealing with death, especially in a small town where the officers are expected to do a little bit of everything.

There are no full-time desk jobs where an officer can investigate crime from the comfort of an air-conditioned office and a cushy chair. In rural towns like Buena Vista, officers are out on patrol without a partner so when they approach a potential volatile situation, each officer must take the long and lonely walk from the relative safety of their patrol car into an unpredictable and frequently dangerous situation.

October 2018

"You are correct, I do have a gun. I have it to keep you guys safe," explained Officer DiGirolamo. She had all the students' attention in Mrs. Thompson's second grade class.

She was presenting the "what's on my belt" section of the School Resource Officer education program which helps explain to the kids who she was and why she was there. "This is a dangerous weapon; it is not a toy and will only be used when it is absolutely necessary."

"Does anyone know what this is?" the officer asked.

"That's easy, it looks like a flashlight," one of the students replied.

"Correct, we have lots of things on our belt, and it can weigh up to twenty pounds. And that's in addition to wearing a ten-pound vest," Officer DiGirolamo stated.

"What is the other thing that looks like a gun, do you have two of them?" asked another student.

"That's called a taser, and it is used to temporarily shock somebody and slow them down if they need to be arrested," she replied and continued, "I'm guessing you all know what this is?"

"Handcuffs," replied several of the students.

"Can you handcuff me?" asked one of the students.

"No, again, the items on my belt are not toys, so I only use the handcuffs if I have to arrest somebody.

Officer DiGirolamo imagined letting one of the kids examine the handcuffs and somehow a kid gets chained to a desk. She could see the headline now: *Police officer handcuffs second grader for no reason.* No handcuff demonstration for today.

"What are those other things?" a different student asked.

"I also have a tourniquet that is used to stop someone from bleeding, and a radio to talk to other police officers."

"And this thing that looks like a stick is used in case I have to break a window," the officer said and showed them her collapsible baton. With the flick of her wrist, the baton expanded from 12 to 21 inches in less than a second.

"Whoa, that's cool," responded one of the students.

"I have a key fob and an extra pair of handcuffs," Officer DiGirolamo continued. "I also have a second heavy-duty protective vest," the officer described. "Would anyone like to try to lift it up?" she asked. Several of the boys raised their hands and she called on one of them to come up to the front of the classroom.

"This is easy!" Ruben explained as he struggled to lift the 40 plus pound vest in the air, "I could hold this all day," he proclaimed as his arms started to shake from the weight of the vest. The heavier vest was designed to protect an officer from powerful rifle rounds.

"Yes, I'm sure you could, but why don't you give it to me and go sit back down," she said with a slight chuckle. "Are there any more questions?"

"So why are you at the school, Ms. D?" a student asked.

"Well, I have this really cool job as a police officer where I get to hang out with you guys all day. Doesn't that sound like fun? Of course, I am here to keep you safe. Sometimes I'm in the high school and middle school too, so you won't see me every day, but you will see me often."

"Thank you for joining and educating our class," Mrs. Thompson said.

"Like I said before, you can come to me if there's any kind of trouble, or you can visit just to talk. I'd like to get to know you, and you can get to know me too. This might be the first time that you've ever met a police officer, and you need to know that we're here to help you," Officer DiGirolamo recapped and left the classroom.

***

Recess was over and the kids started returning back into the school building, shuffling to form a single-file line. As usual Officer DiGirolamo was holding the door open for them, giving many of them "high-fives" as they entered the school. The students were supposed to enter the school quietly and the officer would silently greet the students with a smile.

Then one of the students spoke out. "Don't shoot me," said Jake, a second grader, while he walked towards the officer with his hands up.

"Why would you say that?" asked Officer DiGirolamo, a bit surprised and taken aback by the comment. She then said, "We were just playing tag on the playground not 15 minutes ago." It didn't matter.

Jake's expression did not project the message that he was trying to be funny or was making some kind of joke. His concern for his safety was genuine in the moment. *Where does a second grader learn that?* A second grader typically does not watch the news or see political commentary, so he must have heard it from family members, most likely his parents.

Officer DiGirolamo involuntarily took a deep breath, as the boy's quick but meaningful action sunk in and she was at a loss on how to react. He walked by her without saying anything else.

Is this boy actually afraid of her? Does Jake think that an officer is going to shoot second graders, and him specifically? Where was this kid headed if he had such a mistrust of the police at such an early age?

Do his parents carry such a negative view of police officers that it has now permeated and probably permanently infected this seven-year-old? He wasn't joking; he wasn't jesting, as if he'd heard an adult tell a story and laughed about it. No, this was a kid who was serious about what he was feeling in that moment.

219

The officer believed that kids are not born suspicious or fearful of police, it was learned behavior from an outside influence. Officer DiGirolamo slowed down her breathing, drooped her shoulders and felt a strong sense of sadness. This is not what policing is all about. This is a little slice of what's wrong with our society. *Her heart was a little bit broken.*

***

The elementary school kids were once again finishing their recess and funneling into a single-file line back into the school. Officer DiGirolamo was standing just outside the building, holding the door open and continuing her routine of giving the kids "high fives." Jake said nothing and didn't give the officer a high-five as he walked by.

However, there were three boys towards the back of the line that were goofing off as they were getting closer to the school building.

"Boys, you need to be quiet; recess is over," Officer DiGirolamo advised. The boys continued to joke around, and one of them pushed another second grader out of line, who then countered with punching the other kid in the arm.

"Hey, stop that. It's time to settle down and get back inside. Please be quiet," the officer instructed, only to be ignored once again by the rambunctious elementary school kids.

As the boys approached Officer DiGirolamo, she gave them a *look* which conveyed her unhappiness with their behavior. They glanced back at her and laughed it off. Her best parental-inspired *death stare* didn't work. The kids continued to be noisy once they got into the school. Officer DiGirolamo said a third time, "Boys you need to start listening and be quiet when you are going back into the classroom."

While the officer reprimanded the kids without a change in behavior, Mrs. Thompson was standing just outside her classroom and noticed the ongoing shenanigans.

"That's the third time I've told them to settle down, but they aren't listening today," the officer told the teacher.

"Boys settle down now and go back to your seats," Mrs. Thompson said with a no-nonsense attitude. The boys quietly went to their seats.

The next day

Mrs. Thompson asked Officer DiGirolamo to come into her classroom while the kids were at lunch.

"Some of those kids sure do try to push the limits. I'm sorry that they didn't behave properly yesterday," Mrs. Thompson told her.

"That's OK, I'll keep trying to work on them, but sometimes it seems as if they are *trying to get in trouble*," replied Officer DiGirolamo with a smile.

"Yes, I know what you mean," Mrs. Thompson said with a laugh, and then continued, "I had a talk with the class yesterday about showing respect for the police, and specifically about listening to you."

"Oh, how did that go?"

"I had that discussion with the entire class even though it was for the benefit of those three boys. I had them make this," she said and handed three pieces of paper to Officer DiGirolamo.

The papers were apology notes from the boys, saying that they were sorry for not respecting the officer. "Thank you so much for supporting me, and thanks for having a talk with these kids," the officer replied.

"Of course. They are a good bunch of boys, but sometimes they like to push the envelope. They shouldn't treat you like that."

"Well, I do appreciate the apology notes," Officer DiGirolamo replied. She decided to see if those boys wanted to hang out during lunch.

***

Middle School

All middle school teachers should be paid double and wear a badge of courage, awarded for putting up with sixth, seventh and eighth graders five days a week. The principal had asked Officer DiGirolamo on Thursday to come to the middle school to discuss the newest eighth grade trend. New trends were hardly ever good, and this one was no exception; it was called "Slap-Ass Friday", and it was as bad as it sounded.

"For some reason, a few eighth graders decided to start a tradition, where a bunch of the boys go around slapping a girl's butt in the hallway or classroom on Fridays. Two weeks ago, it was just a couple of times, but last week it was happening throughout the day," the principal said in an exasperated tone. She continued, "Many teachers observed this in the hallway and during lunch."

"I've heard of this happening in some schools in the Denver area," Officer DiGirolamo commented.

"I've already talked to the kids, but I think it would be great if you can reinforce that this behavior won't be tolerated. Maybe you can have a discussion with all the grades, but especially with the eighth graders," the principal suggested.

"I'd be happy to, we need to stop this before it gets out of control."

"I agree. One of the girls, Ariana Dollymomus was standing by her locker and was encouraging a lineup of boys to spank her rear end!" the principal said with disdain. "They all thought it was a big joke, and I think it emboldened the boys to do the same thing to the other girls."

"Yes, I know that girl and, unfortunately, she is headed for trouble in my opinion," the officer stated and continued, "I will talk to the class this afternoon."

"I've already heard complaints from several kids and their parents and this needs to be stopped before any other kids are harassed. Thanks."

Thirty minutes later, Officer DiGirolamo was addressing one of the eighth-grade classes. "So, I understand there's a new disturbing trend going on at the school. Some of the students had a look of confusion, while others reacted with guilt.

The officer continued, "I've heard that in between classes on Friday, there are some students slapping another student's butt. That is not acceptable behavior," she said in a stern manner.

"I don't care if you personally are OK with it or not, that's not something done in the hallway and especially if it's unwanted," Officer DiGirolamo explained. Many of the students started snickering. Their reaction was completely expected.

"This is not funny, just last week I arrested someone in high school for unlawful sexual contact, because he kept doing a similar type of touching that was completely unwanted. *This is not a joke*," she said in a most serious tone and paused to let it sink in with the students.

"Do you want to get arrested? I don't want to have to charge you with a felony, but guess what, I will," she emphasized and paused again to communicate the seriousness. The snickering vanished. The officer continued, "Don't try to push the envelope or tell me it was an accident or that you didn't mean to touch the other person. I'm not buying it."

All eyes were glued to Officer DiGirolamo. She was on a roll, "Do you want to have a juvenile record? That would be a *criminal* juvenile record. I don't care what the reason is, but if I see you inappropriately touching someone, I will charge you and I will bring in your parents and you will be driven several hours to the juvenile detention center."

Chaffee County did not have a juvenile detention center, with the closest one being several hours away in Pueblo, CO. The class was silent, and it looked like the message had gotten through, so she ended the discussion.

Officer DiGirolamo looked around the classroom and no one raised their hand or had a question. She momentarily thought about her previous SRO interactions with the middle schoolers.

She'd be walking down the hallway and one of the kids would say something like, "hey, why don't you taser me." Or one of the boys would push his friend, and the one who was shoved would say, "Hey Officer D, he assaulted me! Can you arrest him?" It seemed like the middle schoolers entire goal in life was to get under the skin of as many adults as possible.

The girls of course had their own way of being annoying and trying to be as difficult as possible. Just last week there was a girl arguing with her friend and was about to be late for class, and the officer told her to get going and hurry up to class. The student just rolled her eyes and Officer DiGirolamo replied with "Don't you dare roll your eyes at me like that!"

She wondered if she was like that when she was in middle school. The officer already knew the answer and realized that some things don't change from generation to generation.

"Slap-Ass Friday" abruptly ended and there were no further incidents the rest of the school year.

***

A few weeks later, Officer DiGirolamo started a new SRO tradition for the school by hosting the special-needs kids from the high school. They met in the parking lot to speak with the officer and check out her patrol car.

The Buena Vista High School typically had five to ten special-needs kids each year. It was a miniature field trip for the kids and several students came out to check out the patrol car and some wanted to sit in the passenger-side front seat.

They turned on the flashing lights and the highlight of the session was being able to turn on the siren. These kids became more comfortable with the officer and it started to build a relationship with them. Officer DiGirolamo took several pictures of the event and posted it to the Buena Vista Police Department Facebook page, and it was positively received by the community.

Thirty minutes later, the kids headed back to the classroom.

***

July 2019

Snapchat messaging:

Rick: Wait, that's not really you is it?

Jillian: It is, is something wrong?

Rick: No, nothing's wrong, I just can't believe that you're sooo beautiful. You didn't tell me that you're a model!

Jillian: Thanks, but I'm not a model.

Rick: Well you should be, you are definitely pretty enough. A cousin of mine knows some people at Teen Vogue magazine, maybe I can talk to him about getting you a photo shoot. What do you think?

Jillian: IDK, do you really think I'm pretty enough to be a model?

Rick: 100% yes! UR prettier than most of the models out there.

Jillian: U Think so?

Rick: Absolutely! How many boyfriends do you have?

Jillian: None at the moment.

Rick: I don't believe you! You must have at least two or three. Don't lie to me.

Jillian: I'm not lying!

Rick: OK, I believe you. You should change your username to sexy_girl_Jillian

Jillian: What?

Rick: Do you mind if I call you sexy girl?

Jillian: No.

Rick: Do you mind if I call you MY sexy girl?

Jillian: ☺

Rick: That selfie you sent me was totally awesome. Can you send me one with a sexy pose?

Jillian: I don't know. I'm not sure how to do that?

Rick: What are you wearing?

Jillian: Just a T shirt and some shorts.

Rick: What kind of T shirt?

Jillian: PINK

Rick: That will do.

Rick: Pretend you are giving me a kiss. Can you do that?

Jillian: I think so.

Rick: Cool, I can't wait.

Fifteen-year-old Jillian Martin extended her arm and snapped a picture on her iPhone. She looked at it quickly and decided *no, this won't do.* She hit the delete button. She again puckered her lips and leaned her head slightly back to show a little more neckline and snapped a photo for her second try. *Close, but not quite right.*

She looked at herself in the picture, hating her completely straight red hair, and wondering why Rick wanted a picture of her. *She wasn't ugly*, she told herself, but no one ever called her pretty either, let alone beautiful, let alone that she should be a model.

"Well, maybe he's just flirting with me," she said aloud to no one. *That's OK, he can give me compliments, I don't mind.* She smiled at her thoughts and snapped a burst of 10 pictures.

She finally found one she liked and sent it to her new "friend" Rick. Maybe he'd be more than a friend? Who knows, but she liked the idea that a guy would be more than someone in her friend zone. She already had too many of those at high school.

Jillian stared at the picture that she'd just sent Rick. Her hair crossed just in front of her left eye that reminded her of a picture she saw from one of *Snapchat's* influencers. *Maybe I'm not that bad looking after all. Maybe I have a pretty side.* She saw the curve of her nose and her puckered lips. *Her lips looked good, but that chin! Ugh!* She was glad that the *Snapchat* photo would disappear in 10 seconds.

Jillian had been flirting with Rick for three days while she was on vacation in Buena Vista with her family. She'd simply been sitting on a rock watching the Arkansas River flow by on a beautiful summer day, when out of the blue she received a friend request from Rick. *Sure, why not*, she thought to herself.

And there he was, 16-year-old Rick with wavy jet-black hair. He was shirtless and muscular and sported a smile that conveyed "I'm up to no good and wouldn't you like to be part of it." He would be #1 on her shor*t hot-guy* friend list. That was all it took for Jillian to accept the request, and they immediately started messaging each other.

Most good-looking guys never give a second notice to Jillian, so why is he paying attention to her? "No matter," she said aloud to herself, "it's just a summer fling, right?"

His profile picture showed him holding a rafting paddle, so Jillian assumed that he was from the area. All of Chaffee County, including Buena Vista and Salida, is known as a summer destination for river rafting, but is also popular for hiking, mountain biking and fishing. Jillian's family was renting a house for a week and each day they planned to hit up one of those activities.

Yesterday, the family rented mountain bikes and decided to try the Midland Gravel Loop trail. What a disaster, after going about a mile, the trail went straight up! Fifteen seconds later Jillian was pushing her bike up the hill. *You call this fun? This is what you want to do on vacation?*

She shook her head, frustrated that she was unable to convince her parents to try a Caribbean cruise instead. *Now that would be fun!* She could sit poolside all day and relax. That sounded much better than the physical trauma caused by biking and hiking excursions. This place was full of mountains which meant you are *always going uphill.* Her Dad would always tell her that "what goes up must come down." *Dad jokes* really annoyed her. But she was looking forward to tomorrow, that was going to be their rafting trip.

The next morning, she woke up early at 10:30a.m. and before getting out of bed, she decided to check her phone.

Rick: Hey cutey, I missed you.

Rick: I've been dreaming about you all night.

Rick: I'm thinking about you all day long.

Rick: R U there?

Jillian: Sorry, I just woke up!

Rick: I thought you didn't like me anymore.

Jillian: This is the first time I've seen my phone today.

Rick: OK, I forgive you.

Jillian: 🙂

Rick: What are you wearing?

Jillian: Just what I wore to bed.

Rick: Send me a pic.

Jillian: I just woke up; I look awful!

Rick: You are always beautiful to me. Please!

Jillian: OK.

Jillian stretched out her arm to take a picture of herself in the plain powder blue t-shirt she was wearing. She sent Rick the picture and he replied that he wanted another one, this time with her belly button showing. She hesitated a second, but then thought that it wasn't any different than when she was in a swimsuit. She raised her t-shirt to show off her belly button, and the picture also caught the top end of her bikini-style underwear.

Rick: You are even more beautiful than I could imagine.

Jillian: Hey, my parents are calling. I've gotta go. TTYL.

***

"'Cause when you're fifteen
And somebody tells you they love you.
You're gonna believe them"
--**Taylor Swift**, *"15"*

***

Two hours later

Jillian and her family were checking in at the rafting company office. This was her first time rafting, and she was excited to go down the Arkansas River. She couldn't figure out why it was called the Arkansas River when they were vacationing *in Colorado*.

No matter. They would be rafting some "Class 2" rapids which is more than just a lazy float down the river, but definitely not too rough. She guessed that her parents decided that anything more adventurous would be too much for her eight-year-old brother to handle. She had seen some videos on the company website, and it looked like a lot of fun, and the rafting boat could hold up to nine people including the guide.

But, before they would get their quick lesson on paddling, they needed to stand in another line to receive their personal flotation device. One of the guides was explaining that Colorado was the starting point for the Arkansas River, and that the river went southeast, and eventually flowed into the Mississippi River in the state of Arkansas. Jillian decided that the explanation of the river's name wasn't that interesting. But that's when she noticed *her*.

"Mine doesn't fit," the blonde replied, trying to stretch the clips of the personal flotation device so it would fasten, but it wasn't working. "I guess I've got healthy lungs," she quipped and laughed to herself, once again trying to clasp the life jacket over her large bosom.

The hot blonde was wearing a skimpy cheetah patterned bikini top and ripped jean shorts which left no room for the imagination. *Healthy lungs, my ass!* She had perfect body proportions and that body was perfectly tanned. She had a beautiful smooth rounded chin which perfectly framed her smile and perfectly smooth skin. Even her teeth were perfectly white! She was too perfect. *Ugh!*

She looked like she just finished a photoshoot for a sunscreen lotion company. Her wavy blonde hair rested just above her obvious cleavage. Wouldn't want to *cover that up*, now would we? And she looked like she just came out of a salon. Her nails were expertly manicured and colored in turquoise blue. Her makeup was even more *perfect*, of course.

How can I compete with a girl like this? She was just like the girls in Jillian's high school that looked down on her and gave her dirty looks just for existing. I'm sure she's the most popular girl in her school, *and I hate her!* She probably has a thousand followers. And I bet every picture she posts is *liked* by everyone.

Her declaration about the lifejacket not fitting seemed to stump the young man handing out the flotation devices. He stumbled with his words as he watched her try again to clasp the flotation device. She was making a scene on purpose, and it seemed as if every male in the room was staring at her.

Even some of the Dads noticed her antics, and Jillian was half expecting them all to rush over to assist the damsel in distress. She had seen this obvious craving for attention before.

There were plenty of girls at her high school who acted exactly the same, all trying to get the boys to fawn over them. She wasn't really in distress of course, but that wasn't the point. The point was to get their attention.

Jillian surmised that this wasn't the first time this chick tried to divert the attention from the competition. She also concluded that it was working flawlessly. You could almost see the steam coming out of Jillian's ears.

When Jillian got into the same line, no one turned *their* heads, or diverted *their* eyes, not even for a millisecond! *Why can't I get noticed? This girl has everything and has the perfect life and I have nothing. I am totally invisible. Guys are such jerks! Why can't I be popular? What's wrong with me? Well, at least Rick likes me.*

Three hours later

Rick: I think I'm falling in love with you.

Jillian: What? Really?

Rick: Yes, I can't stop thinking about you.

Jillian: Me too, I think about you day and night.

Rick: *You are perfect.* Can I ask you something, and will you promise not to be mad?

Jillian: Uh, OK?

Rick: Will you send me a nude?

Jillian: A what?

Rick: You are sooo sexy and sooo beautiful. I have to see more of you. Please!

Jillian: IDK...

Rick: Please, come on, it's just for me. I promise not to show it to anyone. I want to feel closer to you. I want to feel more connected. Don't you want to be connected with me?

Jillian: Yes...

Rick: I take that back.

Rick: I **need** to feel closer to you.

Jillian: Well, maybe.

Rick: Awesome! You have made me sooo happy!

Jillian: Yeah! ☺

***

"We curate our lives around this perceived sense of perfection because we get rewarded in these short-term signals, hearts, likes, thumbs-up and we conflate that with value and we conflate that with truth. And instead what it really is, is fake brittle popularity that's short-term and that leaves you even more, and admit it, vacant and empty before you did it. Because then it forces you into this vicious cycle where you're like 'What's the next thing I need to do now?'"
—**Chamath Palihapitiyal**, Former Facebook VP of Growth, *"The Social Dilemma"*

***

Jillian stared at the phone while riding in the back seat of her parent's car, heading back to their vacation rental. She was wondering if she should really go through with it. No one had asked her for a picture like that before. She was starting to have real feelings for this guy. It sounded like he had real feelings for her too. *He's the only guy that told me I was beautiful.* Maybe it would be OK. *Probably? Hopefully!*

When they arrived back at the house, Julian headed straight for the bathroom. She stepped inside, closed and locked the door behind her and stared at herself in the mirror. She moved her fingers through her hair, tilted her head and blew a kiss into the mirror. She liked what she saw. The big question is, *would Rick like it?*

Hopefully, it is enough to keep him interested. She took off her T shirt, hesitated a second and then removed her bra, and stared at herself. She put her left arm behind her head, puckered her lips, held the phone out with her right hand and pointed it at herself and snapped a picture. She added the "cat" filter to the picture which gave her cat ears and a cat nose. She was pleased; *she looked cute in the picture, maybe even sexy?* She was a little bit nervous as she touched the send button. *That picture is going to disappear in 10 seconds, so what's the big deal?*

235

Three Months Later

October 2019

"So, how many of you think this ended well?" asked Officer Megan DiGirolamo. No one raised their hand.

"This is a true story of a teen being blackmailed. Raise your hand if you see a problem with what Jillian did," Officer DiGirolamo instructed and was surprised that three people didn't raise their hand.

She was addressing a ninth-grade homeroom class at Buena Vista High School. It was only the second year that the town of Buena Vista had a School Resource Officer, with Officer DiGirolamo as the only SRO in the school's history. She presented multiple training education sessions to kids from elementary school through high school.

"Actually, the story gets worse for Jillian. *Snapchat* as you all know sends a picture that will disappear in ten seconds, but there is a way to take a screenshot which then saves the picture forever," she told them, letting that reality sink in with the freshman class.

"Jillian sent a topless photograph of herself, which is technically a crime because it's child pornography," Officer DiGirolamo stated and continued. "The next day this person who called himself or herself "Rick" asked for her Facebook password. For some reason Jillian gave it to him. Keep in mind that they never met, and never talked on the phone, yet she is trusting this person with inappropriate pictures of herself along her password."

"And this girl was some random person on vacation?" a student asked.

"Yes, it is not someone from the area, so it isn't anyone you know," Officer DiGirolamo explained to the group of thirteen- and fourteen-year-olds.

"He then asked for video of her taking a shower. She didn't want to, but he threatened to send her nude picture to everyone on her Facebook account, including family members if she didn't send something."

"She sent a short clip of herself, but it wasn't good enough," Officer DiGirolamo said and continued. "*Rick* sent the topless picture to several people on her Facebook account."

"You can't take back that kind of embarrassment," Officer DiGirolamo told the students, and many of the ninth graders gasped. She could see the distraught look on their faces as they imagined this happening to them. "Imagine that picture sent to her grandpa!"

"Don't let yourself be a victim," Officer DiGirolamo stated. "Imagine the moment Jillian realized what Rick had done. Imagine the stress and panic this girl must have felt." The expression on the students' faces became even more agitated.

"Eww," one the girls responded, her face scrunched in horror.

Officer DiGirolamo continued, "Jillian then broke down and had to tell her parents, who then came to the police department to report what had happened. It was within our jurisdiction because it occurred while she was in town. Remember, all of this happened in *less than one week*."

"Did they ever catch this guy?" another student asked.

"We were able to determine that Rick's user-account was based in Adapazari, near Istanbul, Turkey. So unfortunately, there's no way to bring him or her to justice and who knows what this person did with the picture.

"So, it wasn't some 16-year-old guy?" a student asked, but the answer was obvious.

"Rick's profile picture was obviously fake, so we have no idea whether Rick was a man or a woman, old or young or anything else about that person, the officer stated and continued.

"It was probably someone who was manipulating a dozen or so unsuspecting girls at the same time."

"It doesn't make it any better if he really was 16. It is still a crime," Officer DiGirolamo stated, and she heard the class murmur. "It can happen to boys too. This is a serious problem."

"Let's review what we learned in this case," she outlined. "Sending, possessing, sharing, exchanging, posting, distributing or displaying nude pictures of anyone under eighteen is child pornography, and is illegal. Internet sexual exploitation of a child can be a felony or misdemeanor depending on what's been done and how many pictures or videos are involved.

She continued, "Colorado law states that if someone is more than four years older than a fourteen-year-old and is asking for nudes, it is a felony. There are also specific statutes increasing charges if the sharing of those photos is intended to harm the person in the picture or video. That "harm" can include non-physical harm like causing emotional distress."

Officer DiGirolamo summarized, "The last thing you want is an embarrassing picture sent to your family or friends. These pictures don't really get deleted. You should treat your social media account as if your grandmother were seeing everything you did. Imagine how horrified Jillian was when she had to tell her parents what had happened, and how humiliated she felt when her friends and family saw pictures of her."

The class went silent and the air suddenly seemed thicker and still. "I know this is an awkward discussion, but it happens all too often," Officer DiGirolamo told them. "If you or one of your friends are ever caught up in this, you should talk to me in private in my office."

"Some websites directed at teens, like *Bedsider*, tell you that sexting is a good way to let your partner know you are in the mood," she continued, "But I'm here to tell you that's the worst advice I ever heard."

No one raised their hands, and it didn't look like anyone was about to make a comment, so Officer DiGirolamo continued, "Stuff on the internet doesn't go away. A picture of you could resurface while you're at your first job as an adult."

"It doesn't have to be a nude picture, it could be a picture or video of you doing something stupid, which could be a hundred different things," she told them and she could see the students imagining many circumstances that you wouldn't want for public consumption.

"You don't want that to happen. It won't be that long before you'll be out of high school and wanting to start a career. Also, if you've got nude pictures of other kids on your phone, you don't wanna have a criminal record of that, which also can follow you into adulthood."

"Imagine trying to explain to your boss why you got busted for having naked pictures of a bunch of freshman," the officer continued. "That's not what you want to be doing when you're 23 years old. Ten years may seem like a long way away, but trust me, it isn't." She saw a lot of heads nodding in understanding and agreement, but would it sink in?

***

Two days later

"Officer DiGirolamo, can we talk to you a minute?" asked Melanie, a ninth-grader. She was accompanied with her best friend Monica, and the two friends were inseparable. Everyone knew them as M&M.

"Sure, close the door," she answered.

"Well, you were talking about sexting and everything in class the other day…" Melanie said, trailed off and looked down at the floor.

"Tell me what happened," Officer DiGirolamo asked softly, getting right to the point.

"Do you know Lucas Mansfield?" Melanie asked.

"I know he's a senior, but I don't know him very well."

"Well..."

"Did he ask you for nudes?" Officer DiGirolamo asked.

"Yes, he asked both of us," Melanie replied and looked over at Monica, who nodded in agreement.

"Did either of you send him anything?"

"Oh, no we didn't! We don't know him at all. I mean, it's kinda cool that a senior boy even noticed me, but..." Melanie stated.

"I don't know why a senior boy would even want to talk with us or would be interested in us," Monica added, "but I didn't send him anything."

"He's also has asked our other friends. He seems to be going around asking everyone," Melanie explained.

"Did any of them send any pictures?" Officer DiGirolamo asked.

"No, not that we know of. He seems to be asking every freshman girl for naked pictures!" Monica exclaimed.

"OK, so the good news is you didn't send anything. And definitely don't do that. I will go talk to Mr. Mansfield."

"Thanks," both girls said in unison.

"Of course, that's what I'm here for. And I won't let him know I heard this from you two."

"That's good," Monica replied.

"Thanks for letting me know," Officer DiGirolamo replied. "Now you girls get back to lunch and let me know if anything else happens."

This is why you need a School Resource Officer, thought Officer DiGirolamo. If there was no one on campus, these girls probably wouldn't walk down to the police station and tell anyone, they'd have nowhere to go except maybe a parent or a teacher, which could be awkward. The subject would likely just get dropped, but that wouldn't mean the behavior would stop.

Officer DiGirolamo was present in the school just about every day, so she was already getting to know even the newer freshman class. By being a regular presence on campus, many students would feel more comfortable coming to her with sensitive or awkward issues, and it also helped that she was a young female police officer as well. It looks like giving these regular education presentations to the students was having an impact.

The next day, Officer DiGirolamo had the front office call Lucas during his free period to go to her office. Generally, the SRO was free to talk to any of the students and if a minor is a victim or a witness, parental consent was not required.

However, it was Officer DiGirolamo's standard practice to let parents know if she was talking to one of the kids who was a victim or witness. Parental consent would be required before interrogating a minor who was arrested. Lucas was eighteen, so he was no longer a minor, and he wasn't being arrested.

"What is going on?" Lucas asked.

"Let me be direct, I've heard that you've been asking a bunch of girls for nude pictures, is that correct?"

"Well, it wasn't me," he lied.

"Then who was it?" she asked. Since the M&M girls said they didn't send any pictures, there was no probable cause to confiscate his phone.

"I don't know," Lucas replied.

"Well let's just say, hypothetically of course, that you received naked pictures from your classmates. If you showed anyone or posted it anywhere or saved it to your computer, as you know from listening to my presentation, that would be child pornography. You're eighteen, right?" Officer DiGirolamo asked a question she already knew the answer to.

"Yeah," Lucas answered without direct eye contact.

"Well, some of the freshman girls at this school are thirteen, and if you have nude pictures of someone who is under fourteen, it automatically makes it a felony."

"What, that can't be right," Lucas replied with surprise.

"It is. It certainly doesn't look good when an eighteen-year-old man is charged with sexually exploiting a thirteen-year-old girl, now does it?"

"No, I guess not," he answered, and his face turned red with shame and embarrassment.

"You haven't gotten in trouble around here, so it would be a real shame for you to start now. I'm pretty disappointed in you," Officer DiGirolamo stated flatly.

"Well..."

"Well, what? You need to get your act together. This is not a joke. If I hear any more talk of you harassing anyone for pictures at this school, I will personally make it my mission to get the evidence to arrest you. Do you understand?" Officer DiGirolamo stated emphatically.

"Yes, but you don't have to worry about me, I'm not doing that kind of stuff." That really meant from that moment on, he was *no longer going to be doing that kind of stuff.*

"Don't ruin any of these girls' future, *or your own.*"

"OK."

"This is unacceptable behavior, and I am not going to tolerate that," she said with a stern voice and a serious look on her face. Her expression slightly softened when she realized she sounded just like her parents.

"I got it," Lucas replied and stood up and she motioned him towards the door.

This kid's actions were definitely creepy. Was he a sexual predator? It was too early to tell. He might be the kind of person that will continue harassing young women once he's out of high school, or maybe he was merely a teenager trying to show off to his friends.

He might have simply wanted to see what he could get from these girls, pushing the envelope and trying to figure out how far they would go, without really thinking about the consequences. He may have thought it was just a big joke. Lucas' path could go either way, and Officer DiGirolamo felt like she gave her best Olivia Benson of *Law & Order* impersonation, trying to scare this kid straight. She hoped it worked.

***

November 3, 2019

"Let's go grab some lunch at the Chinese place, what do you think?" Deputy Roy Williams asked.

"Sure, how about 12:30," Officer Megan DiGirolamo suggested.

"See you there," he said and hung up the phone. Twenty-seven-year-old Deputy Roy Williams had been with the Chaffee County Sheriff's Office for about two years, after serving in the army. He and his girlfriend had become friends with Officers Megan DiGirolamo and Jesse Mitchell.

"So, do you still like babysitting those kids?" asked Deputy Williams with a smirk as he looked at his restaurant menu.

"Very funny Mr. Williams," she answered with a frown.

"You know, I would be a better school resource officer than you," the deputy stated, clearly in the mood to agitate his friend.

"Oh, is that so? You wouldn't last one day doing my job," shot back Officer DiGirolamo.

"How hard could the job be? If they act up, all you have to do is knock their heads together!" Deputy Williams said laughing in jest.

"Oh, that's a great solution. Did they teach you that at the academy?" Officer DiGirolamo countered.

"Yeah, you're right, those kids would make me crazy."

"You have no idea about everything that goes on in the school, and how there are so many dynamics and personalities, let alone the maturity level between elementary school and high school. Well sometimes the maturity level doesn't change from second grade to the twelfth grade!" Officer DiGirolamo joked.

"Better you than me dealing with those kids," Deputy Williams responded.

"That's for sure. Leave the SRO job to me. So, Roy, how are you doing" Megan asked, changing the subject and mood of the conversation.

It was only a couple of days since Roy and his longtime girlfriend had broken up. Megan was going to miss those double dates, hanging out with Jesse, Roy and his former girlfriend, talking and playing games such as Yahtzee and Monopoly. Megan made a mental note to try to summit another 14er mountain with Roy, like they accomplished this past summer when they hiked up Mount Princeton with their dogs.

"Yeah, it's fine. I've already found this new woman on Tinder in Colorado Springs. She's a veterinarian and I think I might ask her out," Roy stated.

"Oh really?" Megan asked, a bit surprised that he was moving quickly into another relationship. It was hard to figure out what was going on inside of Roy's head. He was rather good at putting up an emotional wall, even with his closest friends.

It had been a tough couple of weeks, beginning when he put down his old dog which he'd owned since his army days. The bad news continued when a few days ago, Roy's girlfriend broke up with him.

Everything hit the fan that evening, and the girlfriend went over to Megan's house to talk and Jesse went over to Roy's. It wasn't clear if Jesse and Megan were playing referee or relationship counselor. It was a bit of both.

After Megan talked with the girlfriend for several hours, it was obvious that Roy was more smitten with her than she was with him. During their "girl talk," Megan concluded that she had commitment issues. Since they were dating over a year, Megan suspected that she didn't want the relationship to get more serious, especially if she didn't have strong feelings for Roy and was nowhere ready to make a marital commitment.

Neither Roy nor his girlfriend were good at communication. She told Megan about some of their relationship problems, but none of them seemed insurmountable. Any suggestions she offered were shot down, which was frustrating because Megan thought they were fixable, but only if both parties wanted to fix it.

That night she was texting back and forth with Jesse and the ultimate question was posed to her: *Was there a chance they could get back together? Could they work it out?* It was obvious that Roy wanted to work on their relationship but based upon Megan's conversation with his girlfriend, she could only come to one conclusion: it wasn't in the cards.

They were already living together when they broke up, which created an awkward living situation when you're not together as a couple. Maybe that put pressure on Roy, and it must have been difficult to see his former girlfriend day in and day out.

***

While Megan was having the "girl talk," Jesse Mitchell was with Roy who was visibly angry. His girlfriend had cheated on him; but rather than ask for forgiveness, she decided to end the relationship. She made her true feelings clear and it was a double punch of rejection for Roy. That pain and anger led Jesse and Roy to start taking shots of whiskey, and Roy let his guard down for a moment.

Occasionally Roy would talk about his good experiences from the army, the friends he'd made and the camaraderie of his unit. But he also carried a burden from his time in Iraq and the alcohol allowed a glimpse of Roy's burden.

Roy's unit was on patrol in a small Iraqi town and several people had blocked the street. They didn't clear out as instructed and the standoff quickly became intense with the uncertainty of what was going to happen next.

The townspeople appeared to be regular Iraqi people, including children, but American soldiers knew that looks could be deceiving and insurgents could be hiding amongst the population. A scuffle broke out and several soldiers fired with less lethal munitions. These types of rounds are a ballistic bag with stabilizing tails filled with tiny shot that forms an extremely accurate "bean bag."

Roy shot the bean bag and saw it hit a boy in the chest and he was knocked down to the ground. The child did not initially get up, and Roy's convoy did not stay long, so he didn't know if the child survived or was indeed killed. Roy beat himself up over the incident and assumed the worst-case scenario, that this child was killed by an American soldier, Roy Williams.

Roy admitted to Jesse that it had been several years, but he could not let this incident go, and like a cancer, it ate at Roy and resulted in a combination of guilt and anger. The anguish was tortuous for Roy because he was unable to confirm what ultimately happened to this kid, even with Jesse pointing out that the less lethal munitions were designed to stun people, and not to kill them. But Roy was convinced that he was morally responsible for this kid's death. He was stuck with the guilt and time had not healed this wound.

Jesse was hoping that this rare incidence where Roy talked about his moral injury would help him get the pain off his chest. But Roy could be a stubborn man and it wasn't clear whether his admission of his true feelings was going to be therapeutic or not. The evening ended with Roy still hurt, angry, frustrated and inebriated.

***

Is he really moving on, or is he just putting on a show? Megan hoped her friend was moving on, but with Roy it was so hard to tell. He was always guarded with his emotions and rarely revealed the difficulties of his past. His wall was always tall and strong. Long-term breakups are never easy and simple, and perhaps Roy was trying to find some new woman to fill the void and forget his past relationship.

Roy spent most of his childhood bouncing around from one foster home to another and never connected with a family. Maybe that's why he didn't want to have any children. His girlfriend didn't want kids either, so that wasn't one of their relationship issues.

Soon after high school Roy joined the army, and he was sent overseas. His friends didn't know the details of his experience in the Middle East. Roy didn't talk about it, and he made it pretty clear that he didn't want to talk about it, so the subject rarely came up. Megan suspected that he suffered from PTSD which added to the stress of being a new deputy.

Roy had a brash personality and was like a bull-in-a-china-shop, who didn't care whether people liked him or not, or whether he hurt someone's feelings when he said what was on his mind. Roy wasn't afraid to tell anyone that they were wrong, in his opinion. He was known to argue with people just for the sake of arguing. He would ruffle *anyone's* feathers. He wasn't doing it to be mean or spiteful, that's just how he was. It was always obvious where you stood with Roy.

However, Roy's interactions could rub some people the wrong way. He was never going to be a diplomat. Some peers weren't fond of Roy, and recently he was looking to join the Chaffee County SWAT team, so he was concerned that some of the current members wouldn't support him. Joining the SWAT team was prestigious, and he was stressed that he'd be excluded from the team due to personality conflicts.

On the other side of the coin, a friendship with Roy was a true gift. He'd be the best friend you ever had and would always have your back. He valued loyalty and he'd support his friends in any way when he was needed. Megan was trying to be that kind of friend to Roy while he was facing difficulties, but since he rarely opened up, it was a tricky balance to provide support and comfort.

"So, your Tinder girl is a veterinarian dealing with wild animals all day? That's perfect for you, maybe she'll tame you," she said joking.

"Ha ha you're so funny," Roy answered.

"Did her Tinder profile say that she liked gingers?" Megan continued to joke, referring to his reddish color hair.

"I am not a ginger. Even the guy who cuts my hair says I'm more of a strawberry blonde. Maybe your two different colored eyes are screwing up your vision," he countered.

"Ha ha, now you're the one that's so funny," Megan said and paused a moment. "So, how are you *really* doing?" Megan asked again. She was concerned about her friend who was dealing with the death of his dog, to the death of his romantic relationship, stress at work and the uncertainty of joining the SWAT team.

"This is much better than the crap they used to give us in the dorms isn't it?" he said, ignoring her question and referring to the time they attended Western State Colorado University. They were at the school at the same time, but they didn't run in the same circles, so they didn't know each other. He put his menu down and said with a tinge of annoyance, "I told you, I'm fine." Cleary they were done talking about his *feelings*.

***

Author's note: PTSD, depression, anger and other mental health afflictions are more common with veterans of war, first responders and people living in small communities. The following section is the author's attempt to illustrate the struggles against the darkness and is not intended to specifically apply to anyone mentioned in this book.

The Power of Darkness

"Hello, darkness, my old friend
I've come to talk with you again
Because a vision softly creeping
Left its seeds while I was sleeping
And the vision that was planted in my brain
Still remains
Within the sound of silence"
—**Simon and Garfunkel**, *The Sound of Silence*

***

When I wake up in the morning, I'm alright in that first moment. Then I remember all of it and it comes flooding back. I remember the sadness, the despair and all that's spoiled. Everything is ruined. I am swimming against a current that's too strong and I can't make any progress. The current brings me backwards and it's taking me under.

I keep hearing the screams and I can't get the noise out of my head. They keep screaming and won't shut up. It is a tortured sound, and it won't stop. Then I feel a chill when I realize who is making that horrible noise: *I am the one screaming*. I am trapped inside a box, and it is shrinking.

You say there is light, and I should follow it, but it is faint. And it is fading. Sometimes the darkness seems too powerful. I can't do anything right. Sometimes it seems easier to succumb. I am so tired. Let it take over; let it win.

I know that there are people that love me. Family and friends. They do so unconditionally, but there is a little voice inside that keeps telling me that their love isn't real. Maybe it's not enough. My head says they love me. My heart knows it, but something darker is pushing those thoughts out. Maybe it isn't love, maybe it's their pity. I am consumed with dread, which is much, much worse than fear.

The darkness is winning, and I know it, but I can't stop it. No one can help. It is too late. I am on the edge of a cliff, and I just need a little push. It is all fading fast, but the one thing I can hold onto is knowing that it will soon be over. I can finish something. At least I can accomplish something.

I know some will feel bad and I am sorry about that, and a distant voice says that I shouldn't do it. But there is that nagging doubt which doesn't leave my head. And there is another voice, a much stronger voice that tells me to just get it done. The darkness has told me that I'm broken, unwanted and worthless, *and I believe it.* And that I need to end it. I must stop the pain once and for all.

***

"Jumping at shadows that come up from behind
Scared of the darkness that's there in your mind
You're frightened to move because of what you might find"
—**The Alan Parsons Project,** *The Voice*

***

I had to pretend to be happy. I lied about being OK. It is what they wanted to hear. It is what I wanted to hear too. We were all hoping for it, but if I admitted that I wasn't OK, then I would be forced to face the darkness. Face the problems, but I really don't want to do that. Why would I when it is all hopeless anyway?

Sad songs make me sad because they describe me. Happy songs make me sad because I know I can't have it. Jokes are not funny, and smiles seem wicked. I don't want tomorrow to come. What would be the point? It would just mean more torment and torture. I just want everyone to leave me alone.

That voice is stronger than anything I have known. I hate to admit it, but it rules my life. I am sorry, really and truly sorry, but being sorry won't be enough to stop me. Everyone will go on, and soon I will just be a memory. I don't want this life, and this life doesn't want me. I just want to give up. I have nothing to say and no one to say it to. People say that life is a journey to find your purpose and how you fit in. I have looked, and have determined that I have no purpose and I don't fit in. *At all.*

***

"All the lonely people
Where do they all come from?
All the lonely people
Where do they all belong?"
—The Beatles, -*Eleanor Rigby*

***

There is a sense of calm. It will all be over soon. The pain will end. *Finally*, it will end. There is a sense of reassurance because there will be an ending. I've thought about it many times, gone over it in my mind, how it will happen, what I will be thinking the moment when there is no turning back. There will be a brief moment when I realize that I can't change my mind.

It sounds frightening, but I have gone through it enough times in my mind that I now feel a sense of peace. I know, it sounds backwards, and warped, that the last violent moment will be peaceful. But it will finally be over. That's all I want. That is all I think about. I just want it done. I can't wait to have the bad thoughts finally stop.

I know how they will react. They will try not to believe. They will be sad, and they will be angry. Their friends will try to console them and fill up the refrigerator with casseroles for a week. Then they will stop, *and I will be forgotten.* I feel even worse about this, but I can't stop it. It is inevitable. I am fighting the tide and the tide is winning. If I am being honest, the darkness has already won.

***

"I've stood here before inside the pouring rain
With the world turning circles running 'round my brain.
I guess I'm always hoping that you'll end this reign,
But it's my destiny to be the king of pain..."
—The Police, *King of Pain*

***

253

The pain is at least something to feel. Feeling pain is hard. Feeling *nothing is unbearable*. It wasn't my problems that were causing me pain. It was *the nothingness.* I am so utterly alone, and I am so tired, and it is hard to stay awake. The darkness clings and consumes me. I have no choice but to embrace the darkness and let it win.

***

"Sometimes you tell the day
By the bottle that you drink
And times when you're all alone
All you do is think
--**Bon Jovi**, *Wanted Dead or Alive*

***

November 5

11:16p.m.

"Where are you?"

"I'm standing outside your front door."

"What's going on?"

"Just come outside."

Megan put down her phone and got out of bed, adjusted her pajamas, and walked to the door and unlocked it. Standing in the doorway was Jesse Mitchell who was on duty in his police uniform. He had a shell-shocked look on his face. Whatever the news he was about to deliver, it wasn't going to be good.

Jesse licked his lips and struggled to talk, finally uttering, "It's Roy."

"What happened with him? He's not on duty tonight," Megan replied and searched for hope on Jesse's face. She didn't find any.

"He and his ex-girlfriend got into an argument. They were drinking and Roy got upset," Jesse said and trailed off. His throat felt dry and he struggled to continue. It was going to be hard to say the words.

Megan felt the pit of her stomach instantly tighten up. Her heart started to beat rapidly, and her breathing became erratic, with both short and long breaths. She was afraid to ask the question. She didn't want to hear the answer, but there was no way to avoid it. She just stared at Jesse and before she even knew the details, she started to cry.

"He shot himself," Jesse said in a low and hoarse voice and then instantly leaned in to give Megan a hug.

***

Four days later

Roy didn't have any family to give his possessions to, so his ex-girlfriend asked Megan and Jesse to come to the home and help decide what items would be given away to charity. The atmosphere was chilly and not because it was in November. Jesse was trying to keep his emotions in check because he blamed the ex-girlfriend for contributing to Roy's fatal decision to take his own life.

Both Megan and Jesse felt uneasy looking through their friend's possessions, but it had to be done or else all of it would be given away or thrown out. The last few days seemed unreal and seeing his clothes especially brought back memories.

"This is for you," Roy's ex-girlfriend replied without emotion. "Roy bought this for you a month ago for Christmas."

It was an unwrapped *Doctor Who* monopoly set. As a big fan of the *Doctor Who* television series, she immediately recognized the box cover and saw many of the characters from the show and of course, the *Tardis*. Megan felt a rush of emotion and wiped a tear. Leave it to Roy to figure out the perfect gift. It would be treasured.

There would be days of sadness and frustration filled with unanswered questions. Why did Roy take his own life at that particular moment? What was he feeling and thinking in the hours and minutes before ending it? If only he had asked Megan for help, the outcome could have been different.

Those were questions that would never be answered. Why he didn't give anyone a chance to help was speculative and such speculation only fueled more frustration for Megan and Roy's other friends and coworkers.

At a department meeting, it was reminded that if any officer wanted to have a conversation with a licensed counselor, the sessions were free and confidential. It was also noted that in America, more officers die from suicide than from being killed in the line of duty. The situation ultimately left Megan with the simple longing for her friend and with no choice but to carry on.

Jesse Mitchell and Roy Williams rafting on the Arkansas River

"Grief, I've learned, is really just love.
It's all the love you want to give but cannot.
All that unspent love gathers up in the corners of your eyes,
the lump in your throat, and in that hollow part of your chest.
Grief is just love with no place to go."
—Jamie Anderson

Five Fun Facts About Megan DiGirolamo

1. Has a *Doctor Who* tattoo.

2. Raised $1,100 for diabetes Tour de Cure and rode a bicycle 31 miles at age 11.

3. Won family "Chopped" cooking competition at age 22 and 24.

4. Won "best pizza" at an Italian Culinary school at age 19.

5. Started a business to sell baked goods door-to-door in middle school.

VI.

It's Not Mayberry

November 15, 2020

He didn't sleep at all last night. His mind was racing and although his body was tired, thoughts constantly popped into his head, and would not allow for restful slumber. Today was going to be the day. After this day, his life would never be the same. It would be the start of a new beginning. It had been a long time coming and he was going to ask a question that he'd never asked anyone before.

Perhaps he would have slept better if he didn't have such an elaborate plan. There were a lot of moving pieces which meant there were a lot of different things that could go wrong. All these variables kept him tossing and turning.

Could his friends really keep a secret? Could they pull off an Emmy-Award-winning acting performance and not accidentally give away the plan?

His roommate Damon was assigned to manage the seven family members and friends who would be hiding and waiting to witness the big moment. That was the easy part.

The hard part was convincing her that the circumstances were real and selling that would be dependent on the Chaffee County Sheriff's Department.

<u>On a separate radio frequency:</u>

Sergeant Cortese: I'm about to pick up the package.

<u>Actual open band police radio chatter:</u>

Sergeant Cortese: I've got Buena Vista #7 on board and we are in route to your location.

Sergeant Mullenax: She's really upset. I can't get much from her. She won't give me a name and she's kinda walking around right now.   No threats, but really agitated and will not speak to any male officer.

Sergeant Cortese: Copy that. Will you let her know that a female officer is ready to talk to her.

Sergeant Mullenax: I'll let her know that she's coming.

Sergeant Cortese: We're eight minutes out.

<u>On a separate radio frequency, nine minutes later:</u>

Sergeant Cortese: The package has arrived.

That means she's here. She thinks there's a distraught woman behaving so strangely that the police were called. The female officer is going to have to use her crisis intervention training to help deescalate the situation. Little does she know the situation is going to be escalated, but for all the right reasons.

He can still remember when he first saw her three years ago and the second thing he noticed, after her good looks, was that she was just too damn happy. How could somebody be that bubbly and happy all the time?

For a while he couldn't stand her chipper attitude, but later realized the reason he reacted that way was because he was not in a good place in his own life. He had recently broken up with his longtime girlfriend and the thought of dating *Miss Happy* was the furthest thing from his mind. But, over time he transitioned to a better state of mind, and eventually *Miss Always-in-a-Good-Mood* started to look like a good thing. Maybe some of that happiness would rub off on him.

The relationship began as a friendship and the two of them enjoyed hanging out with Roy Williams and his girlfriend, having dinner and playing board games. It didn't take long before the friendship turned into stronger feelings. He got to know her better and was pleasantly surprised that their values, long term goals and outlook on life were similar.

Then one night he decided to lay his cards on the table. He told her that he wanted more than friendship. It was a risk, but he was compelled to take it. He was pleased that she felt the same way. Nineteen months of dating led up to this moment, a moment that he'd planned for several months, a moment that he wanted to be perfect.

It was that upcoming moment which caused him to be tossing and turning without sleep the night before. It almost didn't happen when the ring he'd ordered was left on his front porch instead of the driver getting the required signature. That would have been a disaster, but luckily it was sitting there when he arrived home.

He was ready and wanted the moment to be special and memorable, to reflect his true feelings and to solidify their future together. All she had to do was give him the correct one-word answer.

He saw her walk from the parking lot to the edge of Wright's Lake in the small town of Nathrop. He'd chosen this spot since it was a picturesque small mountain lake with the Chalk Cliffs and Mount Princeton in the background. And because they'd been there many times to fish and picnic.

This was a place he went to relax and find peace and solace. This was a place he enjoyed sharing with her. It was their spot.

She was wearing her service gun on her hip, along with her badge, heading towards Sergeant Mullenax, who was standing at the end of the lake shore where the "distraught woman" was located. She was focused and ready to do her job and he suddenly appeared from behind some bushes just as she arrived.

"This is a bogus call," he said.

"Yeah, I know, what's going on?" she asked, thinking that this woman was being overly dramatic about her personal problems, and it was not likely a serious police matter.

A nice way to spend her day off. She was reviewing in her mind all that she had recently learned from her training. But when he made his move, she stopped thinking about the "woman in distress" and focused on his face.

That's when he dropped to one knee, and tried to say in a calm voice, "Will you marry me?"

She said "yes."

***

Meet Jesse Mitchell, age 31

Follower of Christ

Man

Son

Brother

Uncle

Soon to be a husband

American

High School Wrestler

Fisherman

Corporal, Police Department, Town of Buena Vista, CO

Member of Chaffee County SWAT team

5,332 days earlier

April 2006

"Why don't you just leave him alone?" Jesse asked in a stern tone. The final bell had just rung, and he was headed towards the exit when he noticed two guys picking on a smaller kid at the end of a dead-end hallway.

"What's it to you?" asked Beck, a junior at the school with whom Jesse had a few prior encounters and brawls.

"Yeah, buzz off Mitchell," chimed in Cameron and he turned back around and grabbed Jarrod's chest and gave him a painful purple nurple. Jarrod was being restrained by Beck and Cameron against the painted cinder-block wall and Cameron inflicted another painful twist of the freshman's skin.

"Ow," he wailed and started to cry from the agonizing pinch as well as the embarrassing method of torment.

"Shut up doofus," Cam stated to Jarrod and this time went in with both hands, ready to torture the underclassman some more.

"Why don't you pick on someone your own size?" Jesse stated more than he was asking a question, and yanked Cam's shoulder backwards, moving him several feet away from Jarrod. He was staring down Beck.

"Why don't you go play with your jock friends?" Beck sneered while still restraining Jarrod with one arm forced against his upper body.

"At least I'm not an idiot stoner like you two," Jesse countered.

"Why do you care what happens to him?" Beck asked as Jesse took a step closer, forcing him to make a decision of whether to defend himself or continue restraining Jarrod.

Beck quickly gazed beyond Jesse and saw Cam taking a few steps backwards with a facial expression communicating that that he was in no mood to fight. The same couldn't be said for Beck.

Beck chose to prioritize his own well-being and decided that restraining Jarrod would only slow him down. He let him go and within a second, Jarrod was starting to remove himself from the situation. That left Jesse and Beck in a standoff to determine who was going to back down first.

"You need to..." Jesse started to say but stopped in mid-sentence as Beck threw the first punch. But Jesse knew Beck's fighting style and was ready for him. Beck preferred brute force without much strategy, quickness or finesse and Jesse easily dodged his blow. Leave it to a bully like Beck to project his punch with the arrogance that it'd land easily, but instead his momentum moved him forward after whiffing the punch and that was all Jesse needed.

Beck was momentarily off balance and Jesse put both arms around Beck's upper body and easily made a wrestling move to throw him to the floor. But this floor was not a padded mat in the gym, but instead was hard tile and Beck landed with a solid thud.

Cam slinked off further into the background and had no intention of helping his friend. Jesse quickly got on top of Beck and put his forearm on his upper back and leaned in hard with all 170 pounds pressing against the other junior. Beck wasn't going anywhere.

Next, with ease and precision, Jesse put his right arm underneath Beck's neck and began to squeeze him. He wasn't looking to do permanent harm but rather to completely restrain and dominate Beck. Jesse wanted this fight to end quickly; he got his wish.

"OK," Beck was able to say in a raspy voice and slapped his hand on the ground indicating that he was done. And just as quickly as it had started, the fight was over. Both Jarrod and Cam were long gone, and Jesse slowly let Beck out of his grasp.

It would be an overstatement to say that Jesse and Jarrod were friends, but he knew Beck and Cam's habit of picking on younger kids in school. It wasn't the first time he'd seen it, but for some reason on this day it struck a nerve with him. Who else was going to stop it? Who else was going to protect Jarrod? Who else was going to help Jarrod when he needed it?

"Let it go Beck," Jesse said and allowed him to stand up. Beck was not known for "letting it go" but for now, he was willing to live to fight another day. It would not be the last time that he'd get into it with Beck, and it felt good to have the upper hand this time.

***

11 years later

Officer Jesse Mitchell recognized the address that dispatch provided. As he arrived, he saw Sergeant Jesse Cortese getting out of his patrol car. He was expecting a bad situation, for it wasn't the first time the police were called to this address. Over the past eleven years their paths had diverged significantly to where Jarrod was practically a stranger. But that didn't make this situation any easier or less disturbing.

Jesse and Jarrod hardly spoke after the high school incident in the hallway with Beck and Cameron. That day solidified Jesse's instinctual need to help and protect people, especially someone vulnerable. He had several more fights with Beck throughout high school, including ones protecting his little brother and sister. Maybe the instinct to help and protect came from being an older brother, but it wasn't the only source.

If you're helping and protecting people, then logic would dictate that you are doing good in this world. Taking that thought process further, by doing good for the community you are, by definition, making something of yourself. Although he didn't know it at the time, that instinct to help people and make something of himself would lead him to choose law enforcement as a career.

That seed was planted in his early childhood with the failings of his biological father. Before Jesse entered the second grade, his father was out of his life and involved with drugs. Soon his father was no longer capable of taking care of his family, forcing Jesse's mother, Debbie, to raise the children alone.

Jesse's father, Charles, stopped being "Dad" and became "Chuck." Chuck was not around to protect him, and Chuck was not there to help him. Chuck was a longtime resident of Buena Vista and was well liked and known throughout the small community, so when he chose the destructive path of methamphetamine use, it was not a secret.

In addition to using drugs, he was getting arrested for running a meth laboratory and driving under the influence. When Chuck's name was mentioned in the local newspaper, it always included police involvement. Being "Chuck's kid" ceased being a compliment.

Debbie was honest with her children and didn't sugarcoat Chuck's lifestyle. Even at a young age Jesse recognized Chuck's self-destructive behavior and he avoided his tornado-like path of bad choices.

Not only did his self-preservation instinct kick in, but it created a gut level promise that his name wouldn't be in the paper for the same reasons as Chuck's. He loathed the thought of the community thinking, "what did you expect from Chuck's kid?"

As a teenager this led Jesse to have a singularly focused goal: Don't end up like your father, you can do better than that. The thought of taking drugs became repulsive and that helped him stay away from guys like Beck and Cameron and out of trouble.

In early adulthood, the life goal of being better than his father was obviously achieved. He realized that was a low measurement bar and he started to focus on more meaningful and challenging goals. He knew several of the local police officers and was bored working as a cable installer, so he made the decision to enter the police academy. This was the final proof to himself, the town of Buena Vista and the world that he was no longer Chuck's kid.

Unfortunately, Jarrod didn't choose a positive life path after high school and quickly became an alcoholic. Jarrod was known to the local police after he earned the reputation of a violent drunk. He never lasted a long time at various jobs and still lived with his mother in the house he grew up in.

The police were called when Jarrod's mother and sister could not revive him. Officer Jesse Mitchell and Sergeant Jesse Cortese were quickly escorted into the garage once they entered the house.

Jarrod was sprawled out on several blankets on the garage floor and appeared to be passed out, or worse. After checking for a pulse and not finding any, the officers decided to perform CPR.

Even though Officer Mitchell was young at 26 years old and had a strong frame at 6 feet tall and 225 pounds, performing CPR could be tiring. So, both he and Sergeant Cortese would switch off every few minutes while Jarrod's mother and sister waited inside the house.

Unfortunately, there wasn't a chance of reviving Jarrod because he'd consumed both a toxic level of alcohol and barbiturates.

Officer Mitchell wondered what had happened to Jarrod over the years. He seemed to come from a nice and stable middle-class family, had several friends, as well as an attractive and personable longtime girlfriend. From the outside it appeared that Jarrod should be enjoying his life instead of someone with so many problems that needed to be drowned with alcohol and drugs.

But the outside cursory view obviously didn't tell the full story. Somehow Jarrod must have perceived himself as someone with unsolvable problems which weighed on his state of mind over the past several years.

And once he started dulling his senses with alcohol and drug use, it became a situation that he was unable to turn around. Officer Mitchell would never know how deliberate Jarrod's decision was to take the lethal combination of drugs and alcohol that eventually led to him dying in his mother's garage.

Officer Mitchell had conflicting emotions, and from his initial perspective, he was frustrated with Jarrod's mother and sister for not checking on him, but he also understood that this was not the first time that Jarrod was severely intoxicated; he'd usually sleep it off in the garage. It was sad and seemed like a waste of life. He opened the door to the house and stepped inside.

Jarrod's mother and sister were in the kitchen and quickly looked over to Officer Mitchell and interpreted the look on his face; he wasn't going to deliver good news.

"He's gone," Officer Mitchell told the family and both the mother and sister started crying. Although Jarrod wasn't the officer's friend, it was always more difficult to witness the death of someone you knew. When you've grown up and become a police officer in a small town like Buena Vista, chances were high that you'd previously crossed paths with someone present at a local crime scene.

Sergeant Cortese had already called the coroner who was in route. But Officer Mitchell's work was not done, and he remembered what his supervisor Sergeant Dean Morgan had told him about situations such as this. Jarrod was no longer able to talk for himself so officer Mitchell would have to create a detailed report of the facts and circumstances.

Small details needed to be captured, such as how many blankets were in the garage? Were there any physical marks on Jarrod that could indicate a struggle? What was the temperature in the garage? Were the lights on? What was the position of the body when they arrived?

Jarrod had a lifestyle of abusing alcohol and drugs, and they didn't have the toxicology report at that time, but there was no proof that Jarrod didn't die from foul play. Although that wasn't the likely scenario, the details needed to be captured in case the investigation went in a different direction. By being factually accurate, not only was the officer correctly doing his job, but he was also doing right by the victim. Officer Jesse Mitchell became the voice of the dead.

***

June 2016

"This place is a dump," Gloria stated.

"It's not that bad and what's it to you anyway?" Stacey responded with sarcasm. She never could take much of Gloria and her nagging attitude. According to Stacey, the most appealing thing about Gloria was that she lived several states away.

"What's it to me? My son lived here. Why he ever decided to live with you I'll never understand," Gloria retorted. Gloria couldn't imagine what attracted her son to this woman. She wasn't pretty on a good day, and even less so when she hadn't showered or applied makeup. She looked older than her thirty years of age and sported the stereotypical overweight unkept look of a trailer trash woman.

"He left Dayton to get away from you. And why wouldn't he, considering the way you treat him. We were very happy together, except for the times you came around," Stacey clapped back.

"The way I treat him? You're the one with piles of cat litter everywhere, a ton of dishes in the sink, trash on the floor and God knows what other gross stuff you've got in in this apartment," Gloria exclaimed and was pointing to various messes in the apartment. "I'm surprised you don't have any mice. Or maybe you do?"

"I haven't cleaned up today, so what?"

"Cleaned up *today*? It looks more like you haven't cleaned up all year," Gloria complained and continued, "You don't have a job, so what do you do all day? It certainly isn't housekeeping!"

"Well, I don't need you coming in here and ragging on me," Stacey complained. "Especially today. This is not your apartment so why don't you just get out."

"You know why I'm here. I'll get out as soon as I get my son's belongings."

"You'll get them when I'm good and ready," she stated defiantly.

"They don't belong to you. You'll give them to me right now," Gloria demanded with her voice rising.

"I'll put them in a box and ship it to you," Stacey countered.

"Do you think I trust you to do that?"

"You don't have a choice, this is my home and not yours," Stacey retorted with her voice escalating too.

"You call this a home? It looks more like the town dump. My son has been hurt and on workers comp for six months, so the least you could have done was to clean apartment once in a while and not sit on your butt playing video games all day long," Gloria seethed.

"What we do is our business not yours. I'm his wife, so all this stuff belongs to me anyway. That means *I decide* if you get any of it," Stacey replied with an arrogant tone.

"Wife? You mean more like shack up girlfriend. You two never got married, so you have no claim whatsoever."

"I'm a common law wife if you must know. I'm sick and tired of you insulting me," Stacey shot back and continued, "Why don't you just leave."

"I'm not going anywhere. I have every right to be here," Gloria countered.

"We'll see about that. Maybe I'll call the police."

"I'll do you one better, I'm going to call them right now," Gloria snapped and dialed 9-1-1. She explained to the operator about Stacey's refusal to hand over her son's belongings and was told that the police would be there in a few minutes.

"When the police get here, I'm going to have them throw you out!" Stacey shouted.

"Good luck with that. You are a cruel and dark person," Gloria hissed with hatred. "You have some nerve refusing to hand over my son's remaining possessions. It's your fault that he's dead."

***

Officer Jesse Mitchell already knew where Troy and Stacey's apartment was located. A few days ago, Stacey found a suicide note and reported that Troy, along with his handgun and ammunition were missing. The note specified the location where Troy was planning to shoot himself.

After interviewing Stacey, he and Officer Abrams went into the mountainous foothills just outside of Buena Vista to look for Troy. It was past midnight when they arrived at a popular trailhead, wondering how far up the trail Troy may have gone.

It was a potentially dangerous and volatile situation with an unstable person threatening to take his own life. Troy had a loaded firearm in the cover of darkness, so anything could happen.

The officers were hoping to reach Troy and have a chance to talk him down, but they had no idea what kind of reaction they would receive. Would he listen to them? Would he get angry and take a shot at the officers? Was he going to create an altercation that would force an officer to shoot back, hoping to end his life by the police instead of his own hands?

It was a dark night, so not only would the trail be challenging to follow, but if Troy were a mere 20 yards off the trail, he would be impossible to see. After looking for over an hour, they were unable to find Troy. Unfortunately, the next morning, county deputies searched the area and found that Troy had taken his own life.

Officer Mitchell and Officer Abrams headed to Stacey's apartment to diffuse the squabble between Troy's mother, Gloria, and his common law wife, Stacey. Officer Mitchell was hoping that the argument hadn't turned violent.

Most of the time it's inappropriate for someone to yell at a police officer, but in this situation Officer Mitchell was anticipating that both women would view him as the enemy. He expected both to take their anger out on him. *He was OK with that.*

Both women were hurting and upset after Troy's death, and their emotions would be raw and ragged. Add the squabble over what little remained of Troy's possessions and it could be a recipe for disaster. He was preparing himself to walk into a very volatile situation with two angry women.

If they wanted to yell at him, and that might make them feel better, Officer Mitchell was prepared to take it. Maybe that was what would keep the peace between the two women. He knew it wasn't personal, and he'd let them vent if it didn't become an officer safety issue.

The two officers knocked on the apartment door and Stacey answered it. "This woman is unlawfully trespassing in my apartment. I demand that you make her leave," she immediately told them.

"Well, *this woman* is unlawfully retaining my son's possessions and I'm not leaving until I get them. I'm the one who called the police," Gloria interjected.

"Hold on a minute ladies. Let's see if we can sort this out," Officer Mitchell replied and took a small step forward to separate the women. "I know this is a difficult time for both of you. I'm sorry for your loss," he continued while Officer Abrams was silent.

"I just want you to throw her out!" exclaimed Stacey, still highly agitated. Turning to Gloria she said, "You're lucky I even called you."

"Lucky? You think I'm lucky to get a call that my son has taken his life? You think my son was *lucky to have you?* You're the one who drove him to do it!" She was exasperated and started to cry and breath unevenly.

"It's not my fault," Stacey said defensively. "Why do you think Troy moved far away from home?"

"Look officer, she called me a few days ago. At first, I thought it was a sick joke. And my head has been reeling ever since," Gloria stated, and more tears streamed down her face. "I don't even know what happened to Troy!" she exclaimed, and the officers could see that her eyes were already turning red and puffy. She looked for her purse and fumbled for a tissue.

"We were called here a few days ago when Troy went missing, and he left a suicide note. Officer Mitchell and I went to go find him," interjected Officer Abrams with an impatient tone.

"What did the note say?" Gloria asked.

"Not much, it just said that he couldn't take it anymore and he was heading into the forest that evening."

"So, you two went to look for him that night?"

"Yes, we hiked up the trail. We did everything we could for a couple of hours to look for his dumb ass," Officer Abrams stated without emotion. His comment seemed to just hang in the air for a few seconds.

"Hey, I've got this," Officer Mitchell stated with authority and glanced over at Officer Abrams with a face that sent the clear message; *your comment was not appropriate.* Even though he was the junior officer in terms of years on the job, he was going to take over the situation. "Why don't you go outside and check in with dispatch."

Officer Abrams looked at both ladies and then replied, "Sure." He silently left the apartment. Although Officer Abrams was skilled on legal situations and was considered a good cop for many years, his people skills sometimes were lacking.

"I'm sorry, that was not OK to say to you," Officer Mitchell stated directly to Gloria, but her face was unresponsive as she was still trying to process the comment and situation.

"What happened when you went to look for him?" she said in a croaked voice.

"The note described a specific trailhead about 15 minutes from here and where he was planning to, well you know, so we went to look for him and talk him out of it. But it was already past midnight so it was very dark, and we went up the trail a mile or two but couldn't find him," Officer Mitchell said in a calm and reassuring tone.

"I didn't know he went all the way out there."

"The trail was well outside of town limits, so in the morning several county deputies went out to the same spot and they found him on a ledge a few yards from the trail. I'm sorry," he stated with empathy.

"Yeah OK, thanks for telling me. I appreciate you trying to help Troy. I flew in from Dayton as soon as I heard. I just wanted to get some of his things," Gloria stated and had stopped crying.

"I understand," Officer Mitchell replied and slightly nodded his head in agreement. The tension in the air was starting to dissipate.

"My son didn't have much, and there can't be more than a box or two of his things. There are some pictures and clothes that I'd like to keep. I especially want his T-shirts, there are a few from when we went on vacation with him before he moved to Buena Vista. They don't have any monetary value, but they have a lot of sentimental value to me."

"Do you think that's something that could be worked out?" Officer Mitchell directed the question to Stacey.

"Well maybe, but she can't be rummaging around my apartment."

"How about this, why don't you find a hotel for the night and try to calm down. And you, Stacey, round up all of Troy's things, especially the clothes and pictures that his mother really wants. Do you think you could do that?"

"I think so," she replied.

"Does that sound reasonable to you?" he asked to Gloria.

"Yes. We're having his service tomorrow in the early afternoon so maybe I can pick up his things in the morning?"

"That will be fine," Stacey answered, and the situation was completely diffused.

***

A formal complaint was later filed against Officer Abrams and an internal affairs investigation was initiated. This was not the first complaint against Officer Abrams. The incident was easy to verify because it was all captured on body camera video. Soon after, Officer Abrams decided to leave the Buena Vista Police Department to "pursue other interests."

***

August 2018

Mackenzie didn't mind, in fact, she didn't mind *anything* at that moment. In the smoke-filled car she was breathing secondhand marijuana smoke as well as the direct hits she was inhaling from the bong. The marijuana produced a relaxed and easy feeling, the ultimate "chill" disposition.

Her boyfriend Brett was eager to provide the weed that created the 'I don't care about anything attitude', for he knew that the more relaxed she was, the more likely she wouldn't resist any of his advances. Not that she had resisted in the past, but it simply made things easier if she went along. Besides, Brett was chilled out as well while they parked in the darkness on a dirt road near the Arkansas River, just outside of the Buena Vista town limits.

It was past midnight and Mackenzie and Brett were expecting their friends Taylor and Ethan to show up any minute. In the meantime, he offered Kenzie another toke and offered her a shoulder massage, hoping to expand it to a few more body parts. But before he could get too far, they saw a car's headlights coming down the quiet road. They hoped it wasn't the police and this time they got lucky.

Out of the truck jumped Taylor and Ethan. Mackenzie got out of their car to greet her best friend.

"Hey girl!" sixteen-year-old Mackenzie squealed in delight, almost jumping up and down and gave her best friend a big hug. "You got anything to eat? I'm starving."

"Don't worry Kenzie, I got you covered," replied seventeen-year-old Taylor as she opened up the grocery sack to reveal a large bag of *Spicy Sweet Chili Doritos.* Both girls were going to be juniors when school started in a week. The fun days of summer were coming to an end and all four of the teenagers wanted to party hard before school started, not that being in school was going to slow them down.

As Mackenzie was opening the large *Doritos* bag, Ethan was already out of his truck, lighting up his bong. He inhaled deeply and held his breath for a second, then exhaled with a mischievous grin, brazenly allowing the marijuana smell to permeate the air.

"What's up dude?" seventeen-year-old Ethan asked.

"Not much, just chilling out," replied sixteen-year-old Brett.

"Damn, your girl sure likes those chips," Ethan commented as Mackenzie rapidly ate one *Dorito* after another.

"Yeah, she's got the munchies and those are her favorite," Brett answered and continued, "Did you bring the other stuff?"

"Oh yeah, I think these girls are going to like this piece of glass," Ethan answered.

"We're going to like what?" Mackenzie asked.

"You'll see," Brett answered, "Let's go in the truck," he stated and everybody went in without giving it another thought.

Ethan took out a small meth pipe and turned around to show the girls in the backseat, "Weed will get you chilled, but this stuff will blow your mind," he stated with confidence.

"How long have you been smoking meth?" Mackenzie asked.

"Just a couple of times, and Brett said you girls might want to try it," Ethan answered.

"It'll be my first time too," Taylor chimed in.

"I don't know," Kenzie answered, suddenly having a hard time concentrating and making a decision.

"Suit yourself, losers," Ethan stated and lit up a small piece of glass in the pipe. "Whoa," he replied and let out a cough. He handed the pipe to Brett.

"Oh man!" Brett said after his first inhale. "What's the big deal Kenzie, I think your mom's on this stuff anyway."

"Yeah maybe, I don't know, but..." she said and trailed off without finishing.

"Give me some of that," Taylor said and held out her hand to Brett. He handed her the pipe and she lit it up. Taylor continued, "All that weed makes me pig out, but with this stuff you don't need to eat for days."

"Geez, you finished half of that *Doritos* bag already," Brett stated with disdain in Mackenzie's direction.

"Are you saying I'm fat?" Mackenzie asked.

"No of course not baby, I'm just giving you crap," Brett answered with a grin and laughed, making his answer less convincing.

Mackenzie didn't believe him. While she wasn't fat, no one would accuse Mackenzie of being skinny. A typical teenage girl's self-esteem was usually on shaky ground, and a comment from her boyfriend, whether joking or not, was going deflate her confidence and stick with her for a long time.

"You in?" Taylor asked extending her hand with the pipe still smoldering.

Mackenzie looked around and her face grew annoyed, but then she broke out in a small smile and said, "Oh, what the hell?"

***

Two Years Later

> "I've been to the edge
> And then I stood and looked down
> You know I lost a lot of friends there, baby
> I've got no time to mess around"
> **--Van Halen,** *Ain't Talkin' 'Bout Love*

"Come on Harlow, the paperwork can wait," Corporal Jesse Mitchell said. Harlow was currently employed at the county jail and was going to the police academy in a few months; this evening he was riding along with the corporal. It was just after 6:30p.m., the beginning of the corporal's shift.

It only took two minutes from the BVPD to U.S. Highway 24 and the patrol car headed north. The town limit was only another mile away, but Corporal Mitchell had a route that he liked which covered all parts of the town, starting with the north side. A few minutes later, he turned left on Harrison Avenue where the Love's gas station and mini mart were located.

He typically drove around to check the back of the gas station because often there was suspicious activity, although not usually this early in the evening. He didn't see anything except for an old Nissan Sentra parked in the corner under several trees. Harlow wrote down the license plate number, but because the angle of the sun and the car being in the shade, it was hard to tell if anyone was in there. They exited the parking lot and continued driving.

Corporal Mitchell called dispatch to run the plates and a minute later they came back with an answer.

"QVR-182. A 1989 Nissan Sentra belonging to Mackenzie Stratton. Registration is current and no outstanding warrants or violations."

281

"I know that girl," Corporal Mitchell stated and looked for a place to make a U turn. His stomach tightened with anticipated dread.

"Oh really?" Harlow asked.

"She's been arrested for meth possession since she's been 16. Her mother too."

"Let's see what's going on," Harlow stated, and as they got close to the car, he could see someone in there.

"Oh geez, I think that's her," the corporal stated. He quickly got out of the car, turned on his flashlight and peered into the car. Mackenzie Stratton was the only person in the car, and she appeared to have passed out.

Luckily, the driver's side door was open, and Corporal Mitchell opened the door and confirmed what he saw through the window. There was still leftover heroin in a needle along with a spoon and a white powder.

"Get EMS out here, we have a possible overdose," he radioed to dispatch. "Don't come any closer, I don't know if that stuff is fentanyl," he stated to Harlow.

Fentanyl is a potent synthetic opioid that is often prescribed to relieve severe chronic pain. Fentanyl is odorless, and because it is often mixed with other substances, it doesn't have a distinctive or unique appearance. Improper handling or inadvertent exposure to fentanyl can be highly toxic and has put police officers in the hospital.

Corporal Mitchell checked for a pulse and found a heartbeat and slow breathing. A heroin overdose can shut down the respiratory system, so extremely weak breathing can precede dying from a drug overdose. Police officers usually carry and are trained to administer a shot of Narcan (Naloxone), a quick acting drug which can reverse the effects of an opioid overdose. At the moment, Makenzie's breathing was stable enough that the corporal held off giving her the Narcan.

Within a few minutes EMS arrived, and Corporal Mitchell had carefully moved the drugs and needle out of the way so they could retrieve Mackenzie and put her in an ambulance. After she was in route to the hospital, the corporal investigated the remaining contents of the vehicle.

Corporal Mitchell found additional drugs, but it was under the four-gram legal limit, which means that if McKenzie survived, she would not be immediately taken to jail. She possessed about half that amount which would justify giving her a citation for drug possession.

The corporal surmised that she probably had more than four grams initially but was below the legal limit only because the rest of it was in her system. He didn't find much else in the car but then noticed a small notebook stuck in between the window and the dashboard. He opened it and read the handwritten page.

I hope you're happy. I hope you got what you wanted. You beat me down so much that I just can't take it anymore. You're no better than I am, Mom. And stupid Brett, how dare he called me a tweaker when he's the one that got me into it. He's just as bad as I am, so who the hell is he to call me a druggie and look down on me? He's such a piece of crap.

I lost all that weight, but he still didn't want me. How could he do that to me? The only time I feel pretty is when I'm using, so I'd lose weight and be skinny to be more attractive for him. And then he dumps me?

I'm so sick of all the crap you put me through Mom. You're too busy with your own stuff, and don't care about me. I have no place in your life and you've abandoned me. What kind of mother is that? Where is the motherly love? What I'm doing today, let's be honest, is all your fault!

I've almost taken enough to end it all. I'm going to keep going until it's over. So, I hope you'll be happy to be rid of your problem child. I can't stand it anymore. Well, you're not going to have me to kick around anymore. You can find some other loser to rag on day and night.

> *--Kenzie*

***

Two days later

"Is Mackenzie home?" asked Corporal Mitchell.

"No, she left this morning and didn't say when she'll be back," answered Britney Stratton, Mackenzie's mother.

"So, I guess she's OK?"

"Yes, they let her out of the hospital the next day. She's never done something like that. I don't know how this could have happened. Do you know who found her and called it in?

"Actually, it was me, I found her while I was on patrol and the way her car was parked looked peculiar, so when I went to investigate; I found her in the car."

"You rescued her!" Brittany exclaimed and started to cry with the weight of what might have happened to her only daughter. "You saved my baby."

"Well, I'm glad that she's alright and..." Corporal Mitchell said but before he could get any more words out Brittney cut him off.

"Can I give you a hug?" she asked but didn't wait for an answer and embraced the officer and continued to bawl. It was a bit awkward for the officer to have such an emotional moment with someone that he'd previously arrested, as well as her daughter.

"She needs to get some help, so I've spoken to the District Attorney to assign her court date in a week so she can get into a rehab program right away. Normally for this kind of infraction, a court date could be in six to eight weeks, but I think she needs help right away. Do you think she'll want to do that?"

"Maybe? I hope so. I know she was pretty scared about how close she came to overdosing."

"Can you call me when she gets back? I need to give her this summons."

"I can give it to her," Brittany offered.

"Now that she's eighteen I have to give it to her directly," the corporal stated and handed her his business card.

***

Six days later

"Where's my car?" Mackenzie asked while peering out the trailer window and seeing nothing in the small gravel driveway.

"Beats me, Taylor drove it somewhere last night," Hank responded.

"Last night?" she asked, trying to remind herself what had happened last night and how she ended up in this trailer. And who the heck is Hank anyway?

"Yeah, she took it just after you passed out," he replied.

"Well, that's just great," Mackenzie said and folded her arms in annoyance. She was getting a little tired of Taylor's antics. They just spent a weeklong bender of drugs and alcohol in Colorado Springs and she had to pay for almost all of it.

Taylor was being selfish and didn't seem to care one iota that Mackenzie was in the hospital just a few days earlier. What kind of a friend was that? Mackenzie made a promise to herself to find a better set of friends, but first she needed to find her car. It was tiring to be Taylor's friend. She sent Taylor a text and a few minutes later she responded.

Taylor:	I need a new pair of shoes and an iPad.
Mackenzie:	So?
Taylor:	You want your car back, don't you?
Mackenzie:	WTF?
Taylor:	Well, don't you?
Mackenzie:	Bring back my car right now!
Taylor:	Are you going shopping for me?
Mackenzie:	Are you out of your mind?
Taylor:	I won't get much for this POS, but it should be enough.
Mackenzie:	Don't you dare.
Taylor:	Anyone dumb enough to leave their title in the car doesn't deserve to keep it.
Mackenzie:	But it's my car!
Mackenzie:	RU there?
Mackenzie:	Hello???
Mackenzie:	I'm going to call the police.

After waiting a couple of hours without any response from Taylor, Mackenzie was forced to walk three miles back to her mother's house. The next day Corporal Mitchell showed up.

"Are you doing OK?" he asked.

"Yeah, I guess so," Mackenzie answered.

"You didn't have drugs above the legal limit to be arrested when I found you, but you had enough to get a citation, so you've got a court date in a few days."

"You're the one that found me?"

"Yes, and I've talked to the District Attorney about getting you into a rehab program."

"You're my Guardian Angel," she said and immediately gave Corporal Mitchell a hug. After two long seconds he was ready to end the embrace, but she was still holding on tight, and it started to get to an awkward point. She finally let go and said, "Thank you so much."

"I was glad to be there, you're welcome."

"Do you know how long this rehab program will be?"

"It depends on what the court assigns, but it will probably be several months," he said.

"Thanks, I really need to kick this stuff, you know?"

"Yes, that would be good. Oh, and by the way, we found your car. It looks like your friend Taylor forged your signature on the title and sold it to somebody for $500."

"That bitch!" she exclaimed, paused and then said, "That's good news I suppose; when can I pick it up?"

"You should be able to get it out of impound in a couple of days," the corporal answered.

As Corporal Mitchell was driving away from Mackenzie's house, he wondered what was in store for this young woman's future. What direction would she go? Would she really stick to the rehab program?

With her mom and friends being drug users, he wasn't going to place any bets. But he'd been surprised before by people he had arrested, so maybe she'd be one of the success stories. At least Mackenzie had a chance, but her story still had several chapters to be written.

***

100 days later

"Wait, who is he dating?" Corporal Jesse Mitchell asked?

"We just picked up Roberto Salazar last night on an illegal weapons charge," said Officer Holly Boxura of the Salida Police Department. "She was there when we arrested him. Didn't you find her overdosed at the gas station a few months ago?"

The two officers were talking after clearing up an accident on U.S. Highway 24 near the Buena vista town limits.

"That girl was Mackenzie Stratton," he answered.

"Yeah, that's her. She was strung out pretty bad. He was too. We were called out because he was brandishing a stolen gun at one of the local bars," she stated.

"I haven't seen much of her lately," Corporal Mitchell replied.

"Yeah, that's probably because she is living with him in Salida."

"That guy is bad news," he stated, knowing that forty-one-year-old Roberto had a lengthy history of distributing methamphetamines and heroin.

"No doubt about that," Officer Boxura stated flatly.

"That's disappointing," the corporal exclaimed and the small flame of hope he had for Mackenzie was quickly extinguished.

"St. Michael the Archangel,
defend us in battle.
Be our protection against the wickedness
and snares of the Devil.
May God rebuke him, we humbly pray,
and do thou,
O Prince of the heavenly hosts,
by the power of God,
thrust into hell Satan,
and all the evil spirits,
who prowl about the world
seeking the ruin of souls.
Amen"
—Prayer to St. Michael

***

January 1, 2019

1:08a.m.

So maybe it wasn't sophisticated to guzzle wine, but that thought didn't prevent Baird from quickly finding the bottom of his glass. It'd been a difficult week, and he needed a release.

Fifty-one-year-old Baird Wallsdum was a construction supervisor in Grand Junction, CO and he was forced to have the painful conversation with the company's owner that his project wasn't going to be finished on time, nor was it going to be on budget. The worst of both worlds.

Two days ago, he broke the news about the delay which would not only incur additional labor, but due to some miscues with one of the subcontractors, over $10,000 worth of materials had to be scrapped. And of course, the owner was furious at Baird for letting this happen.

The owner was not an easy person to get along with, let alone take bad news in a calm and measured manner, and Baird delayed telling him by several days. Baird's only accomplishment was postponing the inevitable fury.

The late communication did not soften the wrath and verbal beating that Baird took from the owner. When the conversation ended, he wasn't sure if he'd have a job to come back to in the new year.

He was happy when the stressful work week ended, and he surprised himself by actually looking forward to attending the wedding. His wife's niece was getting married and decided to have a destination wedding in the small town of Buena Vista.

He had only met her niece a few times previously but had never met the groom. He didn't have an emotional connection with the "happy couple," but he rapidly developed an emotional connection with the bartender at the wedding reception.

An open bar was a beautiful thing. With his job future in doubt, he wasn't thrilled to be spending money on a trip out of town, so he was going to make damn sure that he drank enough alcohol to make this trip well worth it.

His wife, fifty-year-old Sheila, was also his frequent drinking partner and was eager for the challenge to get their money's worth at the open bar. Attending a wedding can remind a couple of the beauty and virtue of a good marriage. Or it can remind them of what they are missing. Their six-year marriage, both on their second spouse, was inconsistent from the start.

Shelia and Baird fought about little things, petty things, things that they let fester and get under their skin. He was better at letting go after an argument, whereas she typically held the grudge longer. She tended to keep pecking at him even when he admitted he was wrong. That wasn't good enough for her and she'd keep complaining even after he asked for forgiveness.

Their arguments started the same way. She would find a flaw in his behavior or his forgetfulness, like not picking up an item from the grocery store on the way home from work. She would harp on it and not accept that he made a simple mistake.

The tension would escalate until one of them got mad and blew up. Maybe it was because she was a bank manager and was used to dealing with specific regulations and rules, where everything had to be precise. Maybe it was unreasonable to expect that level of precision in her personal life too.

They frequently enjoyed a few bottles of wine at home, so it was no surprise that they were fast becoming friends with the bartender. Some people become goofy or funny when they drink, others melancholy, while some turn into a mean drunk. Unfortunately, Baird and Sheila both could get nasty and dramatic when they drank too much.

But so far, they'd kept their emotions in check and were delighted when they convinced the bartender to give him an already opened, almost full bottle of red wine.

He showed Sheila the bottle proudly and they were one of the last ones to leave the reception hall just after midnight. They headed back to their room for their own little private party.

After a drunken romp with her husband, Sheila decided to take a relaxing bath while Baird sat on the small couch flipping through the television channels. But as soon as she received the text message, her state of relaxation was over.

"Baird, what's wrong with you?" she asked with noticeable sarcasm.

"What?" he asked, stumbling into the bathroom.

"I said, *what the hell is wrong with you?*" she repeated in a nasty tone yet continuing to exclude any details.

"I don't know what you're talking about," he stated, with his voice starting to rise.

"My son has been waiting for a text from you for over an hour."

"About what?"

"You said you were going to text him to wish him a happy new year, remember?" she scowled.

"Oh, yeah. Whatever," he fired back, suddenly reminded of his work-related angst over the future of his job, so the last thing he wanted was her implying that he wasn't living up to her expectations.

"You two haven't gotten along ever since we first met, let alone got married, and you specifically promised me you'd start a real relationship with him in the new year. You said you'd text him about your new year's resolution," Shelia exclaimed.

"Yeah well, I guess I can send him a message in the morning."

"You were supposed to start off the year on the right foot, and here you go failing in the first hour of the new year. You didn't even try!" she exclaimed and started crying. *"What's wrong with you?"* she yelled, quickly going from sad to mad.

"I'm sorry," he growled back, "I'll text him later, what's the big deal?" he said and threw his hands up in disgust.

"Not a big deal?" she hissed, "You had one thing to do, to get along with my son, and you screwed it up. You had a chance to actually be a stepdad, and you just blew it off."

This isn't how Baird planned to end the evening. "I said I'm sorry, how many times do I have to say that?" Baird yelled back at her, "Can't you just give me a break? Just once? Can't you be on my side for once in your life?"

"I would if you weren't such a loser," she spouted with venom.

That was the last straw. When she uttered those hurtful words, he just reacted. He was tired of being her punching bag and he snapped. He took the wine bottle that was placed on a nearby dresser and hurled it at his wife with all his might.

The intention was clearly to express his anger. But using every ounce of strength also caused his aim to be off and it landed square at the foot of the bathtub.

Sheila screamed in fright as the glass shattered in all directions, cutting her dangling arm in the process. He turned around without even bothering to check on her and left the hotel room. He needed to get out of there fast.

***

"Everyone has a plan until they get punched in the mouth."
—Mike Tyson

***

It was just over a month since Officer Mitchell spent an entire day being evaluated for the SWAT team. SWAT had a few openings, and five other people were also applying. Officer Mitchell wasn't confident he'd make the cut. He'd been training and diligently preparing himself both physically and mentally, although he viewed it as a practice run for being accepted next year.

He changed his diet and exercised to lose 45 pounds to get down to 220 pounds. Getting in better shape would help him prepare physically for the grueling SWAT tryouts consisting of sit-ups, planking, pull-ups, pushups, vertical-jump and an obstacle course wearing full tactical gear. There was also a shooting qualification that allowed only a 4% error rate as well as oral boards, which consisted of the entire SWAT team peppering him with questions.

He also would be asked about the priority-of-life model which stipulated specific action to take in a threatening situation. The code required an officer to protect or attempt to save a life in an explicit priority, putting at the top the innocents (children, victims, hostages), civilians, bystanders, partners (other officers and other first responders), the suspect and evidence, in that order.

At the end of the session, he was pleased to be the SWAT team's first choice. He'd underestimated the extent that his hard work had paid off, which was a boost of confidence for the officer.

Officer Mitchell was first to arrive at the hotel, and he expected Officer Rusty Barnes to be a few minutes behind him. He exited and took the long and lonely walk from the relative safety of his patrol car towards a potentially unpredictable and volatile situation.

Statistically the most dangerous situation for a police officer are calls involving a domestic violence incident. Therefore, in small towns like Buena Vista, all available officers are called to the scene of domestic violence.

As a recent addition to the Chaffee County SWAT team, Officer Mitchell was tactically prepared as he walked down the hallway towards Sheila's hotel room. He heard a woman's scream coming from down the hallway and he ran in that direction.

He drew his gun and was ready for anything as he approached the room and found the door wide open. *And there she was, on the bed and covered in blood, completely naked.*

Officer Mitchell immediately scanned the room and then asked, "Where are you hurt?

"My arm is sliced open!" she wailed. "I think I'm going to bleed out; this tourniquet isn't working," she exclaimed and was referring to a phone charger cord wrapped around her upper bicep trying to stop the bleeding.

Officer Mitchell had to quickly determine the extent of her injury. Although there was blood on the bed and all over the victim, she didn't appear to have sliced a major artery so her life wouldn't be immediately threatened. But first, he needed to make sure the perpetrator wasn't still in the room.

"Hold on, I need to check this room," the officer stated and started with the balcony to see if anyone was there.

"My husband left a few minutes ago, he's gone," she replied in a slurred tone.

"OK, but I still need to verify that," Officer Mitchell responded.

Regardless of what the victim claimed, before Officer Mitchell would holster his weapon, he needed to know that the potential threat was no longer in the room or nearby. Tactically, inspecting a small space such as a hotel room would be quick and easier to secure compared to a rental house.

After finding no one on the balcony, he walked back into the room and quickly checked the bathroom. The walls had red splotches everywhere and there was broken glass covering the floor and inside of the bathtub. No one was in there and as he walked back into the main part of the hotel room, Officer Rusty Barnes arrived.

"We're all clear," Officer Mitchell stated.

Officer Barnes, a former medic in the army, quickly assessed the situation and started to apply pressure to the wound.

"Do you want me to you get a towel or a robe or something?" Officer Mitchell asked the woman who seemed to forget she was still totally naked.

"What about my arm? I don't want to die. Please save me," she moaned.

"Here's EMT now," the officer said, and the technician entered the hotel room and immediately opened her medical bag and applied a temporary bandage on her. With the medical technician working on her, Shelia's stress level came down a notch.

"Can you tell us what happened?" Officer Mitchell asked.

"My husband and I came back from the ballroom where we were attending my cousin's wedding. We brought a bottle of wine back to the room. Are we in trouble for this?"

"Please continue, I just need to know what happened tonight before I decide if anyone is in any trouble," he stated without any intention of answering her question.

"I went to go take a bath and we got in an argument, and he got mad. Then he became even angrier and threw the bottle of wine at me," she wailed and then looked at her arm starting to bleed through the bandage.

"I'm feeling lightheaded, can you please just stop my bleeding?" she asked to the technician and continued, "I'm going to die."

"We'll take care of you, don't worry," the EMT interjected. The dried blood on her arm made the injury look worse than it actually was, and the technician started to clean it.

Officer Mitchell then concluded that the red stains on the bathroom wall were mostly from the broken wine bottle, rather than her blood. It was hard to tell whether the bottle shattered and then cut her or whether she cut herself trying to get out of the bathtub.

"What's your husband's name?"

"Baird."

"You said he left. Did he take the car keys?"

"I think so, I called 9-1-1 right after he left," she replied and lifted her arm slightly so the EMT could continue to work on her arm.

"What kind of car do you have?"

"It's a...is he going to get in trouble?" she said with hesitation. "I don't want him to be arrested."

"First we need to find him so we can get his side of the story." It was clear that Sheila was intoxicated, and it was likely that her husband Baird was too, which meant that her version of what happened had to be thoroughly checked out and compared against the evidence, as well as any testimony that her husband might provide.

"Your car's make and model?" Officer Mitchell pushed the question.

"I don't want you to ruin his life, or our marriage for that matter," she said and seemed more lucid. Just then her cell phone rang and displayed *Husband* on the screen.

Officer Barnes picked up the phone and said, "Is this Baird?"

"Yeah, who is this? Where is my wife?"

"This is Officer Barnes with the Buena Vista Police Department. I'm here with Shelia and EMS is about to take her to the hospital.

"The hospital?"

"Her arm got cut from a broken wine bottle. She's got a gash that needs stiches," Officer Barnes answered. "Mr. Wallsdum, we need to talk to you about what happened earlier. Where are you now? We can come to you so we can talk."

"I don't think I want to talk to you," Baird replied somewhat slurring his words.

"Mr. Wallsdum, we need to get your side of the story, and find out about what happened in the hotel room."

"I don't wanna talk. This is a private matter between husband and wife," he replied.

"Where are you now?" the officer asked, but Baird had hung up.

"Just leave us alone, we can resolve it ourselves," Sheila said.

"Are you sure you don't want a towel ma'am?" the EMS technician asked again now that she was finished prepping Shelia's arm.

"Yeah OK," she finally relented, and the second technician went into the bathroom to look for a clean towel and Sheila awkwardly grabbed it from him.

"OK, we are ready to go," the EMT said breaking the uncomfortable moment, and wheeled Sheila into the hallway and down to the ambulance that would take her to the hospital in Salida.

"Well, Baird was uncooperative," Officer Barnes stated.

"He sure was, and he's not doing himself any favors by refusing to give us his side of the story. We need to figure out what make and model of car he has and put out a BOLO (be on the lookout)."

"They were both intoxicated so who knows what really happened."

"Yup, we'll see where the facts lead us," stated Officer Mitchell.

Officer Barnes called into dispatch while Officer Mitchell informed the Chaffee County Sheriff's Department, Colorado State Patrol and the Salida Police Department about the situation. Twenty-three minutes later, Officer Mitchell's cell phone rang. It was the Colorado State Patrol.

"Baird Wallsdum showed up at the hospital and we have him in custody. He never made it through the front door. He is definitely intoxicated."

"Thanks, that's good news," Officer Mitchell replied.

"He was mostly cooperative and claimed that he threw the wine bottle at the wall because of their argument and had no intention to hit his wife, let alone hurt her."

"A jury can decide whether that story holds up."

"We arrested him for driving under the influence as well as criminal mischief because of the damage to the hotel room."

"We're in the process of securing the room and will follow up to collect more evidence," Officer Mitchell stated.

The officers needed to secure the hotel room so that no hotel staff or anyone else would enter the room and possibly disturb the scene. Under the circumstances, it was still unclear whether Baird showed up at the hospital because of concern for his wife, or with intent to inflict more harm.

Officer Mitchell went back to the BVPD to write up a warrant request to search the hotel room for evidence that could help determine what had happened during that early morning dispute. He'd also have to wake up the district attorney on duty, and later a county judge.

Because the victim was no longer in the hotel room, which is considered the equivalent of the couple's residence, a warrant was required to continue searching for evidence that may corroborate the victim's story or lead the investigation in another direction.

There's always something happening on New Year's Eve. Why did these tourists have to bring their problems to Buena Vista?

It was more proof that no matter where you go, when people reach their breaking point and snap, someone can land up in the hospital, even in this idyllic town, which had its share of problems and criminal activity.

It's not Mayberry.

The officer slightly shook his head and made a mental note to never get married on New Year's Eve.

**

August 2019

"People need to be reminded
more often than they need to be instructed."
—**Samuel Johnson**, 18th century writer and poet

"How was your weekend?" asked Sergeant Jesse Cortese.

"It was good, I went fishing at Wrights Lake. I really needed to escape, and forget about the world for a little bit," Officer Jesse Mitchell answered. The two men arrived early at the Clearview Church for the weekly men's bible group that was organized by Chaffee County Sergeant Jesse Cortese.

"Did you catch anything?"

"Just a couple of small ones, but I go there just to relax, and not really worry about how many or what size of fish I catch. But I kept thinking of Micah," Jesse replied.

"You know it's not your fault, right?" Cortese replied.

"Yes, but he did it on my property, and used my gun."

"That still doesn't make it your fault. Micah's decision to take his own life was just that, his decision."

"I hear what you're saying, but I can't shake feeling responsible," Jesse replied.

"That's normal."

"For a while, I was called "officer suicide" because I seem to always be on call when a death happens. Even my ex-girlfriend's sister died in Arizona, she was texting and walked into traffic. I don't know why those situations find me," Jesse stated and breathed out a long sigh.

"That means now is the time to ask for God's strength. Whether it's work stuff or personal, you can lean on him for anything," Cortese commented.

"That's why I like coming to this group, I know that he hasn't lost his attention for me, even though there were times that I stopped giving my attention to him," Jesse admitted.

"I hear you brother, you're not the only one struggling with things and this is a great support system. It helps knowing that other guys have similar battles."

"Sometimes the battle is with yourself. It's uncanny how many times someone else says exactly what I am thinking," Jesse replied.

"Especially lately. Just the other day, I felt like I made the wrong career decision. Especially, considering what's going on in our country politically, as well as in Colorado."

"Well, just like we talked about last week, we have to be reminded that this is all earthly stuff, and you have a future through Christ. This is just noise."

"But sometimes that noise is pretty loud!" Cortese replied and chuckled.

"I know what you mean," Jesse commented, also smiling.

"But you're right, we don't always learn something new in this group, but instead we're reminded of thoughts that were pushed to the back of our mind," Cortese said.

"It's not always easy to keep things in perspective, sometimes seeing things in this job can be bewildering, whether it's death or someone ruining their life with drugs, you know what I mean?" Jesse asked.

"I do. Sometimes I have to stop myself from getting hardened when I see all this stuff. Although in one sense you need to have thick skin and not let it get to you, otherwise you'll go crazy."

"And that's where it comes back to this men's group, trying to find our place in God's eyes and reigniting that relationship," Jesse replied.

"All of us are human, and we all are distracted by life and have to be reminded there's something greater beyond this earthly journey," Cortese commented.

"It's about finding your value in God and knowing in your heart that God loves you," Jesse told him.

"I couldn't agree more. Well, I guess we better get a seat," Cortese said as a few other guys walked in.

***

Five Fun Facts About Jesse Mitchell

1. His drawing of a favorite cartoon was published in a magazine at age 10.

2. Accidently burned down his family garage at age 12.

3. Almost blew up a deputy's house while installing TV cable by drilling through a natural gas meter.

4. Cooking specialty is pancakes.

5. Refuses to watch cop-themed television shows or movies.

It's Not Mayberry

Chaffee County, Colorado

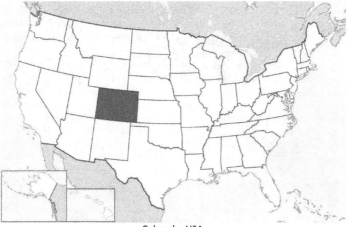

Colorado, USA

Chaffee County, Colorado

Chaffee County Demographics

- **Population** (2019 estimate): 20,356
- **County Seat**:
  - Salida
    Population (2019 estimate) 6,082
- **Towns**:
  - Buena Vista
    Population (2019 estimate) 2,866
  - Poncha Springs
    Population (2019 estimate) 956

Mountain Views
Courtesy of Phreckles Photography LLC, Salida, CO

Chaffee County Geography

- **Area**: 1,015 square miles
- **Terrain**:
  - The Upper Arkansas River Valley is located in the geographic center of Colorado
  - Surrounded by three mountain ranges rising 7,000 feet above the valley floor to an elevation of over 14,000 feet.
  - There are fifteen 14,000-foot peaks in the Sawatch Mountain Range; more than anywhere else in Colorado.

Acknowledgements

In addition to the six officers portrayed in this book, I'd also like to thank Catherine Cortese, Andrea Morgan, Tiffany Murray and Averi Mullenax for sharing their perspective on their spouse's police work. Also, I appreciated feedback, encouragement and support from Doug and Geraldine Frost, Ted and Martha Montoya and Jeff and Lynn Klopstad.

I'd also like to thank my publishing team of Mark Swanson and Andrew Duffy for their support.

And finally, to thank my wife Kathy for reviewing all of my work and being a first-line editor.

Acknowledgements

About the Author

John DiGirolamo is a columnist for the *Winter Park Times* in Colorado and previously published a collection of short stories, *#12 Suicide*. DiGirolamo is a retired CPA whose career spanned over 32 years in various management positions at both small and large technology companies.

He lives with his wife, Kathy, in Chaffee County, CO along with their dog Emmie.

About the Author

CPSIA information can be obtained
at www.ICGtesting.com
Printed in the USA
FSHW022310040421
80036FS

9 781736 508817